Birnbaum's

Paris

A BIRNBAUM TRAVEL GUIDE

Alexandra Mayes Birnbaum
EDITORIAL CONSULTANT

Lois Spritzer
Executive Editor

Laura L. Brengelman
Managing Editor

Mary Callahan
Senior Editor

Patricia Canole
Gene Gold
Jill Kadetsky
Susan McClung
Beth Schlau
Associate Editors

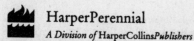

HarperPerennial
A Division of HarperCollinsPublishers

To Stephen, who merely made all this possible.

FIRST EDITION

ISSN 0749-2561 (Birnbaum Travel Guides)
ISSN 1056-4438 (Paris)
ISBN 0-06-278144-8 (pbk.)

93 94 95 96 97 CC/CW 10 9 8 7 6 5 4 3 2 1

Cover design © Drenttel Doyle Partners
Cover photograph © Nancy Henriksson/Bruce Coleman Inc.

BIRNBAUM TRAVEL GUIDES

Bahamas, and Turks & Caicos
Berlin
Bermuda
Boston
Canada
Cancun, Cozumel & Isla Mujeres
Caribbean
Chicago
Disneyland
Eastern Europe
Europe
Europe for Business Travelers
France
Germany
Great Britain
Hawaii
Ireland
Italy
London
Los Angeles
Mexico
Miami & Ft. Lauderdale
Montreal & Quebec City
New Orleans
New York
Paris
Portugal
Rome
San Francisco
Santa Fe & Taos
South America
Spain
United States
USA for Business Travelers
Walt Disney World
Walt Disney World for Kids, By Kids
Washington, DC

Contributing Editors

Paul Century
Stephanie Curtis
Hélène Dupont
William Echikson
Emily Emerson
Joan Gannij
Tracy Smith

Maps

B. Andrew Mudryk

Contents

Getting Ready to Go

Practical information for planning your trip.

Useful Words and Phrases

The City

Thorough, qualitative guide to Paris that offers a comprehensive report on the city's most compelling attractions and amenities — highlighting our top choices in every category.

Diversions

A selective guide to a variety of unexpected pleasures, pinpointing the best places in which to pursue them.

Directions

Seven of the most delightful walks through Paris.

Foreword

My first trip to the City of Light coincided with *Bastille Day*. I was 15 years old, and I will never forget watching the Algerian troops (remember, Algeria was French back then) on camelback clomping down the Champs-Elysées as part of the celebrations; nor my first evening in Paris when I was taken to the *Lido* — no easy entertainment for a naive 1950s American teen.

To say that my first look at l'Etoile and Les Invalides forever made a difference is to understate the impact. On many a subsequent foray with my husband, Steve Birnbaum — whether staying in an intimate pension on the left bank or luxuriating at the *Ritz* — we agreed that it wouldn't be the worst thing if we spent a significant portion of the rest of our lives learning what all was out there. Even after dozens of visits to Paris, we never failed to find something we missed last time through.

Obviously, any guidebook to Paris must keep pace with and answer the real needs of today's travelers. That's why we've tried to create a guide that's specifically organized, written, and edited for the more demanding modern traveler, one for whom qualitative information is infinitely more desirable than mere quantities of unappraised data.

For years, dating back as far as Herr Baedeker, travel guides have tended to be encyclopedic, seemingly much more concerned with demonstrating expertise in geography and history than with a real analysis of the sorts of things that actually concern a typical modern tourist. I think you'll notice a different, more contemporary tone to our text, as well as an organization and focus that are distinctive and more functional. Early on, we realized that giving up the encyclopedic approach precluded our listing every single route and restaurant, a realization that helped define our overall editorial focus. Similarly, when we discussed the possibility of presenting certain information in other than strict geographic order, we found that the new format enabled us to arrange data in a way that we feel best answers the questions travelers typically ask.

Travel guides are, understandably, reflections of personal taste, and putting one's name on a title page obviously puts one's preferences on the line. But I think I ought to amplify just what "personal" means. I don't believe in the sort of personal guidebook that's a palpable misrepresentation on its face. It is, for example, hardly possible for any single travel writer to visit thousands of restaurants (and nearly as many hotels) in any given year and provide accurate appraisals of each. And even if it were physically possible for one human being to survive such an itinerary, it would of necessity have to be done at a dead sprint, and the perceptions derived therefrom would probably be less valid than those of any other intelligent individual visiting the same establishments. It is, therefore, impossible (especially in a large, annually revised and updated guidebook *series* such as we offer) to have only one person provide all the data on the entire world.

I also happen to think that such individual orientation is of substantially less value to readers. Visiting a single hotel for just one night or eating one hasty meal in a random restaurant hardly equips anyone to provide appraisals that are of more than passing interest. We have, therefore, chosen what I like to describe as the "thee and me" approach to restaurant and hotel evaluation and, to a somewhat more limited degree, to the sites and sights we have included in the other sections of our text. What this really reflects is a personal sampling tempered by intelligent counsel from informed local sources, and these additional friends-of-the-editor are almost always residents of the city and/or area about which they are consulted.

In addition, very precise editing and tailoring keep our text fiercely subjective. So what follows is the gospel according to Birnbaum, and it represents as much of our own taste and instincts as we can manage. It is probable, therefore, that if you like your cities stylish and prefer small hotels with personality to huge high-rise anonymities, we're likely to have a long and meaningful relationship.

I also should point out something about the person to whom this guidebook is directed. Above all, he or she is a "visitor." This means that such elements as restaurants have been specifically picked to provide the visitor with a representative, illuminating, stimulating, and above all pleasant experience. Since so many extraneous considerations can affect the reception and service accorded a regular restaurant patron, our choices can in no way be construed as an exhaustive guide to resident dining. We think we've listed all the best places, in various price ranges, but they were chosen with a visitor's enjoyment in mind.

Other evidence of how we've tried to tailor our text to reflect modern travel habits is most apparent in the section we call DIVERSIONS. Where once it was common for travelers to spend an urban visit seeing only the obvious sights, the emphasis today is more likely to be directed toward pursuing some special interest. Therefore, we have collected these exceptional experiences so that it is no longer necessary to wade through a pound or two of superfluous prose just to find unexpected pleasures and pleasures.

Finally, I also should point out that every good travel guide is a living enterprise; that is, no part of this text is carved in stone. In our annual revisions, we refine, expand, and further hone all our material to serve your travel needs better. To this end, no contribution is of greater value to us than your personal reaction to what we have written, as well as information reflecting your own experiences while using the book. Please write to us at 10 E. 53rd St., New York, NY 10022.

We sincerely hope to hear from you.

Alexandra Mayes Birnbaum

ALEXANDRA MAYES BIRNBAUM, editorial consultant to the Birnbaum Travel Guides, worked with her late husband, Stephen Birnbaum, as co-editor of the series. She has been a world traveler since childhood and is known for her lively travel reports on radio on what's hot and what's not.

Paris

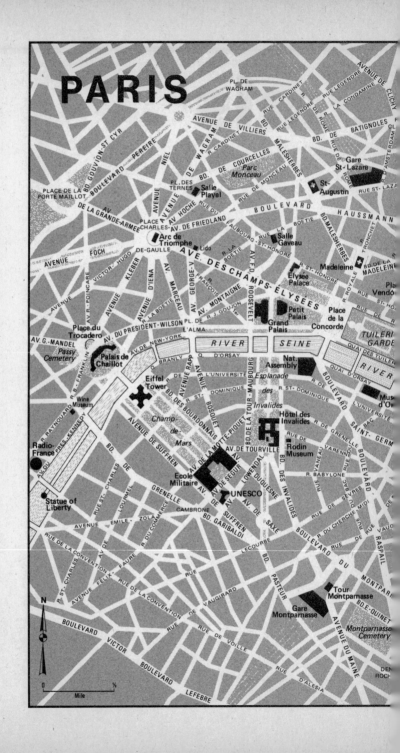

How to Use This Guide

A great deal of care has gone into the special organization of this guide-book, and we believe it represents a real breakthrough in the presentation of travel material.

Our text is divided into five basic sections in order to present information in the best way on every possible aspect of a Paris vacation. Our aim is to highlight what's where and to provide basic information — how, when, where, how much, and what's best — to assist you in making the most intelligent choices possible.

Here is a brief summary of what you can expect to find in each section. We believe that you will find both your travel planning and en route enjoyment enhanced by having this book at your side.

GETTING READY TO GO

A mini-encyclopedia of practical travel facts with all the precise data necessary to create a successful trip to Paris. Here you will find how to get where you're going, plus selected resources — including useful publications, and companies and organizations specializing in discount and special-interest travel — providing a wealth of information and assistance useful both before and during your trip.

USEFUL WORDS AND PHRASES

Though most hotels and restaurants in Paris have at least one English-speaking staff member, at smaller establishments a little knowledge of French will go a long way. This collection of often-used words and phrases will help you to make a hotel or dinner reservation, order a meal, mail a letter — and even buy toothpaste.

THE CITY

The individual report on Paris offers a short-stay guide, including an essay introducing the city as a historic entity and a contemporary place to visit; *At-a-Glance* material is actually a site-by-site survey of the most important, interesting, and sometimes most eclectic sights to see and things to do; *Sources and Resources* is a concise listing of pertinent tourism information, such as the address of the local tourist office, which sightseeing tours to take, where to find the best nightspot or hail a taxi, which shops have the finest merchandise and/or the most irresistible bargains, and where the best museums and theaters are to be found. *Best in Town* lists our choices of the best places to eat and sleep on a variety of budgets.

DIVERSIONS

This section is designed to help travelers find the best places in which to engage in a variety of exceptional — and unexpected — experiences, without having to wade through endless pages of unrelated text. In each case, our particular suggestions are intended to guide you to that special place where the quality of experience is likely to be highest.

DIRECTIONS

Here are seven walks that cover the city, along its main thoroughfares and side streets, past its most spectacular landmarks and magnificent parks. DIRECTIONS is the only section of the book that is organized geographically; itineraries can be connected for longer sojourns or used individually for short, intensive explorations.

———————————

To use this book to full advantage, take a few minutes to read the table of contents and random entries in each section to get a firsthand feel for how it all fits together. You will find that the sections of this book are building blocks designed to help you put together the best possible trip. Use them selectively as a tool, a source of ideas, a reference work for accurate facts, and a guidebook to the best buys, the most exciting sights, the most pleasant accommodations, and the tastiest foods — *the best travel experience* that you can possibly have.

Getting
Ready to Go

When to Go

Paris maintains fairly moderate temperatures year-round. It rains rather often, however, with winter being the wettest season.

The peak travel period generally is from mid-May to mid-September, but travel during the off-season (roughly November to *Easter*) and shoulder seasons (the months immediately before and after the peak months) also offers relatively fair weather and smaller crowds. During these periods, travel also is less expensive.

The *Weather Channel* (2600 Cumberland Pkwy., Atlanta, GA 30339; phone: 404-434-6800) provides current weather forecasts. Call 900-WEATHER from any touch-tone phone in the US; the 95¢ per minute charge will appear on your phone bill.

Traveling by Plane

SCHEDULED FLIGHTS

Leading airlines offering flights between the US and Paris include *Air France, American, British Airways, Continental, Delta, KLM, Lufthansa, Northwest, SAS, SwissAir, Tower Air, TWA, United,* and *USAir.*

FARES The great variety of airfares can be reduced to the following basic categories: first class, business class, coach (also called economy or tourist class), excursion or discount, and standby, as well as various promotional fares. For information on applicable fares and restrictions, contact the airlines listed above or ask your travel agent. Most airfares are offered for a limited time period. Once you've found the lowest fare for which you can qualify, purchase your ticket as soon as possible.

RESERVATIONS Reconfirmation is strongly recommended for all international flights. It is essential that you confirm your round-trip reservations–*especially the return leg* — as well as any flights within Europe.

SEATING Airline seats usually are assigned on a first-come, first-served basis at check-in, although you may be able to reserve a seat when purchasing your ticket. Seating charts often are available from airlines and are included in the *Airline Seating Guide* (Carlson Publishing Co., PO Box 888, Los Alamitos, CA 90720; phone: 310-493-4877).

SMOKING US law prohibits smoking on flights scheduled for 6 hours or less within the US and its territories on both domestic and international carriers. These rules do not apply to nonstop flights between the US and international destinations. A free wallet-size guide that describes the rights of nonsmokers is available from *ASH (Action on Smoking and Health;* DOT Card, 2013 H St. NW, Washington, DC 20006; phone: 202-659-4310).

SPECIAL MEALS When making your reservation, you can request one of the airline's alternate menu choices for no additional charge. Call to reconfirm your request 24 hours before departure.

BAGGAGE On a major international airline, passengers usually are allowed to carry on board one bag that will fit under a seat or in an overhead bin. Passengers also can check two bags in the cargo hold, measuring 62 inches and 55 inches in combined dimensions (length, width, and depth) with a per-bag weight limit of 70 pounds. There may be charges for additional, oversize, or overweight luggage, and for special equipment or sporting gear. Note that baggage allowances may vary for children (depending on the percentage of full adult fare paid) and on domestic and intra-European routes abroad. Check that the tags the airline attaches are correctly coded for your destination.

CHARTER FLIGHTS

By booking a block of seats on a specially arranged flight, charter operators frequently offer travelers bargain airfares. If you do fly on a charter, however, read the contract's fine print carefully. Charter operators can cancel a flight or assess surcharges of 10% of the airfare up to 10 days before departure. You usually must book in advance (no changes are permitted, so invest in trip cancellation insurance); also make your check out to the company's escrow account. For further information, consult the publication *Jax Fax* (397 Post Rd., Darien, CT 06820; phone: 203-655-8746).

DISCOUNTS ON SCHEDULED FLIGHTS

COURIER TRAVEL In return for arranging to accompany some kind of freight, a traveler may pay only a portion of the total airfare and a small registration fee. One agency that matches up would-be couriers with courier companies is *Now Voyager* (74 Varick St., Suite 307, New York, NY 10013; phone: 212-431-1616).

Courier Companies
Courier Travel Service (530 Central Ave., Cedarhurst, NY 11516; phone: 516-763-6898).

Discount Travel International (169 W. 81st St., New York, NY 10024; phone: 212-362-3636; and 940 10th St., Suite 2, Miami Beach, FL 33139; phone: 305-538-1616).

Excaliber International Courier (c/o *Way to Go Travel*, 6679 Sunset Blvd., Hollywood, CA 90028; phone: 213-466-1126).

F.B. On Board Courier Services (10225 Ryan Ave., Suite 103, Dorval, Quebec H9P 1A2, Canada; phone: 514-633-0740).

Halbart Express (147-05 176th St., Jamaica, NY 11434; phone: 718-656-8279).

International Adventures (60 E. 42nd St., New York, NY 10165; phone: 212-599-0577).

Midnight Express (925 W. High Park Blvd., Inglewood, CA 90302; phone: 310-672-1100).

Publications

Insider's Guide to Air Courier Bargains, by Kelly Monaghan (The Intrepid Traveler, PO Box 438, New York, NY 10034; phone: 212-304-2207).

Travel Secrets (PO Box 2325, New York, NY 10108; phone: 212-245-8703).

Travel Unlimited (PO Box 1058, Allston, MA 02134-1058; no phone).

World Courier News (PO Box 77471, San Francisco, CA 94107; no phone).

CONSOLIDATORS AND BUCKET SHOPS These companies buy blocks of tickets from airlines and sell them at a discount to travel agents or to consumers. Since many bucket shops operate on a thin margin, before parting with any money check the company's record with the Better Business Bureau.

Bargain Air (655 Deep Valley Dr., Suite 355, Rolling Hills, CA 90274; phone: 800-347-2345).

Council Charter (205 E. 42nd St., New York, NY 10017; phone: 800-800-8222 or 212-661-0311).

International Adventures (60 E. 42nd St., New York, NY 10165; phone: 212-599-0577).

Travac Tours and Charters (989 Ave. of the Americas, New York, NY 10018; phone: 800-872-8800 or 212-563-3303).

Unitravel (1177 N. Warson Rd., St. Louis, MO 63132; phone: 800-325-2222 or 314-569-0900).

LAST-MINUTE TRAVEL CLUBS For an annual fee, members receive information on imminent trips and other bargain travel opportunities. Despite the names of these clubs, you don't have to wait until literally the last minute to make travel plans.

Discount Travel International (114 Forest Ave., Suite 203, Narberth, PA 19072; phone: 215-668-7184).

Last Minute Travel (1249 Boylston St., Boston, MA 02215; phone: 800-LAST-MIN or 617-267-9800).

Moment's Notice (425 Madison Ave., New York, NY 10017; phone: 212-486-0500, -0501, -0502, or -0503).

Spur-of-the-Moment Cruises (411 N. Harbor Blvd., Suite 302, San Pedro, CA 90731; phone: 800-4-CRUISES in California; 800-343-1991 elsewhere in the US; or 310-521-1070).

Traveler's Advantage (3033 S. Parker Rd., Suite 900, Aurora, CO 80014; phone: 800-548-1116 or 800-835-8747).

Vacations to Go (1502 Augusta, Suite 415, Houston, TX 77057; phone: 713-974-2121 in Texas; 800-338-4962 elsewhere in the US).

Worldwide Discount Travel Club (1674 Meridian Ave., Miami Beach, FL 33139; phone: 305-534-2082).

GENERIC AIR TRAVEL These organizations operate much like an ordinary airline standby service, except that they offer seats on not one but several scheduled and charter airlines. One pioneer of generic flights is *Airhitch* (2790 Broadway, Suite 100, New York, NY 10025; phone: 212-864-2000).

BARTERED TRAVEL SOURCES Barter is a common means of exchange between travel suppliers. Bartered travel clubs such as *Travel World Leisure Club* (225 W. 34th St., Suite 909, New York, NY 10122; phone: 800-444-TWLC or 212-239-4855) offer discounts to members for an annual fee.

CONSUMER PROTECTION

Passengers with complaints who are not satisfied with the airline's response can contact the US Department of Transportation (DOT; Consumer Affairs Division, 400 7th St. SW, Room 10405, Washington, DC 20590; phone: 202-366-2220). If you have a complaint against a local travel service, contact the French tourist authorities. Also see *Fly Rights* (Publication #050-000-00513-5; US Government Printing Office, PO Box 371954, Pittsburgh, PA 15250-7954; phone: 202-783-3238).

On Arrival

FROM THE AIRPORT TO THE CITY

Paris has two airports: **Charles de Gaulle Airport** is located 14 miles (23 km) northeast of the center of Paris; **Orly** is 8 miles (13 km) south of the city center. To travel from either airport to central Paris takes between 30 and 45 minutes by taxi. The fare is about 150F to 250F (about $27 to $45), with an extra charge of about 5F (90¢) for each bag.

The *RER* (suburban train) runs between the city and the airports. From Charles de Gaulle Airport, take the *B* train (sometimes designated Roissy-Rail); you can buy a ticket for 31F (about $6) at the airport. From Orly, take the *C* train (sometimes designated Orly-Rail); the fare is 23F (approximately $4). From either airport, you also can take the *Air France* coach service to the Montparnasse, Port Maillot, or Les Invalides bus terminals in the city. The coach service also operates between the two airports. For more information, check at the *Air France* counter at the airport.

CAR RENTAL

Although useful for day trips outside Paris, cars usually are more trouble than they are worth for touring within the city. You can rent a car through a travel agent or international rental firm before leaving home, or from a regional or local company once in Paris. Reserve in advance.

Most car rental companies require a credit card, although some will accept a substantial cash deposit. The minimum age to rent a car is set by the company; some impose special conditions on drivers above a certain age. Electing to pay for collision damage waiver (CDW) protection will add to the cost of renting a car, but releases you from financial liability for the vehicle. Additional costs include drop-off charges or one-way service fees. One way to keep down the cost of car rentals is to deal with a car rental consolidator, such as *Connex International* (phone: 800-333-3949 or 914-739-0066).

International Car Rental Companies

Auto Europe (phone: 800-223-5555).

Avis (phone: 800-331-1084).

Budget (phone: 800-472-3325).

Dollar Rent A Car (known in Europe as *Eurodollar Rent A Car;* phone: 800-800-4000).

Europe by Car (phone: 212-581-3040 in New York State; 800-223-1516 elsewhere in the US).

European Car Reservations (phone: 800-535-3303).

Foremost Euro-Car (phone: 800-272-3299).

Hertz (phone: 800-654-3001).

Kemwel Group (phone: 800-678-0678).

Meier's World Travel (phone: 800-937-0700).

National (known in Europe as *Europcar;* phone: 800-CAR-EUROPE).

Thrifty (phone: 800-367-2277).

French Car Rental Companies

Citroën (phone: 1-43-55-39-63).

Dergi Location (phone: 1-45-87-27-04).

Package Tours

A package is a collection of travel services that can be purchased in a single transaction. Its principal advantages are convenience and economy — the cost is usually lower than that of the same services bought separately. Tour programs generally can be divided into two categories: escorted or locally hosted (with a set itinerary) and independent (usually more flexible).

When considering a package tour, read the brochure *carefully* to determine what is included and other conditions. Check the company's record with the Better Business Bureau. The *United States Tour Operators Association* (*USTOA;* 211 E. 51st St., Suite 12B, New York, NY 10022; phone: 212-944-5727) also can be helpful in determining a package tour operator's reliability. As with charter flights, always make your check out to the company's escrow account.

Many tour operators offer packages focused on special interests such as the arts, food and wine, and sports and other recreations. *All Adventure*

Travel (PO Box 4307, Boulder, CO 80306; phone: 800-537-4025 or 303-499-1981) represents such specialized packagers; some also are listed in the *Specialty Travel Index* (305 San Anselmo Ave., Suite 313, San Anselmo, CA 94960; phone: 415-459-4900 in California; 800-442-4922 elsewhere in the US).

Package Tour Operators

Abercrombie & Kent (1520 Kensington Rd., Oak Brook, IL 60521; phone: 708-954-2944 in Illinois; 800-323-7308 elsewhere in the US).

American Airlines FlyAAway Vacations (phone: 800-832-8383).

American Express Vacations (offices throughout the US; phone: 800-241-1700 or 404-368-5100).

AutoVenture (425 Pike St., Suite 502, Seattle, WA 98101; phone: 800-426-7502 or 206-624-6033).

Blue Marble Travel (c/o *Odyssey Adventures,* 89 Auburn St., Suite 1199, Portland, ME 04103; phone: 800-544-3216 or 207-878-8650).

Brendan Tours (15137 Califa St., Van Nuys, CA 91411; phone: 800-421-8446 or 818-785-9696).

British Airways Holidays (phone: 800-AIRWAYS).

Cityrama (347 Fifth Ave., Suite 709, New York, NY 10016-5098; phone: 800-225-2595 or 212-683-8120).

Contiki Holidays (300 Plaza Alicante, Suite 900, Garden Grove, CA 92640; phone: 800-466-0610 or 714-740-0808).

Continental Grand Destinations (phone: 800-634-5555).

Delta's Dream Vacations (phone: 800-872-7786).

DER Tours (11933 Wilshire Blvd., Los Angeles, CA 90025; phone: 800-937-1234).

DMI Tours (14340 Memorial Dr., Suite 117, Houston, TX 77079; phone: 800-553-5090 or 713-558-9933).

Especially France (1398 Diamond Mountain Rd., Calistoga, CA 94515; phone: 800-FRANCE-X or 707-942-4582).

Extra Value Travel (683 S. Collier Blvd., Marco Island, FL 33937; phone: 800-336-4668 or 813-394-3384).

Five Star Touring (60 E. 42nd St., New York, NY 10165; phone: 800-792-7827 or 212-818-9140).

The French Experience (370 Lexington Ave., New York, NY 10017; phone: 212-986-1115).

Globus and Cosmos (5301 S. Federal Circle, Littleton, CO 80123; phone: 800-221-0090 or 800-556-5454).

Grand Slam Tennis Tours (222 Milwaukee St., Suite 407, Denver, CO 80206; phone: 800-289-3333 or 303-321-1760).

H.S.A. Voyages (formerly *H.S. & Associates,* 160 E. 26th St., Suite 5H, New York, NY 10010; phone: 800-927-4765 or 212-689-5400).

In Quest of the Classics (316 Mission Ave., Oceanside, CA 92054; phone: 800-227-1393 or 619-721-1123 in California; 800-221-5246 elsewhere in the US).

Jet Vacations (1775 Broadway, New York, NY 10019; phone: 800-JET-0999 or 212-247-0999).

KLM's Vacation Center (phone: 800-777-1668).

Northwest WorldVacations (phone: 800-727-1400).

Odyssey Adventures (89 Auburn St., Suite 1199, Portland, ME 04103; phone: 800-544-3216 or 207-878-8650).

Pleasure Break (701 Algonquin Rd., Suite 900, Rolling Meadows, IL 60008; phone: 708-670-6300 in Illinois; 800-777-1885 elsewhere in the US).

Solrep International (3271 W. Alabama St., Houston, TX 77098; phone: 713-529-5547 in Texas; 800-231-0985 elsewhere in the US).

STS (24 Culloden Rd., Enfield, London EN2 8QD, England; phone: 44-81-363-8202; US Office: 795 Franklin Ave., Franklin Lakes, NJ 07417; phone: 800-752-6787 or 201-891-4143).

Take-A-Guide (11 Uxbridge St., London W8 7TQ, England; in the US call 800-825-4946).

Thomas Cook (Headquarters: 45 Berkeley St., Piccadilly, London W1A 1EB, England; phone: 44-71-408-4191; main US office: 2 Penn Plaza, 18th Floor, New York, NY 10121; phone: 800-846-6272 or 212-967-4390).

Travcoa (PO Box 2630, Newport Beach, CA 92658; phone: 800-992-2004 in California; 800-992-2003 elsewhere in the US; or 710-476-2800).

TWA Getaway Vacations (phone: 800-GETAWAY).

Unitours (8 S. Michigan Ave., Chicago, IL 60603; phone: 800-621-0557 or 312-782-1590).

X.O. Travel Consultants (38 W. 32nd St., Suite 1009, New York, NY 10001; phone: 800-262-9682 or 212-947-5530).

Insurance

The first person with whom you should discuss travel insurance is your own insurance broker. You may discover that the insurance you already carry protects you adequately while traveling and that you need little additional coverage. If you charge travel services, the credit card company also may provide some insurance coverage (and other safeguards).

Types of Travel Insurance

Baggage and personal effects insurance: Protects your bags and their contents in case of damage or theft anytime during your travels.

Personal accident and sickness insurance: Covers cases of illness, injury, or death in an accident while traveling.

Trip cancellation and interruption insurance: Guarantees a refund if you must cancel a trip; may reimburse you for the extra travel costs incurred for catching up with a tour or traveling home early.

Default and/or bankruptcy insurance: Provides coverage in the event of default and/or bankruptcy on the part of the tour operator, airline, or other travel supplier.

Flight insurance: Covers accidental injury or death while flying.

Automobile insurance: Provides collision, theft, property damage, and personal liability protection while driving your own or a rented car.

Combination policies: Include any or all of the above.

Disabled Travelers

Make travel arrangements well in advance. Specify to all services involved the nature of your disability to determine if there are accommodations and facilities that meet your needs.

The French Government Tourist Office in the US distributes the *Paris Hotel Guide* and *Paris Guide to Monuments and Museums,* which list wheelchair accessibility. The *Comité National Français de Liaison pour la Réadaptation des Handicapés* (38 Bd. Raspail, Paris 75007, France; phone: 1-45-48-90-13) provides information about accessibility and transportation for the disabled in Paris. For information on accessibility in Paris airports, contact the *Paris Airport Authority* (10 E. 21st St., Suite 600, New York, NY 10010; phone: 212-529-8484). Hotel and restaurant guides, such as the *Michelin Red Guide to France* (Michelin Guides and Maps, PO Box 3305, Spartanburg, SC 29304-3305; phone: 803-599-0850 in South Carolina; 800-423-0485 elsewhere in the US), use a symbol of access (person in a wheelchair) to point out accommodations suitable for wheelchair-bound guests.

Organizations

ACCENT on Living (PO Box 700, Bloomington, IL 61702; phone: 309-378-2961).

Access: The Foundation for Accessibility by the Disabled (PO Box 356, Malverne, NY 11565; phone: 516-887-5798).

American Foundation for the Blind (15 W. 16th St., New York, NY 10011; phone: 800-232-5463 or 212-620-2147).

Holiday Care Service (2 Old Bank Chambers, Station Rd., Horley, Surrey RH6 9HW, England; phone: 44-293-774535).

Information Center for Individuals with Disabilities (Ft. Point Pl., 1st Floor, 27-43 Wormwood St., Boston, MA 02210; phone: 800-462-5015 in Massachusetts; 617-727-5540 or 617-727-5541 elsewhere in the US; TDD: 617-345-9743).

Mobility International USA (*MIUSA;* PO Box 3551, Eugene, OR 97403; phone: 503-343-1284, both voice and TDD; main office: 228 Borough High St., London SE1 1JX, England; phone: 44-71-403-5688).

National Rehabilitation Information Center (8455 Colesville Rd., Suite 935, Silver Spring, MD 20910; phone: 301-588-9284).

Paralyzed Veterans of America (*PVA;* PVA/ATTS Program, 801 18th St. NW, Washington, DC 20006; phone: 202-872-1300 in Washington, DC; 800-424-8200 elsewhere in the US).

Royal Association for Disability and Rehabilitation (*RADAR;* 25 Mortimer St., London W1N 8AB, England; phone: 44-71-637-5400).

Society for the Advancement of Travel for the Handicapped (*SATH;* 347 Fifth Ave., Suite 610, New York, NY 10016; phone: 212-447-7284).

Travel Information Service (MossRehab Hospital, 1200 W. Tabor Rd., Philadelphia, PA 19141-3099; phone: 215-456-9600; TDD: 215-456-9602).

Tripscope (The Courtyard, Evelyn Rd., London W4 5JL, England; phone: 44-81-994-9294).

Publications

Access Travel: A Guide to the Accessibility of Airport Terminals (Consumer Information Center, Dept. 578Z, Pueblo, CO 81009; phone: 719-948-3334).

Air Transportation of Handicapped Persons (Publication #AC-120-32; US Department of Transportation, Distribution Unit, Publications Section, M-443-2, 400 7th St. SW, Washington, DC 20590).

The Diabetic Traveler (PO Box 8223 RW, Stamford, CT 06905; phone: 203-327-5832).

Directory of Travel Agencies for the Disabled and *Travel for the Disabled,* both by Helen Hecker (Twin Peaks Press, PO Box 129, Vancouver, WA 98666; phone: 800-637-CALM or 206-694-2462).

Guide to Traveling with Arthritis (Upjohn Company, PO Box 989, Dearborn, MI 48121).

The Handicapped Driver's Mobility Guide (*American Automobile Association,* 1000 AAA Dr., Heathrow, FL 32746; phone: 407-444-7000).

Handicapped Travel Newsletter (PO Box 269, Athens, TX 75751; phone: 903-677-1260).

Handi-Travel: A Resource Book for Disabled and Elderly Travellers, by Cinnie Noble (*Canadian Rehabilitation Council for the Disabled,* 45 Sheppard Ave. E., Suite 801, Toronto, Ontario M2N 5W9, Canada; phone: 416-250-7490, both voice and TDD).

Incapacitated Passengers Air Travel Guide (*International Air Transport Association,* Publications Sales Department, 2000 Peel St., Montreal, Quebec H3A 2R4, Canada; phone: 514-844-6311).

Ticket to Safe Travel (*American Diabetes Association,* 1660 Duke St., Alexandria, VA 22314; phone: 800-232-3472 or 703-549-1500).

Travel for the Patient with Chronic Obstructive Pulmonary Disease (Dr. Harold Silver, 1601 18th St. NW, Washington, DC 20009; phone: 202-667-0134).

Travel Tips for Hearing-Impaired People (*American Academy of Otolaryngology,* 1 Prince St., Alexandria, VA 22314; phone: 703-836-4444).

Travel Tips for People with Arthritis (*Arthritis Foundation*, 1314 Spring St. NW, Atlanta, GA 30309; phone: 800-283-7800 or 404-872-7100).

Traveling Like Everybody Else: A Practical Guide for Disabled Travelers, by Jacqueline Freedman and Susan Gersten (Modan Publishing, PO Box 1202, Bellmore, NY 11710; phone: 516-679-1380).

Package Tour Operators

Accessible Journeys (35 W. Sellers Ave., Ridley Park, PA 19078; phone: 215-521-0339).

Accessible Tours/Directions Unlimited (Lois Bonnani, 720 N. Bedford Rd., Bedford Hills, NY 10507; phone: 800-533-5343 or 914-241-1700).

Beehive Business and Leisure Travel (1130 W. Center St., N. Salt Lake, UT 84054; phone: 800-777-5727 or 801-292-4445).

Classic Travel Service (8 W. 40th St., New York, NY 10018; phone: 212-869-2560 in New York State; 800-247-0909 elsewhere in the US).

Evergreen Travel Service (4114 198th St. SW, Suite 13, Lynnwood, WA 98036-6742; phone: 800-435-2288 or 206-776-1184).

Flying Wheels Travel (143 W. Bridge St., PO Box 382, Owatonna, MN 55060; phone: 800-535-6790 or 507-451-5005).

Good Neighbor Travel Service (124 S. Main St., Viroqua, WI 54665; phone: 608-637-2128).

The Guided Tour (7900 Old York Rd., Suite 114B, Elkins Park, PA 19117-2339; phone: 800-783-5841 or 215-782-1370).

Hinsdale Travel (201 E. Ogden Ave., Hinsdale, IL 60521; phone: 708-325-1335 or 708-469-7349).

MedEscort International (ABE International Airport, PO Box 8766, Allentown, PA 18105; phone: 800-255-7182 or 215-791-3111).

Prestige World Travel (5710-X High Point Rd., Greensboro, NC 27407; phone: 800-476-7737 or 919-292-6690).

Sprout (893 Amsterdam Ave., New York, NY 10025; phone: 212-222-9575).

Weston Travel Agency (134 N. Cass Ave., PO Box 1050, Westmont, IL 60559; phone: 708-968-2513 in Illinois; 800-633-3725 elsewhere in the US).

Single Travelers

The travel industry is not very fair to people who vacation by themselves—they often end up paying more than those traveling in pairs. Services catering to singles match travel companions, offer travel arrangements with shared accommodations, and provide useful information and discounts. Also consult publications such as *Going Solo* (Doerfer Communications, PO Box 123, Apalachicola, FL 32329; phone: 904-653-8848) and *Traveling on Your Own,* by Eleanor Berman (Random House, Order Dept., 400 Hahn Rd., Westminster, MD 21157; phone: 800-733-3000).

Organizations and Companies

Club Europa (802 W. Oregon St., Urbana, IL 61801; phone: 800-331-1882 or 217-344-5863).

Contiki Holidays (300 Plaza Alicante, Suite 900, Garden Grove, CA 92640; phone: 800-466-0610 or 714-740-0808).

Gallivanting (515 E. 79th St., Suite 20F, New York, NY 10021; phone: 800-933-9699 or 212-988-0617).

Globus and Cosmos (5301 S. Federal Circle, Littleton, CO 80123; phone: 800-221-0090 or 800-556-5454).

Insight International Tours (745 Atlantic Ave., Suite 720, Boston, MA 02111; phone: 800-582-8380 or 617-482-2000).

Jane's International and Sophisticated Women Travelers (2603 Bath Ave., Brooklyn, NY 11214; phone: 718-266-2045).

Marion Smith Singles (611 Prescott Pl., N. Woodmere, NY 11581; phone: 516-791-4852, 516-791-4865, or 212-944-2112).

Partners-in-Travel (11660 Chenault St., Suite 119, Los Angeles, CA 90049; phone: 310-476-4869).

Singles in Motion (545 W. 236th St., Riverdale, NY 10463; phone: 718-884-4464).

Singleworld (401 Theodore Fremd Ave., Rye, NY 10580; phone: 800-223-6490 or 914-967-3334).

Solo Flights (63 High Noon Rd., Weston, CT 06883; phone: 203-226-9993).

Suddenly Singles Tours (161 Dreiser Loop, Bronx, NY 10475; phone: 718-379-8800 in New York City; 800-859-8396 elsewhere in the US).

Travel Companion Exchange (PO Box 833, Amityville, NY 11701; phone: 516-454-0880).

Travel Companions (Atrium Financial Center, 1515 N. Federal Hwy., Suite 300, Boca Raton, FL 33432; phone: 800-383-7211 or 407-393-6448).

Travel in Two's (239 N. Broadway, Suite 3, N. Tarrytown, NY 10591; phone: 914-631-8301 in New York State; 800-692-5252 elsewhere in the US).

Older Travelers

Special discounts and more free time are just two factors that have given older travelers a chance to see the world at affordable prices. Many travel suppliers offer senior discounts — sometimes only to members of certain senior citizen organizations, which provide other benefits. Prepare your itinerary with one eye on your own physical condition and the other on a topographical map, and remember that it's easy to overdo when traveling.

Publications

Going Abroad: 101 Tips for Mature Travelers (Grand Circle Travel, 347

Congress St., Boston, MA 02210; phone: 800-221-2610 or 617-350-7500).

The Mature Traveler (GEM Publishing Group, PO Box 50820, Reno, NV 89513-0820; phone: 702-786-7419).

Take a Camel to Lunch and Other Adventures for Mature Travelers, by Nancy O'Connell (Bristol Publishing Enterprises, PO Box 1737, San Leandro, CA 94577; phone: 510-895-4461 in California; 800-346-4889 elsewhere in the US).

Travel Tips for Older Americans (Publication #044-000-02270-2; Superintendent of Documents, US Government Printing Office, PO Box 371954, Pittsburgh, PA 15250-7954; phone: 202-783-3238).

Unbelievably Good Deals & Great Adventures That You Absolutely Can't Get Unless You're Over 50, by Joan Rattner Heilman (Contemporary Books, 180 N. Michigan Ave., Chicago, IL 60601; phone: 312-782-9181).

Organizations

American Association of Retired Persons (*AARP;* 601 E St. NW, Washington, DC 20049; phone: 202-434-2277).

Golden Companions (PO Box 754, Pullman, WA 99163-0754; phone: 208-858-2183).

Mature Outlook (Customer Service Center, 6001 N. Clark St., Chicago, IL 60660; phone: 800-336-6330).

National Council of Senior Citizens (1331 F St. NW, Washington, DC 20004; phone: 202-347-8800).

Package Tour Operators

Elderhostel (PO Box 1959, Wakefield, MA 01880-5959; phone: 617-426-7788).

Evergreen Travel Service (4114 198th St. SW, Suite 13, Lynnwood, WA 98036-6742; phone: 800-435-2288 or 206-776-1184).

Gadabout Tours (700 E. Tahquitz Canyon Way, Palm Springs, CA 92262; phone: 800-952-5068 or 619-325-5556).

Grand Circle Travel (347 Congress St., Boston, MA 02210; phone: 800-221-2610 or 617-350-7500).

Grandtravel (6900 Wisconsin Ave., Suite 706, Chevy Chase, MD 20815; phone: 800-247-7651 or 301-986-0790).

Insight International Tours (745 Atlantic Ave., Suite 720, Boston, MA 02111; phone: 800-582-8380 or 617-482-2000).

Interhostel (UNH Division of Continuing Education, 6 Garrison Ave., Durham, NH 03824; phone: 800-733-9753 or 603-862-1147).

OmniTours (104 Wilmont Rd., Deerfield, IL 60015; phone: 800-962-0060 or 708-374-0088).

Saga International Holidays (222 Berkeley St., Boston, MA 02116; phone: 800-343-0273 or 617-262-2262).

Money Matters

The basic unit of currency in France is the French **franc**, which is divided into 100 **centimes**. The franc is distributed in coin denominations of 10F, 5F, 2F, 1F, and ½F, and 20 centimes, 10 centimes, and 5 centimes. Paper money is distributed in denominations of 500F, 200F, 100F, 50F, and 20F. Although the French use a comma in expressing numerical values where Americans use a decimal point (and vice versa), throughout this book we use the American decimal style.

Exchange rates are posted in international newspapers such as the *International Herald Tribune.* Foreign currency information and related services are provided by banks and companies such as *Thomas Cook Foreign Exchange* (for the nearest location, call 800-621-0666 or 312-236-0042), *Harold Reuter and Company* (200 Park Ave., Suite 332E, New York, NY 10166; phone: 212-661-0826), and *Ruesch International* (for the nearest location, call 800-424-2923 or 202-408-1200). In Paris, you will find the official rate of exchange posted in banks, airports, money exchange houses, hotels, and some shops. Since you will get more francs for your US dollar at banks and money exchanges, don't change more than $10 for foreign currency at other commercial establishments. Ask how much commission you're being charged and the exchange rate, and don't buy money on the black market (it may be counterfeit). Estimate your needs carefully; if you overbuy, you lose twice — buying and selling back.

TRAVELER'S CHECKS AND CREDIT CARDS

It's wise to carry traveler's checks while on the road, since they are replaceable if stolen or lost. You can buy traveler's checks at banks and some are available by mail or phone. Although most major credit cards enjoy wide domestic and international acceptance, not every hotel, restaurant, or shop in Paris accepts all (or in some cases any) credit cards. Note that some cards may be issued under different names in Europe; for example, *MasterCard* may go under the name *Access* or *Eurocard,* and *Visa* often is called *Carte Bleue.* When making purchases with a credit card, note that the rate of exchange depends on when the charge is processed; most credit card companies charge a 1% fee for converting foreign currency charges. Keep a separate list of all traveler's checks (noting those that you have cashed) and the names and numbers of your credit cards. Both traveler's check and credit card companies have international numbers to call for information or in the event of loss or theft.

CASH MACHINES

Automated teller machines (ATMs — called "Minibanques" in France) are increasingly common worldwide. Most banks participate in one of the international ATM networks; cardholders can withdraw cash from any machine in the same network using either a "bank" card or, in some cases, a credit card. At the time of this writing, most ATMs belong to the *CIRRUS* or *PLUS* network. For further information, ask at your bank branch.

SENDING MONEY ABROAD

Should the need arise, it is possible to have money sent to you via the services provided by *American Express* (*MoneyGram;* phone: 800-926-9400 or 800-666-3997 for information; 800-866-8800 for money transfers) or *Western Union Financial Services* (phone: 800-325-4176). If you are down to your last cent and have no other way to obtain cash, the nearest US Consulate will let you call home to set these matters in motion.

Accommodations

For specific information on hotels, resorts, and other selected accommodations see *Best in Town* in THE CITY. The French Government Tourist Office distributes lists of selected, rated Paris hotels, and the US representatives of French hotels.

RELAIS & CHÂTEAUX

Native to France, the *Relais & Châteaux* association, which consists of two groups of members — *Relais Châteaux* (hotels and other accommodations) and *Relais Gourmands* (restaurants) — has grown to include establishments in numerous countries. All maintain very high standards in order to retain their memberships, as they are reviewed annually. An illustrated catalogue of properties is available from *Relais & Châteaux* (11 E. 44th St., Suite 707, New York, NY 10017; phone: 212-856-0115).

RENTAL OPTIONS

An attractive accommodations alternative for the visitor content to stay in Paris for a week or more is to rent an apartment or a townhouse. For a family or group, the per-person cost can be reasonable. To have your pick of the properties available, make inquiries at least 6 months in advance. The *Worldwide Home Rental Guide* (369 Montezuma, Suite 297, Santa Fe, NM 87501; phone: 505-984-7080) lists rental properties and managing agencies. Those who wish to arrange a rental themselves can write or call the French Government Tourist Office or contact the *Fédération Nationale des Agents Immobiliers* (129 Rue du Faubourg-St-Honoré, Paris 75008, France; phone: 1-44-20-77-00) for a list of real estate agencies handling property rentals in and around Paris.

Rental Property Agents

At Home Abroad (405 E. 56th St., Suite 6H, New York, NY 10022-2466; phone: 212-421-9165).

B & D De Vogue International (140 E. 56th St., Suite 4C, New York,

NY 10022; phone: 800-438-4748) or *La Vie de Châteaux* (PO Box 79, Aubigny-sur-Mer 1870, France; phone: 44-18-95-47).

Blake's Vacations (4918 Dempster St., Skokie, IL 60077; phone: 800-628-8118).

Castles, Cottages and Flats (7 Faneuil Hall Marketplace, Boston, MA 02109; phone: 617-742-6030).

Chez Vous (220 Redwood Highway, Suite 129, Mill Valley, CA 94941; phone: 415-331-2535).

Europa-Let (92 N. Main St., Ashland, OR 97520; phone: 800-462-4486 or 503-482-5806).

The French Experience (370 Lexington Ave., New York, NY 10017; phone: 212-986-1115).

Hideaways International (PO Box 4433, Portsmouth, NH 03802-4433; phone: 800-843-4433 or 603-430-4433).

Hometours International (1170 Broadway, Suite 614, New York, NY 10001; phone: 800-367-4668 or 212-689-0851).

Interhome (124 Little Falls Rd., Fairfield, NJ 07004; phone: 201-882-6864).

Rent a Home International (7200 34th Ave. NW, Seattle, WA 98117; phone: 206-789-9377).

Rent a Vacation Everywhere (*RAVE;* 383 Park Ave., Rochester, NY 14607; phone: 716-256-0760).

Sterling Tours (formerly, *Livingstone Holidays,* 2707 Congress St., Suite 2G, San Diego, CA 92110; phone: 800-727-4359).

Vacances en Campagne (PO Box 297, Falls Village, CT 06031; phone: 800-533-5405).

VHR Worldwide (235 Kensington Ave., Norwood, NJ 07648; phone: 201-767-9393 in New Jersey; 800-633-3284 elsewhere in the US).

Villas International (605 Market St., Suite 510, San Francisco, CA 94105; phone: 800-221-2260 or 415-281-0910).

HOME EXCHANGES

For comfortable, reasonable living quarters with amenities that no hotel could possibly offer, consider trading homes with someone abroad. The following companies provide information on exchanges:

Home Base Holidays (7 Park Ave., London N13 5PG, England; phone: 44-81-886-8752).

Intervac US/International Home Exchange (PO Box 590504, San Francisco, CA 94159; phone: 800-756-HOME or 415-435-3497).

Loan-A-Home (2 Park La., Apt. 6E, Mt. Vernon, NY 10552; phone: 914-664-7640).

Vacation Exchange Club (PO Box 650, Key West, FL 33041; phone: 800-638-3841 or 305-294-3720).

Worldwide Home Exchange Club (138 Brompton Rd., London SW3

1HY, England; phone: 44-71-589-6055; or 806 Brantford Ave., Silver Spring, MD 20904; phone: 301-680-8950).

HOME STAYS

The *United States Servas Committee* (11 John St., Room 407, New York, NY 10038; phone: 212-267-0252) maintains a list of hosts throughout the world willing to accommodate visitors free of charge. The aim of this nonprofit cultural program is to promote international understanding and peace, and *Servas* emphasizes that member travelers should be interested mainly in their hosts, not in sightseeing, during their stays. Another organization offering home stays with French families is *Friends in France* (40 E. 19th St., 8th Floor, New York, NY 10003; phone: 212-260-9820).

Time Zone

France is in the Greenwich Plus 1 time zone — which means that the time is 6 hours later than it is in east coast US cities. Like most Western European nations, France moves its clocks ahead an hour in the spring and back an hour in the fall, corresponding to daylight saving time in the US, although the exact dates of the changes are different from those observed in the US. French timetables use a 24-hour clock to denote arrival and departure times, which means that hours are expressed sequentially from 1 AM.

Business Hours

In Paris, as throughout France, most businesses and shops are open from 9 AM to 5 or 6 PM. Banks usually are open weekdays from 9 or 9:30 AM to 4:30 PM. Many shops also are open on Saturdays from 10 AM to 6PM. Banks generally are open from 9 or 9:30 AM to 4:30 PM.

Department stores and other large emporia are open from about 9:30 AM to 6:30 PM, Mondays through Saturdays, and often stay open until 9 or 10 PM 1 or 2 days a week. Other retail establishments usually are open Tuesdays through Saturdays from 10 AM to noon, and from 2 to 6:30 or 7 PM; some also may be open on Mondays (for a full day or just for the afternoon).

Holidays

France shuts down even more thoroughly than the US on public holidays. Banks, offices, stores, museums, and public monuments — even most gas stations — are closed tight, and banks and some offices may close at *noon* the day before as well. The French national holidays are as follows:

New Year's Day (January 1)
Easter Sunday (April 3)
Easter Monday (April 4)

Labor Day (May 1)
V-E Day (May 8)
Ascension Thursday (May 12)
Whitmonday (May 23)
Bastille Day (July 14)
Feast of the Assumption (August 15)
All Saints' Day (November 1)
Armistice Day (November 11)
Christmas Day (December 25)

GETTING READY TELEPHONE

Mail

Post offices in France are indicated by signs with the letters *PTT (Postes, Télécommunications, et Télédiffusion)* or by a sign with a blue bird on a white disk. The main post office in Paris is located at 52 Rue du Louvre, 1er (phone: 1-40-28-20-00) and is open 24 hours. Other post offices are open weekdays from 8 AM to 7 PM and Saturdays from 9 AM to noon. Stamps can be bought at post offices, at *tabacs* (tobacco shops), or at coin-operated vending machines painted yellow. Letter boxes also are yellow.

Although letters sent to the US from France have been known to arrive in as little as 5 days, allow at least 10 days for delivery in either direction. If your correspondence is especially important, you may want to send it via one of the international courier services, such as *Federal Express (Copyshop,* 44 Rue du Colisée, 8e; phone: 40-85-38-88) or *DHL Worldwide Express* (59 Av. d'Iéna, 16e; phone: 45-01-91-00 or 48-63-70-00).

You can have mail sent to you care of your hotel (marked "Guest Mail, Hold for Arrival") or to a post office (the address should include *Poste Restante*–the French equivalent of "General Delivery"). *American Express* offices also will hold mail for customers ("c/o Client Letter Service"); information is provided in the pamphlet *American Express Travelers' Companion.* US Embassies and Consulates abroad will hold mail for US citizens *only* in emergency situations.

Telephone

Direct dialing within the country, between nations, and overseas; operator-assisted calls; collect calls; and other familiar services all are available in France. In addition, many French homes are equipped with a phone computer called a *minitel,* which offers services ranging from the standard telephone listings to brief descriptions of the films currently playing in Paris.

Public telephones are found in post offices, cafés, and in booths on the street. Although some public telephones still take coins, in Paris and other major cities in France, most accept only plastic phone cards called *télécartes.* These cards can be purchased in the US from *Marketing Challenges*

25

International (10 E. 21st St., Suite 600, New York, NY 10010; phone: 212-529-8484), or in France, at post offices, transportation centers, tobacco shops, and newsstands.

All French telephone numbers have 8 digits. To call the Paris/Ile-de-France area from the US, dial 011 (the international access code) + 33 (the country code) + 1 (the city code) + the local 8-digit number. (To call other areas in France, leave off the 1 before the local number; the city code for these numbers is included in the 8-digit local phone number.) The procedure for making a station-to-station call to the US from anywhere in France is to dial 19 (wait for a dial tone) + 1 (the US country code) + the area code + the local number.

France is divided into two zones: Paris/Ile-de-France and the rest of the country — that is, the provinces. The procedures for dialing within France are as follows:

To call within the Paris/Ile-de-France area: Dial the local 8-digit number (beginning with 4, 3, or 6).

To call from the Paris/Ile-de-France area to the provinces: Dial 16 (wait for a dial tone) + the local 8-digit number.

To call from the provinces to the Paris/Ile-de-France area: Dial 16 (wait for a dial tone) + 1 + the local 8-digit number.

To call between provinces: Dial the local 8-digit number.

Long-distance telephone services that help you avoid the surcharges that hotels routinely add to phone bills are provided by *American Telephone and Telegraph* (*AT&T Communications,* International Information Service, 635 Grant St., Pittsburgh, PA 15219; phone: 800-874-4000), *MCI* (323 3rd St. SE, Cedar Rapids, IA 52401; phone: 800-444-3333), *Metromedia Communications Corp.* (1 International Center, 100 NE Loop 410, San Antonio, TX 78216; phone: 800-275-0200), and *Sprint* (offices throughout the US; phone: 800-877-4000). Some hotels still may charge a fee for line usage.

AT&T's Language Line Service (phone: 800-752-6096) provides interpretive services for telephone communications in French. Also useful are the *AT&T 800 Travel Directory* (available at *AT&T Phone Centers* or by calling 800-426-8686), the *Toll-Free Travel & Vacation Information Directory* (Pilot Books, 103 Cooper St., Babylon, NY 11702; phone: 516-422-2225), and *The Phone Booklet* (*Scott American Corporation,* PO Box 88, W. Redding, CT 06896; phone: 203-938-2955).

Important Phone Numbers

Local information and operator: 12.

International operator: 19, wait for dial tone, then 3311.

For emergency assistance:

15 for an ambulance.

17 for the police.

18 for the fire department.

Electricity

Like most other European countries, France runs on 220- or 230-volt, 50-cycle alternating current (AC). Travelers from the US will need electrical converters to operate the appliances they use at home, or dual-voltage appliances, which can be switched from one voltage standard to another. (Some large tourist hotels may offer 110-volt current or may have converters available.) You also will need a plug adapter set to deal with the different plug configurations found in France.

Staying Healthy

For information on current health conditions, call the Centers for Disease Control and Prevention's *International Health Requirements and Recommendations Information Hotline:* 404-332-4559.

Travelers to France — and to Western Europe in general — do not face the same health risks entailed in traveling to many other destinations around the world. Tap water generally is clean and potable — if the water isn't meant for drinking, it should be marked *eau non potable.* Bottled water is readily available in stores. Milk is pasteurized throughout France, and dairy products are safe to eat, as are fruit, vegetables, meat, poultry, and fish. Because of Mediterranean pollution, however, all seafood should be eaten cooked, and make sure it is *fresh,* particularly in the heat of the summer, when inadequate refrigeration is an additional concern.

French hospitals fall into three categories, with the *CHRU* (*Centre Hôpital Régional et Universitaire,* or Central Regional University Hospital), a large, full-service hospital associated with a major medical university, at the top of the list. Others are the *CHR,* which designates a full-service regional hospital, and the *CH,* which means that the hospital is the central one in its town or city (and probably has 24-hour emergency service). France has socialized medicine, and all hospitals are public facilities *(hôpitaux publiques).* Although medical care is free (or relatively inexpensive) for French citizens, this does not apply to travelers from the US. There also are some private clinics *(cliniques privées),* which are like small hospitals and can provide medical aid for less serious conditions.

The **American Hospital** in Paris (63 Bd. Victor-Hugo, Neuilly 92202; phone: 1-46-41-25-25) is a major hospital with 24-hour emergency service and advanced equipment, and all of the staff speaks English. The hospital also has a dental service and maintains an extensive network of English-speaking specialists. *SOS Médecins* has 24-hour house calls by doctors (phone: 1-47-07-77-77). English-speaking dentists in Paris include Dr. Edward Cohen (20 Rue de la Paix, 2e; phone: 1-42-61-65-64) or Dr. Gérard Gautier (47 Av. Hoche, 8e; phone: 1-47-66-17-10). You also can ask at your hotel for the house physician or for help in reaching a doctor or dentist or contact the US Consulate.

French drugstores, called *pharmacies,* are identified by a green cross out front. There should be no problem finding a 24-hour drugstore in Paris. One of these is *Pharmacie Dhéry* (in the *Galerie Les Champs,* 84 Av. Champs-Elysées, 8e, Paris 75008; phone: 1-45-62-02-41). Pharmacists who are closed often provide the addresses of the nearest all-night drugstores in the window. In some areas, night duty may rotate among pharmacies.

In an emergency: Go directly to the emergency room of the nearest hospital, dial one of the emergency numbers given above, or call an operator for assistance.

Additional Resources

International Association of Medical Assistance to Travelers (*IAMAT;* 417 Center St., Lewiston, NY 14092; phone: 716-754-4883).

International Health Care Service (440 E. 69th St., New York, NY 10021; phone: 212-746-1601).

International SOS Assistance (PO Box 11568, Philadelphia, PA 19116; phone: 800-523-8930 or 215-244-1500).

Medic Alert Foundation (2323 Colorado Ave., Turlock, CA 95380; phone: 800-ID-ALERT or 209-668-3333).

TravMed (PO Box 10623, Baltimore, MD 21285-0623; phone: 800-732-5309 or 410-296-5225).

Consular Services

The American Services section of the US Consulate is a vital source of assistance and advice for US citizens abroad. If you are injured or become seriously ill, the Consulate can direct you to sources of medical attention and notify your relatives. If you become involved in a dispute that could lead to legal action, the Consulate is the place to turn. In cases of natural disasters or civil unrest, Consulates handle the evacuation of US citizens if necessary.

The US Embassy is located at 2 Av. Gabriel, Paris 75008, France (phone: 1-42-96-12-02 or 1-42-61-80-75). The US consulate is located at 2 Rue St. Florentin, Paris 75001, France; same phone numbers as the Embassy).

The US State Department operates a 24-hour *Citizens' Emergency Center* travel advisory information hotline (phone: 202-647-5225). **In an emergency, call 202-647-4000 and ask for the duty officer.**

Entry Requirements and Customs Regulations

ENTERING FRANCE

The only document a US citizen needs to enter France or to re-enter the US is a valid US passport. Immigration officers in French airports also *may* want to see that you have sufficient funds for your trip and a return or ongoing ticket. As a general rule, a US passport entitles the bearer to remain in France for up to 90 days as a tourist. A visa is required for study, residency, work, or stays of more than 3 months, and US citizens should contact the French Embassy or Consulate well in advance of a proposed trip. Proof of means of independent financial support during the stay is pertinent to the acceptance of any long-term–stay application. Note that individuals for whom a visa is necessary also must obtain a *Carte de Sejour* (residency permit) at the local police prefecture once they arrive in France.

You are allowed to enter France with the following duty-free: 200 cigarettes or 250 grams of tobacco; 50 cigars; up to 2 liters of wine and either 2 liters of liquor under 44 proof or 1 liter over 44 proof; 50 grams of perfume; a quarter of a liter of cologne; 500 grams of coffee; 40 grams of tea; and items designated as gifts and valued at less than 300F (about $55 per item).

RETURNING TO THE US

You must declare to the US Customs official at the point of entry everything you have acquired in France. The standard duty-free allowance for US citizens is $400; if your trip is shorter than 48 continuous hours, or you have been out of the US within 30 days, it is cut to $25. Families traveling together may make a joint declaration. Antiques (at least 100 years old) and paintings or drawings done entirely by hand are duty-free.

A flat 10% duty is assessed on the next $1,000 worth of merchandise; additional items are taxed at a variety of rates (see *Tariff Schedules of the United States* in a library or any US Customs Service office). With the exception of gifts valued at $50 or less sent directly to the recipient, items shipped home are dutiable. Some articles are duty-free only up to certain limits. The $400 allowance includes 1 carton of (200) cigarettes, 100 cigars (not Cuban), and 1 liter of liquor or wine (for those over 21); the $25 allowance includes 10 cigars, 50 cigarettes, and 4 ounces of perfume. To avoid paying duty unnecessarily, before your trip, register the serial numbers of any expensive equipment you are bringing along with US Customs.

Forbidden imports include articles made of the furs or hides of animals on the endangered species list. In addition, you must obtain a permit from *Safico* (*Service for Financial and Commercial Authorization*, 42 Rue de Clichy, Paris 75436, France; phone: 1-42-81-91-44) or the French customs information center in Paris (phone: 1-40-40-39-00) to take archaeological finds or other original artifacts out of France.

For further information, consult *Know Before You Go; International Mail Imports; Travelers' Tips on Bringing Food, Plant, and Animal Products into the United States; Importing a Car; GSP and the Traveler; Pocket Hints; Currency Reporting;* and *Pets, Wildlife, US Customs;* all available from the US Customs Service (PO Box 7407, Washington, DC 20044). For tape-recorded information on travel-related topics, call 202-927-2095 from any touch-tone phone.

DUTY-FREE SHOPS AND VALUE ADDED TAX Located in international airports, duty-free shops provide bargains on the purchase of foreign goods. But beware: Not all foreign goods are automatically less expensive. You *can* get a good deal on some items, but know what they cost elsewhere.

Value Added Tax (VAT) — called *taxe à la valeur ajoutée (TVA)* in France — is a tax added to the purchase price of most goods and services. For most purchases, visitors are entitled to a refund (the exceptions include antiques and works of art worth over 30,000F, gold, food, wine, medicine, and tobacco). For information about minimum purchase requirements and refund procedures, contact the French Government Tourist Office.

For Further Information

In the US, branches of the **French Government Tourist Office** are the best sources of travel information. Offices generally are open on weekdays, during normal business hours, although they do not accept telephone inquiries. Tourist information is available through a "900" number telephone hotline called "France on Call" (phone: 900-990-0040); the cost is 50¢ per minute. (There is no charge for information requested by mail or in person.) A number of free publications also are available through this service, including the 1994 *France Discovery Guide;* the *American Express Welcome Center Directory;* and the *AT&T France Fun Book,* which includes 100 coupons good for discounts on shopping, restaurants, museums, and other tourist attractions. In France, *American Express* provides an English-language toll-free travel information hotline (phone: 05-20-12-02).

French Government Tourist Offices

California: 9454 Wilshire Blvd., Suite 303, Beverly Hills, CA 90212-2967 (phone: 310-271-6665).

Illinois: 645 N. Michigan Ave., Suite 630, Chicago, IL 60611 (phone: 312-337-6301).

New York: *walk-in office on street level:* 628 Fifth Ave., New York, NY 10020 (phone: 212-757-1125); *mail inquiries only:* 610 Fifth Ave., New York, NY 10020-2452.

Texas: 2305 Cedar Springs Rd., Suite 205, Dallas, TX 75201 (phone: 214-720-4010).

NOTE Once you have arrived in France, you can take advantage of a computerized information system called *minitel*. Computer terminals are available in the lobbies of most French hotels rated two stars or above, as well as in many post offices.

Useful Words and Phrases

Useful Words and Phrases

The French as a nation have a reputation for being snobbish and brusque to tourists, and, unfortunately, many Americans have allowed this stereotype to affect their appreciation of France. The more experienced traveler, however, knows that on an individual basis, the French people are usually cordial and helpful, especially if you speak a few words of their language. Don't be afraid of misplaced accents or misconjugated verbs — in most cases you will be understood.

The list below of commonly used words and phrases can help you get started.

Greetings and Everyday Expressions

Good morning! (Hello!)	*Bonjour!*
Good afternoon, good evening!	*Bonsoir!*
How are you?	*Comment allez-vous?*
Pleased to meet you!	*Enchanté!*
Good-bye!	*Au revoir!*
See you soon!	*A bientôt!*
Good night!	*Bonne nuit!*
Yes!	*Oui!*
No!	*Non!*
Please!	*S'il vous plaît!*
Thank you!	*Merci!*
You're welcome!	*De rien!*
Excuse me!	*Excusez-moi* or *pardonnez-moi!*
It doesn't matter.	*Ca m'est égal.*
I don't speak French.	*Je ne parle pas français.*
Do you speak English?	*Parlez-vous anglais?*
Please repeat.	*Répétez, s'il vous plaît.*
I don't understand.	*Je ne comprends pas.*
Do you understand?	*Vous comprenez?*
My name is . . .	*Je m'appelle . . .*
What is your name?	*Comment vous appelez-vous?*
miss	*mademoiselle*
madame	*madame*
mister/sir	*monsieur*
open	*ouvert*
closed	*fermé*
entrance	*l'entrée*

exit	*la sortie*
push	*poussez*
pull	*tirez*
today	*aujourd'hui*
tomorrow	*demain*
yesterday	*hier*
Help!	*Au secours!*
ambulance	*l'ambulance*
Get a doctor!	*Appelez le médecin!*

Checking In

I have (don't have) a reservation.	*J'ai une (Je n'ai pas de) réservation.*
I would like . . .	*Je voudrais . . .*
a single room	*une chambre pour une personne*
a double room	*une chambre pour deux*
a quiet room	*une chambre tranquille*
with bath	*avec salle de bains*
with shower	*avec douche*
with a view of the Seine	*avec une vue sur la Seine*
with air conditioning	*une chambre climatisée*
with balcony	*avec balcon*
overnight only	*pour une nuit seulement*
a few days	*quelques jours*
a week (at least)	*une semaine (au moins)*
with full board	*avec pension complète*
with half board	*avec demi-pension*
Does that price include breakfast?	*Est-ce que le petit déjeuner est inclus?*
Are taxes included?	*Est-ce que les taxes sont comprises?*
Do you accept traveler's checks?	*Acceptez-vous les chèques de voyage?*
Do you accept credit cards?	*Acceptez-vous les cartes de crédit?*

Eating Out

ashtray	*un cendrier*
bottle	*une bouteille*
(extra) chair	*une chaise (en sus)*
cup	*une tasse*
fork	*une fourchette*
knife	*un couteau*
spoon	*une cuillère*
napkin	*une serviette*

plate	*une assiette*
table	*une table*
beer	*bière*
coffee	*café*
black coffee	* café noir*
coffee with milk	* café au lait*
cream	*crème*
fruit juice	*jus de fruit*
lemonade	*citron pressé*
milk	*lait*
mineral water (non-carbonated)	*l'eau minérale*
mineral water (carbonated)	*l'eau gazeuse*
orangeade	*orange pressée*
port	*vin de porto*
sherry	*vin de Xérès*
red wine	*vin rouge*
white wine	*vin blanc*
rosé	*rosé*
tea	*thé*
water	*eau*
cold	*froid*
hot	*chaud*
sweet	*doux*
(very) dry	*(très) sec*
bacon	*bacon*
bread	*pain*
butter	*beurre*
eggs	*oeufs*
soft boiled	* à la coque*
hard boiled	* oeuf dur*
fried	* sur le plat*
scrambled	* brouillé*
poached	* poché*
ham	*jambon*
honey	*miel*
sugar	*sucre*
jam	*confiture*
juice	*jus*
orange	* jus d'orange*
tomato	* jus de tomate*
omelette	*omelette*
pepper	*poivre*
salt	*sel*

| Waiter! | Garçon! |
| Waitress! | Mademoiselle! |

I would like	Je voudrais
a glass of	un verre de
a bottle of	une bouteille de
a half bottle of	une demie-bouteille
a liter of	un litre de
a carafe of	une carafe de

The check, please.	L'addition, s'il vous plaît.
Is the service charge included?	Le service, est-il compris?
I think there is a mistake in	Je crois qu'il y a une erreur
the bill.	dans l'addition.

Shopping

bakery	boulangerie
bookstore	librairie
butcher store	boucherie
camera shop	magasin de photographie
clothing store	magasin de vêtements
delicatessen	charcuterie
department store	grand magasin
drugstore (for medicine)	pharmacie
grocery	épicerie
jewelry store	bijouterie
newsstand	kiosque à journaux
notions (sewing supplies) shop	mercerie
pastry shop	pâtisserie
perfume (and cosmetics) store	parfumerie
pharmacy/drugstore	pharmacie
shoestore	magasin de chaussures
supermarket	supermarché
tobacconist	bureau de tabac

| inexpensive | bon marché |
| expensive | cher |

large	grand
larger	plus grand
too large	trop grand
small	petit
smaller	plus petit
too small	trop petit

long	long
short	court
old	vieux

new	*nouveau*
used	*d'occasion*
handmade	*fabriqué à la main*
Is it machine washable?	*Est-ce que c'est lavable à la machine?*
How much does this cost?	*Quel est le prix?/Combien?*
What is it made of?	*De quoi est-ce fait?*
camel's hair	*poil de chameau*
cotton	*coton*
corduroy	*velours côtelé*
filigree	*filigrane*
lace	*dentelle*
leather	*cuir*
linen	*lin*
silk	*soie*
suede	*suède*
synthetic	*synthétique*
wool	*laine*
brass	*cuivre jaune*
copper	*cuivre*
gold (plated)	*or (plaqué)*
silver (plated)	*argent (plaqué)*
wood	*bois*
May I have a sales tax rebate form?	*Puis-je avoir le formulaire pour la détaxe?*
May I pay with this credit card?	*Puis-je payer par cette carte de crédit?*
May I pay with a traveler's check?	*Puis-je payer avec chèques de voyage?*

Getting around

north	*le nord*
south	*le sud*
east	*l'est*
west	*l'ouest*
right	*droite*
left	*gauche*
Go straight ahead	*tout droit*
far	*loin*
near	*proche*
airport	*l'aéroport*
bus stop	*l'arrêt de bus*

gas station	station service
train station	la gare
subway	le métro
map	carte
one-way ticket	aller simple
round-trip ticket	un billet aller et retour
gate	porte
track	voie
in first class	en première classe
in second class	en deuxième classe
no smoking	défense de fumer

Does this subway/bus   *Est-ce que ce métro/bus*
    go to . . . ?   *va à . . . ?*
What time does it leave?   *A quelle heure part-il?*

gas	essence
regular (leaded)	ordinaire
super (leaded)	super
unleaded	sans plomb
diesel	diesel
Fill it up, please.	Le plein, s'il vous plaît.

| the tires | pneus |
| the oil | huile |

Danger	Danger
Caution	Attention
Detour	Déviation
Dead End	Cul-de-sac
Do Not Enter	Défense d'entrer
No Parking	Défense de stationner
No Passing	Défense de dépasser
No U-turn	Défense de faire demi-tour
One way	Sens unique
Pay toll	Péage
Pedestrian Zone	Zone piétonne
Reduce Speed	Ralentissez
Steep Incline	Côte à forte inclination
Stop	Stop; Arrêt
Use Headlights	Allumez les phares
Yield	Cédez le passage
Where is the . . . ?	Où se trouve . . . ?
How many kilometers are we	A combien de kilomètres
from . . . ?	sommes nous de . . . ?

Personal Items and Services

aspirin	*aspirine*
Band-Aids	*sparadrap*
barbershop	*coiffeur pour hommes*
bath	*bain*
bathroom	*salle de bain*
beauty shop	*salon de coiffure*
condom	*préservatif*
dentist	*dentiste*
disposable diapers	*couches*
dry cleaner	*nettoyage à sec*
hairdresser	*coiffeur pour dames*
laundromat	*laundrette* or *blanchisserie automatique*
post office	*bureau de poste*
postage stamps (airmail)	*timbres (par avion)*
razor	*rasoir*
sanitary napkins	*serviettes hygiéniques*
shampoo	*shampooing*
shaving cream	*crème à raser*
shower	*douche*
soap	*savon*
tampons	*tampons*
tissues	*tissus*
toilet	*toilettes* or *WC*
toilet paper	*papier hygiénique*
toothbrush	*brosse à dents*
toothpaste	*dentifrice*

Where is the men's/ladies' room?   *Où sont les toilettes?*

Days of the Week

Monday	*lundi*
Tuesday	*mardi*
Wednesday	*mercredi*
Thursday	*jeudi*
Friday	*vendredi*
Saturday	*samedi*
Sunday	*dimanche*

Months

January	*janvier*
February	*février*
March	*mars*
April	*avril*
May	*mai*

June	*juin*
July	*juillet*
August	*août*
September	*septembre*
October	*octobre*
November	*novembre*
December	*décembre*

Numbers

zero	*zéro*
one	*un*
two	*deux*
three	*trois*
four	*quatre*
five	*cinq*
six	*six*
seven	*sept*
eight	*huit*
nine	*neuf*
ten	*dix*
eleven	*onze*
twelve	*douze*
thirteen	*treize*
fourteen	*quatorze*
fifteen	*quinze*
sixteen	*seize*
seventeen	*dix-sept*
eighteen	*dix-huit*
nineteen	*dix-neuf*
twenty	*vingt*
twenty-one	*vingt-et-un*
thirty	*trente*
forty	*quarante*
fifty	*cinquante*
sixty	*soixante*
seventy	*soixante-dix*
eighty	*quatre-vingts*
ninety	*quatre-vingt-dix*
one hundred	*cent*
1994	*mille neuf cent quatre-vingt quatre*

Colors

black	*noir*
blue	*bleu*
brown	*marron*

gray	*gris*
green	*vert*
orange	*orange*
pink	*rose*
purple	*violet*
red	*rouge*
yellow	*jaune*
white	*blanc*

Writing Reservations Letters

Restaurant/Hotel Name
Street Address
Postal Code, City
France

Dear Sir:

    I would like to reserve a table for (number of) persons for lunch/dinner on (day and month), 199?, at (hour) o'clock.

or

    I would like to reserve a room for (number of) people for (number of) nights.

    Would you be so kind as to confirm the reservation as soon as possible?

    I am very much looking forward to meeting you. (The French usually include a pleasantry such as this.)

    With my thanks,

(Signature, followed by your typed name and address)

Monsieur:

    Je voudrais réserver une table pour (number) personnes pour le déjeuner/dîner du (day and month) 199?, à (time using the 24-hour clock) heures.

or

    Je voudrais réserver une chambre à (number) personne(s) pour (number) nuits.

    Auriez-vous la bonté de bien vouloir me confirmer cette réservation dès que possible?

    J'attends avec impatience la chance de faire votre connaissance.

    Avec tous mes remerciements,

The City

Paris

Victor Hugo, the great French poet and novelist, captured the true spirit of his native city when he called it "the heir of Rome, the mundane pilgrim's home away from home." If Rome, for all its earthly exuberance, never lets a visitor forget that it is the spiritual home of the West, Paris — with its supreme joie de vivre and its passion for eating, drinking, and dressing well — belongs unabashedly to the material world.

Like a magnet, Paris always has attracted visitors and exiles from all corners of the earth. At the same time, it remains not so much an international city as a very French one, and a provincial one at that. Paris has its own argot, and each neighborhood retains its peculiar character, so that the great capital is still very much a city of 20 villages.

But parochialism aside — and forgetting about the consummate haughtiness of Parisians (someone once remarked that Parisians don't even like themselves) — the main attraction of the City of Light is its beauty. When you speak of the ultimate European city, it must be Paris, if only for the view from the Place de la Concorde or the Tuileries up the Champs-Elysées toward the Arc de Triomphe, or similarly striking sights beside the Seine. Here is the fashion capital of the world and the center of gastronomic invention and execution. Here the men all seem to swagger with the insouciance of privilege, and even the humblest shopgirl dresses with the care of a haute couture mannequin. Paris is the reason "foreign" means "French" to so many travelers.

Paris, roughly elliptical in shape, is in the north-central part of France, in the rich agricultural area of the Seine River Valley. With a population of over 2 million people, it is France's largest city, an industrial and commercial hub, an important river port, as well as an undisputed center for arts and culture. The city has more than doubled in size in the last century; however, the population has decreased in the past decade as residential buildings are converted to offices and the city becomes increasingly too expensive for all but the very rich. Its limits now are the ring of mid-19th-century fortifications that once were well beyond its boundaries. At its western edge is the vast Bois de Boulogne and to the east the Bois de Vincennes — two enormous parks. Curving through Paris, the Seine divides the city into its northern Right Bank (La Rive Droite) and southern Left Bank (La Rive Gauche). The Right Bank extends from the Bois de Boulogne on the far west, through Place Charles-de-Gaulle (l'Etoile), which surrounds the Arc de Triomphe, and farther east to the Tuileries Gardens and the fabulous *Louvre*. North of the *Louvre* is the area of the Grands Boulevards, centers of business and fashion; farther north is the district of Montmartre, built on a hill and crowned by the domed Basilica of Sacré-Coeur, an area that has attracted artists since the days of Monet and Renoir.

The Left Bank sweeps from the Eiffel Tower on the west through the Latin Quarter, with its university and bohemian and intellectual community. Southwest of the Latin Quarter is Montparnasse, once inhabited jointly by artists and intellectuals and laborers, now a large urban renewal project that includes a suburban-style shopping center around the Tour Montparnasse. To the south of Montparnasse are charming, turn-of-the-century, middle class residential districts.

In the middle of the Seine are two islands, the Ile de la Cité and the Ile St-Louis, the oldest parts of Paris. It was on the Ile de la Cité (in the 3rd century BC) that Celtic fishermen known as Parisii first built a settlement they named Lutetia, "place surrounded by water." Caesar conquered the city for Rome in 52 BC, and in about AD 300, Paris was invaded by Germanic tribes, the strongest of which were the Franks. In 451, when Attila the Hun threatened to overrun Paris, a holy woman named Geneviève promised to defend the city by praying. She succeeded — the enemy decided to spare the capital — and Geneviève became the patron saint of Paris. Clovis I, the first Christian King of the Franks, made Paris his capital in the 6th century. Relentless Norman sieges, famine, and plague curtailed the city's development, but at the end of the 10th century peace and prosperity came with the triumph of Hugh Capet over the Carolingians. Capet ascended the throne, the first of a long line of Capetian kings, and Paris became the "central jewel of the French crown," a great cultural center and seat of learning.

The Capetian monarchs contributed much to the growth of the city over the next few centuries. A defensive wall was begun in 1180 by Philip Augustus to protect the expanding Right Bank business and trading center, as well as the intellectual quarter around the newly formed university on the Left Bank. He then built a new royal palace, the *Louvre*, just outside these ramparts, but he never lived there. Medieval Paris was a splendid city, a leader in the arts and in the intellectual life of Europe. The Sorbonne attracted such outstanding scholars as Alexander of Hales, Giovanni di Fidanza (St. Bonaventure), Albertus Magnus, and Thomas Aquinas.

The Ile de la Cité remained a warren of narrow streets and wood and plaster houses, but the banks of the Seine continued to be built up in both directions. Renaissance kings, patrons of the arts, added their own architectural and aesthetic embellishments to the flourishing city. Major streets were laid out; some of Paris's most charming squares were constructed; the Pont-Neuf, the first stone bridge spanning the Seine, was completed; and Lenôtre, the royal gardener, introduced proportion, harmony, and beauty with his extraordinary Tuileries.

Louis XIV, who was responsible for many of the most notable Parisian landmarks, including Les Invalides, moved the court to Versailles in the late 17th century (for more information on Versailles, see *Celebrated Cathedrals and Châteaux Within an Hour of Paris* in DIVERSIONS). Paris nevertheless continued to blossom, and it was under the Sun King's rule that

France and Paris first won international prestige. Visitors were drawn to the city, luxury trades were begun, and the Panthéon, Champ-de-Mars parade ground, and Ecole Militaire were built. In 1785, at age 16, Napoleon Bonaparte graduated from this military school with the notation in his report: "Will go far if circumstances permit!"

French history reflects the conflict between the two extremes of the French character, both equally strong: a tradition of aristocracy and a penchant for revolution. To the French aristocracy we owe magnificent palaces like the *Louvre,* the Luxembourg Palace, and Versailles, with their formal gardens. At the same time, the people of Paris have always been noisily rebellious and independent: from 1358, when the mob rebelled against the dauphin, to the Fronde in 1648–49, the great French Revolution of 1789, the 1830 and 1848 revolutions that reverberated throughout Europe, the Paris Commune of 1870–71, and finally the student rebellion of 1968, which nearly overthrew the Fifth Republic. The most profound one of all was the French Revolution at the close of the 18th century, the bicentennial of which was celebrated in grand style in 1989.

The excesses of the French court, the consummate luxury of the Versailles of Louis XIV, cost the French people dearly in taxes and oppression. The Parisians, fiercely independent, forced the French king to his knees with their dramatic storming of the Bastille in 1789. Inspired by the ideas of the French and English philosophers of the Enlightenment, just like the American founding fathers in 1776, the French subsequently overthrew their monarchy.

During the Revolution, unruly mobs damaged many of the city's buildings, including Ste-Chapelle and Notre-Dame, which were not restored until the mid-19th century. Napoleon, who came to power in 1799, was too busy being a conqueror to complete all he planned, though he did manage to restore the *Louvre,* construct the Carrousel Arch and Place Vendôme victory column, and begin work on the Arc de Triomphe and the Madeleine. Though he was something of a tyrant, Napoleon's conquests spread the new ideas of the Revolution — including the Code Napoléon, a system of laws embodying the ideals of "Liberty, Equality, Fraternity" — to places as far away as Canada and Moscow.

Later in the 19th century, Paris was reorganized and modernized by a great urban planner, Baron Haussmann. He instituted the brilliant system of squares as focal points for marvelous, wide boulevards and roads; he planned the Place de l'Opéra, the Bois de Boulogne and Bois de Vincennes, the railway stations, the boulevards, and the system of 20 *arrondissements* (districts) that make up Paris today. He also destroyed most of the center of the old Cité, displacing 25,000 people.

During the peaceful lull between the Franco-Prussian War and World War I, Paris thrived as never before. These were the days of the Belle Epoque, the heyday of *Maxim's,* the *Folies-Bergère,* and the cancan, whose spirit is captured so well in Offenbach's heady music for *Gaieté Parisienne*. Montmartre, immortalized by Toulouse-Lautrec, was so uninhibited that the foreign press dubbed Paris the "City of Sin."

In the 2 decades before World War II, this free-spirited city attracted politically and socially exiled artists by the dozens: Picasso, Hemingway, Fitzgerald, and Gertrude Stein were just a few. Only in Paris could such avant-garde writers as James Joyce and D. H. Lawrence, and later, Henry Miller, find publishers. And Paris, which witnessed the first Impressionist exhibition in 1874 — introducing Monet, Renoir, Pissarro, and Seurat — heard the first performance of Stravinsky's revolutionary "Sacre du Printemps" (Rite of Spring) in 1913, even though the baffled audience jeered loudly.

As the quintessentially beautiful center of intellectual life and home of the arts, Paris can claim to have earned its City of Light title. Even though it, like other modern cities, is troubled by a rise in crime, its beauty and libertarian atmosphere remain. Its supreme talent for civilized living has made the city beloved by the French and foreigners alike. After all, these are the people who made food preparation a fine art, and despite the unfortunate presence of fast-food vendors on the Champs-Elysées, the French passion for haute cuisine remains unrivaled. And as the undisputed capital of fashion, male and female, Paris continues to be the best-dressed city in the world, and the Rue du Faubourg-St-Honoré remains the standard by which all other shopping streets are measured.

However avant-garde in dress, Parisians are a conservative lot when it comes to any changes in the appearance of their beloved city. When the Eiffel Tower was built in 1889, Guy de Maupassant commented, "I spend all my afternoons on the Eiffel Tower; it's the only place in Paris from which I can't see it." Not long ago, Parisians grumbled about the ultramodern *Centre Georges-Pompidou,* now a focus for every type of applied and performing art, and about *Le Forum des Halles,* a sunken glass structure filled with boutiques in what was once *Les Halles,* the bawdy produce market. Today these are popular tourist attractions, and the symbols of the new, modern Paris. More recent issues that have sparked criticism and controversy include the I. M. Pei glass pyramids that now form the entrance to the *Louvre,* and a project to replace the Bibliothèque Nationale with a giant, glass library. Located on Paris's eastern edge in the redeveloped Bercy district, the library is seen by many as an unnecessary expense, especially in a time of recession. On the brighter side, the now rather tacky Champs-Elysées is undergoing a face-lift, and the recently repaved center of the glorious Place Vendôme, once virtually clogged with cars, is now a pedestrians-only zone.

Parisians accept innovations reluctantly because they want their city to remain as it has always been. They love their remarkable heritage inordinately, and perhaps it is this love, together with the irrepressible sense of good living, that has made Paris so eternally attractive to others.

Paris At-a-Glance

SEEING THE CITY

It's impossible to single out just one perfect Paris panorama; they exist in profusion. The most popular is the bird's-eye view from the top of the Eiffel Tower on the Left Bank; there are several places to have snacks and drinks and enjoy a view (on a clear day) of more than 50 miles. (There also are three restaurants where you can enjoy fine dining; see *Special Places*.) From the top of the towers of Notre-Dame, spectators enjoy close-ups of the cathedral's Gothic spires and flying buttresses, along with a magnificent view of the Ile de la Cité and the rest of Paris (see *Special Places*). Start climbing the steps at the foot of the north tower. On the Right Bank there's a stunning view from the terrace of Sacré-Coeur. The observatory on Tour Montparnasse also offers a striking panorama, as does the landing at the top of the escalator at the *Centre Georges-Pompidou,* and the observation deck of *Samaritaine,* the 6-floor department store at the foot of the Pont-Neuf.

The most satisfying view, if not the highest, is from the top of the Arc de Triomphe. The arch is the center of Place Charles-de-Gaulle, once Place de l'Etoile (Square of the Star), so called because it is the center of a "star" whose radiating points are the 12 broad avenues, including the Champs-Elysées, planned and built by Baron Haussmann in the mid-19th century (see *Special Places*). Another spectacular cityscape can be seen from the Grande Arche de la Défense. Located just to the west of the city, the Grande Arche completes the axis that starts at the *Louvre* and runs through the Champs-Elysées and the Arc de Triomphe. Open Mondays through Fridays, 9 AM to 5 PM, and Saturdays and Sundays from 10 AM to 7 PM; in July and August, open to 7 PM Sundays through Thursdays; to 9 PM Fridays, Saturdays and holidays. Admission charge. 1 Cour de la Défense, Puteaux (phone: 49-07-27-57).

SPECIAL PLACES

Getting around this sprawling metropolis isn't difficult once you understand the layout of the 20 *arrondissements* (districts). We suggest that visitors orient themselves by taking one of the many excellent sightseeing tours offered by *Cityrama* (4 Pl. des Pyramides, 1er; phone: 42-60-30-14) or *Paris Vision* (214 Rue de Rivoli, 1er; phone: 42-60-31-25). Their bubble-top, double-decker buses are equipped with earphones for simultaneous commentary in English and several other languages. Reserve through any travel agent or your hotel's concierge.

Once you have a better idea of the basic layout of the city, buy a copy of *Paris Indispensable* or *Plan de Paris par Arrondissement* at any bookshop or newsstand. These little lifesavers list streets alphabetically and indicate the nearest métro station on individual maps and an overall plan.

Now you're ready to set out by foot (the most rewarding) or by métro (the fastest and surest) to discover Paris for yourself.

Street addresses of the places mentioned throughout the chapter are followed by their *arrondissement* number.

> **NOTE** The *Carte Musées et Monuments* (museum and monuments pass) allows you to avoid ticket-buyer lines and go directly in to view the collections in 65 museums in and near Paris. Available in 1-, 3- or 5-day passes, the carte is sold in métro stations, museums, or at the Paris Tourist Office (see *Tourist Information*). "La Carte" is also available in the US from Marketing Challengers International, 10 E. 21st St., New York, NY 10010 (phone: 212-529-8484). Note that "La Carte" is not valid for certain special exhibits.

LA RIVE DROITE (THE RIGHT BANK)

ARC DE TRIOMPHE AND PLACE CHARLES-DE-GAULLE This monumental arch (165 feet high, 148 feet wide) was built between 1806 and 1836 to commemorate Napoleon's victories. It underwent a major cleanup and restoration for the bicentennial of the French Revolution. Note the frieze and its 6-foot-high figures, the ten impressive sculptures (especially Rude's *La Marseillaise* on the right as you face the Champs-Elysées), and the arches inscribed with the names of Bonaparte's victories, as well as those of Empire heroes. Beneath the arch is the French Tomb of the Unknown Soldier and its Eternal Flame, which is rekindled each day at 6:30 PM. An elevator (or 284 steps) carries visitors to the top for a magnificent view of the city and the 12 avenues radiating from l'Etoile. Open daily from 10 AM to 5:30 PM (in winter to 5 PM; admission charge. Pl. Charles-de-Gaulle, 8e (phone: 43-80-31-31).

CHAMPS-ELYSÉES Paris's legendary promenade, the "Elysian Fields," was swampland until 1616. It once was synonymous with everything glamorous in the city, but the "Golden Arches" and schlocky shops recently have replaced much of the old glamour (happily, restoration of some of the old elegance and the "greening" of what Parisians call the "Champs" is under way). The Champs-Elysées stretches for more than 2 miles between the Place de la Concorde and the Place Charles-de-Gaulle (l'Etoile). The very broad avenue, lined with rows of plane and horse chestnut trees, shops, cafés, and cinemas, still is perfect for strolling, window shopping, and people watching.

The area from the Place de la Concorde to the Rond-Point des Champs-Elysées is a charming park, where Parisians often bring their children. On the north side of the gardens is the Palais de l'Elysée, the official home of the President of the French Republic. Ceremonial events, such as the *Bastille Day Parade* (July 14), frequently take place along the Champs-Elysées.

GRAND PALAIS Off the Champs-Elysées, on opposite sides of Avenue Winston-Churchill, are the elaborate turn-of-the-century *Grand Palais* and *Petit Palais* (Large Palace and Small Palace), built of glass and stone for the *1900 World Exposition.* With its stone columns, mosaic frieze, and flat glass dome, the *Grand Palais* contains a large area devoted to temporary exhibits, as well as the *Palais de la Découverte* (the Paris science museum and the planetarium). Open 10 AM until 8 PM; to 10 PM on Wednesdays. Closed Tuesdays. Admission charge. Av. Franklin-Roosevelt, 8e (phone: 44-13-17-17).

PETIT PALAIS Built contemporaneously with the *Grand Palais,* it has exhibits of the city's history, as well as a variety of fine and applied arts and special shows. Open 10 AM to 5:40 PM. Closed Mondays and holidays. Admission charge. Av. Winston-Churchill, 8e (phone: 42-65-12-73).

PLACE DE LA CONCORDE This square, surely one of the most magnificent in the world, is grandly situated in the midst of equally grand landmarks: the *Louvre* and the Tuileries on one side, the Champs-Elysées and the Arc de Triomphe on another, the Seine and the Napoleonic Palais Bourbon on a third, and the pillared façade of the Madeleine on the fourth. Designed by Gabriel for Louis XV, the elegant square was where his unfortunate successor, Louis XVI, lost his head to the guillotine, as did Marie-Antoinette, Danton, Robespierre, Charlotte Corday, and others. It was first named for Louis XV, then called Place de la Révolution by the triumphant revolutionaries. Ornamenting the square, the eight colossal statues representing important French provincial capitals were polished and blasted clean for the bicentennial celebration in 1989. The 3,300-year-old, 75-foot-high obelisk was a gift from Egypt in 1829.

JARDIN DES TUILERIES Carefully laid out in patterned geometric shapes, with clipped shrubbery and formal flower beds, statues, and fountains, this is one of the finest examples of French garden design (in contrast to an informal English garden, exemplified by the Bois de Boulogne). It is currently undergoing extensive renovations which will be completed in 1996. Along the Seine, between the Place de la Concorde and the *Louvre.*

ORANGERIE A museum on the southwestern edge of the Tuileries gardens, it displays a series of large paintings of water lilies by Monet called the *Nymphéas* and the collection of Jean Walter and Paul Guillaume, with works by Cézanne, Renoir, Matisse, Picasso, and others. Open 9:45 AM to 5:15 PM; closed Tuesdays. Admission charge. Pl. de la Concorde and Quai des Tuileries, 1er (phone: 42-97-48-16).

JEU DE PAUME Renovated and reopened as a gallery for contemporary art in 1991, this is the latest expansion in the Grand *Louvre* project that began with the opening of the I. M. Pei pyramids. Facing the Place de la Concorde on the northeastern corner of the Tuileries opposite the *Orangerie* — and originally an indoor tennis court for royalty — the *Jeu de Paume* is one of the most historic buildings in Paris; in 1789, delegates met here to declare their independence, marking the beginning of the French Revolution. Extensively modernized, the museum now houses exhibitions of contemporary works from 1960 on, including those of Takis, Broodthears, and Dubuffet. Previously home to the *Louvre*'s Impressionist collection (now in the *Musée d'Orsay*; see below), it has video and conference areas available. Open Wednesdays through Fridays from noon to 7 PM; Tuesdays noon to 9:30 PM;) weekends 10 AM to 7 PM. Pl. de la Concorde, 1er (phone: 47-03-12-50).

RUE DE RIVOLI This charming old street has perfume shops, souvenir stores, boutiques, bookstores, cafés, and such hotels as the *Meurice* and the *Inter-Continental* under its 19th-century arcades. The section facing the Tuileries, from the Place de la Concorde to the *Louvre*, is an especially good place to explore on rainy days, although much of the merchandise sold here is not of the highest quality.

LOUVRE This colossus on the Seine, born in 1200 as a fortress and transformed over the centuries from Gothic mass to Renaissance palace, served as the royal residence in the 16th and 17th centuries. It was then supplanted by suburban Versailles, becoming a museum when François I donated a dozen masterpieces from his private collection. Napoleon later turned it into a glittering warehouse of artistic booty from the nations he conquered. Today, its 200 galleries cover some 40 acres; to view all 297,000 items in the collections in no more than the most cursory fashion, it would be necessary to walk some 8 miles. In addition to the *Mona Lisa, Venus de Milo,* and the *Winged Victory of Samothrace,* it has many delights that are easily overlooked — Vermeer's *Lace Maker* and Holbein's *Portrait of Erasmus,* for instance; not to mention van der Weyden's *Braque Triptych,* Ingres's *Turkish Bath,* Dürer's *Self-Portrait,* Cranach's naked and red-hatted *Venus,* and the exquisite 4,000-year-old Egyptian woodcarving known as the *Handmaiden of the Dead.* More of our favorites include Michelangelo's *The Dying Slave* and *The Bound Slave,* Goya's *Marquesa de la Solana,* Watteau's clown *Gilles* and his *Embarkation for Cythera,* Raphael's great portrait *Baldassare Castiglione,* Veronese's *Marriage at Cana,* Titian's masterpiece *Man with a Glove,* both *The Penitent Magdalen* and *The Card Sharps* by Georges de la Tour, Rembrandt's *Bathsheba,* and Frans Hals's *Bohemian Girl.* Try to save time for any one of David's glories: *Madame Récamier, The Oath of the Horatii, The Lictors Bringing Back to Brutus the Body of His Son,* or *The Coronation of Napoleon and Josephine.* And don't miss *Liberty Leading the People* and *The Bark of Dante,* both by Delacroix, and Courbet's *The Artist's Studio, Burial at Ornans,* and *Stags Fighting* — just for openers!

Nor is the outside of this huge edifice to be overlooked. Note especially the Cour Carrée (the courtyard of the old *Louvre*), the southwest corner of which, dating from the mid-1550s, is the oldest part of the palace and a beautiful example of the Renaissance style that François I had so recently introduced from Italy; renovation of the Cour Carrée and other sections of the museum are in progress. Note, too, the Colonnade, which forms the eastern front of the Cour Carrée, facing the Place du Louvre; fully classical in style, it dates from the late 1660s, not too long before the Sun King left for Versailles. Newer wings of the *Louvre* embrace the palace gardens, in the midst of which stands the Arc de Triomphe du Carrousel, erected by Napoleon. (Extensive ongoing renovation of the *Louvre* and its gardens — scheduled for early 1996 completion — has uncovered vestiges of Gallo-Roman structures, which will be displayed in the museum.) From here, the vista across the Tuileries and the Place de la Concorde and on up the Champs-Elysées to the Arc de Triomphe is one of the most beautiful in Paris — which says a lot. The glass pyramids — designed by I. M. Pei and opened in 1989 — sit center stage in the *Louvre*'s grand interior courtyard, and the largest of the intrusive trio now is the museum's main entrance. The controversial structure now houses the *Louvre*'s underground galleries and shops, along with an exhibit space that connects the North and South wings, increasing museum exposition space by almost 80%.

Good guided tours in English, covering the highlights of the *Louvre,* are frequently available, although not every day, so be sure to check in advance. Open from 9 AM to 6 PM; Mondays and Wednesdays from 9 AM to 10 PM; closed Tuesdays. Admission charge. Pl. du Louvre, 1er (phone: 40-20-51-51 for recorded information in French and English, or 40-20-50-50 for more detailed information).

NOTE For a modest price ($15 and up at press time), you can also take home a bit of the *Louvre*. The museum's 200-year-old Department of Calcography houses a collection of 16,000 engraved copper plates — renderings of monuments, battles, coronations, Egyptian pyramids, and portraits — dating from the 17th century. Prints made from these engravings come reproduced on thick vellum, embossed with the *Louvre*'s imprint. The Calcography Department (open daily, except Tuesdays, from 2 to 5 PM) is 1 flight up from the Porte Barbet de Jouy entrance on the Seine side of the *Louvre*.

PLACE VENDÔME Just north of the Tuileries is an aristocrat of a square, one of the loveliest in Paris, the octagonal Place Vendôme, designed by Mansart in the 17th century. Now primarily a pedestrian zone, its arcades contain world-famous jewelers, perfumers, and banks, the *Ritz* hotel, and the Ministry of Justice. The 144-foot column in the center is covered with bronze from the 1,200 cannon captured at Austerlitz by Napoleon in 1805. Just off Place Vendôme is the famous Rue du Faubourg-St-Honoré, one of the oldest streets in Paris, which now holds elegant shops selling the world's most expensive made-to-order items. To the north is the Rue de la Paix, noted for its jewelers.

OPÉRA Charles Garnier's imposing rococo edifice stands in its own busy square, its façade decorated with sculpture, including a copy of Carpeaux's *The Dance* (the original is now in the *Musée d'Orsay*). The ornate interior has an impressive grand staircase, a beautiful foyer, lavish marble from every quarry in France, and Chagall's controversially decorated dome. These days, the opera house is home to the *National Ballet,* while almost all operatic performances have been relocated to the *Opéra de la Bastille.* Visitors may explore its magnificent interior and enjoy its special exhibitions daily from 11 AM to 4:30 PM, except on Sundays in August and on days when there are special performances. Admission charge. Pl. de l'Opéra, 9e (phone: 40-01-17-89).

OPÉRA DE LA BASTILLE In sharp contrast to Garnier's *Opéra* is the curved glass façade of 20th-century architect Carlos Ott's new Paris opera house. Set against the historic landscape of the Bastille quarter, this austere, futuristic structure houses over 30 acres of multipurpose theaters, shops, and urban promenades. Inaugurated for the bicentennial of the revolution on July 14, 1989, the opera house opened in March 1990 with a production of Berlioz's *Les Troyens.* It looks a lot like the prison-fortress that started the French Revolution. Pl. de la Bastille, 11e (phone: 40-01-17-89).

LA MADELEINE Starting in 1764, the Church of St. Mary Magdalene was built and razed twice before the present structure was commissioned by Napoleon in 1806 to honor his armies. The newly cleaned and restored church is based on a Greek temple design, with 65-foot-high Corinthian columns supporting the sculptured frieze. From its portals, the view extends down Rue Royale to Place de la Concorde and over to the dome of Les Invalides. Nearby are some of Paris's most tantalizing food shops. Open 1:30 PM to 7:30 PM, as well as during concerts (held at 4 PM on Sundays) and other frequent musical events; closed Sundays and holidays (except for concerts). Pl. de la Madeleine, 8e (phone: 42-65-52-17).

SACRÉ-COEUR AND MONTMARTRE Built on the Butte of Montmartre — the highest of Paris's seven hills — the white-domed Basilique du Sacré-Coeur provides an extraordinary view from its steps, especially at dawn or sunset.

The Byzantine interior is rich and ornate, though light and well proportioned. Note the huge mosaics, one depicting Christ and the Sacred Heart over the high altar; another, the Archangel Michael and the Maid of Orleans; and a third, of Louis XVI and his family. One of the largest and heaviest bells (19 tons) in Christendom is housed in the tall bell tower to the north.

The area around the church was the artists' quarter of late-19th- and early-20th-century Paris. The more garish aspects of Montmartre's notoriously frivolous 1890s nightlife, particularly the dancers and personalities at the *Moulin Rouge,* were immortalized by the paintings of Henri de Toulouse-Lautrec. And if the streets look familiar, chances are you've seen them in the paintings of Utrillo; they still look the same. The Place du Tertre is still charming, though often filled with tourists and overly eager, mostly undertalented artists. Go early in the day to see it as it was when Braque, Dufy, Modigliani, Picasso, Rousseau, and Utrillo lived here. Montmartre has the last of Paris's vineyards — a boisterous fête is held here during October harvest — and still contains old houses, narrow alleys, steep stairways, and carefree cafés enough to provide a full day's entertainment; at night, this is one of the centers of Paris life. Spare yourself most of the climb to Sacré-Coeur by taking the funicular (it has been replaced by a more modern, glass contraption — bringing the *Louvre*'s main pyramid to mind) or the Montmartre bus (marked with an icon of Sacré-Coeur on the front instead of the usual number) from Place St-Pierre. Butte Montmartre, 18e.

LES HALLES Just northeast of the *Louvre,* this 80-acre area, formerly the *Central Market,* "the Belly of Paris," was razed in 1969. Gone are most of the picturesque early-morning fruit-and-vegetable vendors, butchers in blood-spattered aprons, and truckers bringing the freshest produce from all over France. Their places have been usurped by trendy shops and galleries of youthful entrepreneurs and artisans, small restaurants with lots of charm, the world's largest subway station, acres of trellised gardens and playgrounds, and *Le Forum des Halles,* a vast, mainly underground complex of boutiques, ranging from the superchic designer ready-to-wear to more ordinary shops, as well as concert space and movie theaters. Touch-sensitive locator devices, which help visitors find products and services, are placed strategically. A few echoes of the earthy past remain, however, and you can still dine at *Au Pied de Cochon, Le Pharamond,* and *L'Escargot Montorgueil,* or have a drink with the few remaining workmen (before noon) at one of the old brasseries. See *Walk 6: The Beaubourg and Les Halles, and the Hôtel de Ville* in DIRECTIONS.

LE CENTRE NATIONAL D'ART ET DE CULTURE GEORGES-POMPIDOU (LE CENTRE GEORGES-POMPIDOU) Better known as "the Beaubourg," after the street it faces and the *quartier* it replaced, this stark, 6-level creation of steel and glass, with its exterior escalators and blue, white, and red pipes, created a stir the moment its construction began. Outside, a computerized digital clock ticks off the seconds remaining until the 21st century. This wildly popular museum brings together all the contemporary art forms — painting, sculpture, the plastic arts, industrial design, music, literature, cinema, and theater — under one roof, and that roof offers one of the most exciting views of Paris. The old houses and cobbled, tree-shaded streets and squares vie for attention with galleries, boutiques, and the spectacle provided by jugglers, mimes, acrobats, and magicians in the plaza out front. The scene in the courtyard often rivals the exhibits inside. Open weekdays from noon to 10 PM; 10 AM to 10 PM weekends and holidays. Closed Tuesdays; no admission charge on Sundays except for special exhibitions. Entrances on Rue de Beaubourg or Rue St-Martin, 4e (phone: 42-77-12-33).

LE MARAIS Northeast of the *Louvre,* a marshland until the 16th century, this district became the height of residential fashion during the 17th century. But as the aristocracy moved on, it fell into disrepair. Over the last 25 years, the Marais has been enjoying a complete face-lift. Preservationists have lovingly restored more than 100 of the magnificent old mansions to their former grandeur (including the Hôtel du Salé, which now houses the *Picasso Museum*). They are exquisitely beautiful, with muraled walls and ceilings, and the courtyards of many are the sites of dramatic and musical presentations during the summer *Festival du Marais.* Among the houses to note are the Palais de Soubise, now the National Archives, and the Hôtels d'Aumont, de Clisson, de Rohan, de Sens, and de Sully (*hôtel* in this sense means private residence or townhouse). The Caisse Nationale des Monuments Historiques, housed in the latter, can provide maps of the area, as well as fascinating and detailed tours. It also offers lectures on Saturdays and Sundays. 62 Rue St-Antoine, 4e (phone: 44-61-20-00).

PLACE DES VOSGES In the Marais district, the oldest square in Paris — and also one of the most beautiful — was completed in 1612 by order of Henri IV, with its houses elegantly "built to a like symmetry." Though many of the houses have been rebuilt inside, their original façades remain, and the restored square is one of Paris's enduring delights. Corneille and Racine lived here. At No. 6 is the *Maison de Victor-Hugo,* once the writer's home and now a museum. Closed Mondays; admission charge; 4e (phone: 42-72-10-16).

MUSÉE CARNAVALET (CARNAVALET MUSEUM) Also in the Marais, this once was the home of Mme. de Sévigné, a noted 17th-century letter writer, and now its beautifully arranged exhibits cover the history of the city of Paris from the days of Henri IV to the present. Its recent expansion through the *lycée* next door and into the neighboring *Le Peletier de Saint-Fargeau* hotel doubled the exhibition space, making it the largest museum in the world devoted to the history of a single capital city. The expansion was done primarily to house a permanent major exhibit on the French Revolution. Watch for special exhibitions here. The museum also rents out its concert hall to various music groups. Closed Mondays; no admission charge on Sundays. 23 Rue de Sévigné, 3e (phone: 42-72-21-13).

MUSÉE PICASSO Showing works still amazingly modern, this museum is in the Hôtel du Salé, a 17th-century mansion in Paris's oldest neighborhood (the building is as interesting as the artwork it houses). On display here is a portion of the collection with which Picasso could never bring himself to part; it gives a panoramic view of the versatile doyen of this century's art.

His varied career went from the contemplative self-portrait painted in shades of blue in 1921, through the cubist newspapers and guitars, to the 1961 iron-sheet sculpture of a soccer player looking like an ice cream on a stick. Especially interesting is the master's collection of works by other artists (the Cézannes are best). Open from 9:15 AM to 5:15 PM; Wednesdays from 9:15 AM to 10 PM. Closed Tuesdays. Admission charge. 5 Rue de Thorigny, 3e (phone: 42-71-25-21).

CIMETIÈRE PÈRE-LACHAISE (PÈRE-LACHAISE CEMETERY) For those who like cemeteries, this one is a beauty. In a wooded park, it's the final resting place of such illustrious personalities as Oscar Wilde, Edith Piaf, Marcel Proust, and Sarah Bernhardt. Purchase a map at the entrance before trying to find *Doors* rock group star Jim Morrison's grave (Section 27), where there's always a profoundly bizarre parade going on. And note the legions of resident cats. Open daily from 8 AM to 5:30 PM, November to mid-March; from 7:30 AM to 6 PM, mid-March to November. Bd. de Ménilmontant at Rue de la Roquette, 20e (phone: 43-70-70-33).

LA VILLETTE The City of Sciences and Industry, a celebration of technology, stands in its own park on the northeastern edge of the capital and houses a planetarium, the spherical *Géode* cinema, lots of hands-on displays, and a half-dozen exhibitions at any given time. Also here is the *Cinaxe,* a movie theater that simulates a rocket launch. Viewers are strapped into their seats, and watch a film while the theater shakes and vibrates. A must for children, as is a nearby futuristic park with jungle gyms and slides. Restaurants and snack bars. Open 10 AM to 6 PM. Closed Mondays. Admission charge. 30 Av. Cotentin-Cariou, 20e (phone: 40-05-70-00).

BOIS DE BOULOGNE Originally part of the Forest of Rouvre, on the western edge of Paris, this 2,140-acre park was planned along English lines by Napoleon. Ride a horse or a bike, row a boat, shoot skeet, go bowling, smell roses, picnic on the grass, see horse races at *Auteuil* and *Longchamp,* visit a children's amusement park (*Jardin d'Acclimatation*) and a zoo, see a play, walk to a waterfall — and there's lots more. A particularly lovely spot is the Bagatelle château and park; a former residence of Marie-Antoinette, it boasts a magnificent rose garden (on the Rte. de Sevres in Neuilly, 16e; phone: 40-67-97-00). Open daily 9 AM to 4 PM in winter; 8 AM to 7:30 PM in summer; château open mid-March to November. Admission charge. Try to avoid the park after dark, when it becomes a playground for prostitutes and transvestites who actively solicit passersby. Recent attempts by the French government to stop the nighttime activity by banning cars from the park have begun to alleviate the situation (métros: Port d'Auteuil, Pont de Neuilly, Sablons).

BOIS DE VINCENNES As a counterpart to the Bois de Boulogne, a park, a palace, and a zoological garden were laid out on 2,300 acres during Napoleon III's time. Visit the 14th-century château and its lovely chapel; the large and lovely floral garden; and the zoo, with animals in their natural habitat. It's at the southeast edge of Paris (métro: Château de Vincennes).

Located on the eastern edge of the Bois de Vincennes is another fascinating spot, the *Musée des Arts Africains et Océaniens* (Museum of African and Polynesian Art; see *Museums,* below).

PALAIS DE CHAILLOT Built just off the Seine, near the Arc de Triomphe, for the *Paris Exposition of 1937* — on the site of the old Palais du Trocadéro left over from the *Exposition of 1878* — its terraces have excellent views across gardens and fountains to the Eiffel Tower on the Left Bank. Two wings house a theater, a *Cinémathèque,* and four museums — *du Cinéma* (phone: 45-53-21-86), *de l'Homme* (anthropology; phone: 45-53-70-60), *de la Marine* (maritime; phone: 45-53-31-70), and *des Monuments Français* (monument reproductions; phone: 47-27-35-74). Closed Tuesdays and major holidays. Pl. du Trocadéro, 16e.

LA RIVE GAUCHE (THE LEFT BANK)

TOUR EIFFEL (EIFFEL TOWER) It is impossible to imagine the Paris skyline without this mighty symbol, yet what has been called Gustave Eiffel's folly was never meant to be permanent. Originally built for the *Universal Exposition of 1889,* it was due to be torn down in 1909, but it was saved because of the development of the wireless — the first transatlantic wireless telephones were operated from the 1,056-foot tower in 1916. Its centennial was celebrated with great fanfare in 1989. Extensive renovations have taken place (including modernized elevators); and a post office, three restaurants (*Jules Verne* is the best), and a few boutiques have opened up on the first-floor landing. On a really clear day, it's possible to see for 50 miles. Open daily from 10 AM to 11 PM; in the summer from 9:30 AM to midnight. Admission charge. Champ-de-Mars, 7e (phone: 45-50-34-56).

CHAILLOT TO UNESCO From the Eiffel Tower, it is possible to look out over a group of Paris's 20th-century buildings and gardens on both sides of the Seine, including the Palais de Chaillot, the Trocadéro and Champ-de-Mars gardens, and the UNESCO buildings. Also part of the area (but not of the same century) is the huge Ecole Militaire, an impressive example of 18th-century French architecture on Avenue de la Motte-Picquet. The Y-shaped building just beyond it, facing Place de Fontenoy, is the main UNESCO building, dating from 1958. It has frescoes by Picasso, Henry Moore's *Reclining Silhouette,* a mobile by Calder, murals by Miró, and Japanese gardens by Noguchi.

LES INVALIDES Built by Louis XIV as a refuge for disabled soldiers, this vast classical building has more than 10 miles of corridors and a golden dome by Mansart. For yet another splendid Parisian view, approach the building from the Alexandre III bridge. Besides being a masterpiece of the age of Louis XIV (17th century), the royal Church of the Dôme, part of the complex, contains the impressive red-and-green granite Tomb of Napoleon (admission charge). Also at Les Invalides is the *Musée de l'Armée,* one of the world's richest museums, displaying arms and armor together with mementos of French military history. Open daily from 10 AM to 5 PM. Admission charge. Av. de Tourville, Pl. Vauban, 7e (phone: 45-55-37-70).

MUSÉE D'ORSAY (ORSAY MUSEUM) This imposing former railway station has been transformed (by the Milanese architect Gae Aulenti, among others) into one of the shining examples of modern museum curating. Its eclectic collection includes not only the Impressionist paintings decanted from the once-cramped quarters in the *Jeu de Paume,* but also less consecrated academic work and a panorama of the 19th century's achievements in sculpture, photography, and the applied arts. Now Degas, Toulouse-Lautrec, Monet, and Renoir are displayed in specially designed spaces within this former railroad-cathedral, along with the works of 600 other painters and 500 sculptors. No detail of light, humidity, or acoustics has been left to chance, making this voyage around the art world a very comfortable one. Don't miss the museum's pièce de résistance — the van Goghs on the top floor, glowing under the northern Parisian skylight. Open 10 AM to 6 PM in winter; 9 AM to 6 PM in summer and on Sundays all year; 10 AM to 9:45 PM on Thursdays all year; closed Mondays. Admission charge; reduced on Sundays. 1 Rue de Bellechasse, 7e (phone: 40-49-48-14).

MUSÉE RODIN (RODIN MUSEUM) This is one of France's most complete and satisfying museum experiences. Ambling in a leisurely way through one of the great 18th-century Parisian aristocratic homes and its grounds, it's possible to follow the evolution of the career of Auguste Rodin, that genius of modern sculpture. Among the broad terraces and in the serene and elegant gardens are scattered fabled statues like *The Thinker,* the *Bourgeois de Calais,* the superb statues of Honoré de Balzac and Victor Hugo, the stunning *Gate of Hell,* on which the master labored a lifetime, *Les Bavardes,* a sculpture by Rodin's mistress Camille Claudel, and much, much more. The master's celebrated Ugolin group is placed dramatically in the middle of a pond. The museum boutique sells reproductions of the major works. Open from 10 AM to 5:45 PM in summer; 10 AM to 5 PM in winter. Closed Mondays. Admission charge. 77 Rue de Varenne, 7e (phone: 47-05-01-34).

MONTPARNASSE Just south of the Luxembourg Gardens, in the early 20th century there arose an artists' colony of avant-garde painters, writers, and Russian political exiles. Here Hemingway, Picasso, and Scott and Zelda sipped and supped in places like *La Closerie des Lilas, La Coupole, Le Dôme, Le Select,* and *La Rotonde.* The cafés, small restaurants, and winding streets still exist in the shadow of a new shopping center.

TOUR MONTPARNASSE This giant complex dominates Montparnasse. The fastest elevator in Europe whisks Parisians and tourists alike (for a fee) up 59 stories for a view *down* at the Eiffel Tower, from 9:30 AM to 11:30 PM in summer; 10 AM to 10 PM in winter. The shopping center here boasts all the famous names, and the surrounding office buildings are the headquarters of some of France's largest companies. 33 Av. du Maine, 15e, and Bd. de Vaugirard, 14e (phone: 45-38-52-56).

PALAIS ET JARDIN DU LUXEMBOURG (LUXEMBOURG PALACE AND GARDEN) In what once were the southern suburbs, the Luxembourg Palace and Garden were built for Marie de Médici in 1615. A prison during the Revolution, the Renaissance palace now houses the French Senate. The classic, formal gardens, with lovely statues and the famous Médicis fountain, are popular with students meeting under the chestnut trees and with neighborhood children playing around the artificial lake. 15 Rue de Vaugirard, 6e.

MOSQUÉE DE PARIS (PARIS MOSQUE) One of the most beautiful structures of its kind in the non-Muslim — or even in the Muslim — world, it is dominated by a 130-foot-high minaret in gleaming white marble. Shoes are taken off before entering the pebble-lined gardens full of flowers and dwarf trees. Inside, the Hall of Prayer, with its lush Oriental carpets, may be visited daily, except Fridays (the weekly prayer day for Muslims), from 9 AM to noon and 2 to 6 PM. Admission charge. Next door is a restaurant and a patio for sipping Turkish coffee and tasting Oriental sweets. Pl. du Puits-de-l'Ermite, 5e (phone: 45-35-97-33).

PANTHÉON This 18th-century "nonreligious Temple of Fame dedicated to all the gods" has an impressive interior, with murals depicting the life of Ste-Geneviève, patron saint of Paris. It contains the tombs of Victor Hugo, the Résistance leader Jean Moulin, Rousseau, Voltaire, and Emile Zola. Open from 10 AM to 6 PM in summer; 10 AM to 12:30 PM and 2 to 5:30 PM in winter. Admission charge. Pl. du Panthéon, 5e (phone: 43-54-34-51).

QUARTIER LATIN (LATIN QUARTER) Extending from the Luxembourg Gardens and the Panthéon to the Seine, this famous neighborhood still maintains its unique atmosphere. A focal point for Sorbonne students since the Middle Ages, it's a mad jumble of narrow streets, old churches, and academic buildings. Boulevard St-Michel and Boulevard St-Germain are its main arteries, both lined with cafés, bookstores, and boutiques of every imaginable kind. There are also some charming old side streets, such as the Rue de la Huchette, near Place St-Michel. And don't miss the famous *bouquinistes* (bookstalls) along the Seine, around the Place St-Michel on the Quai des Grands-Augustins and the Quai St-Michel.

EGLISE ST-GERMAIN-DES-PRÉS (CHURCH OF ST-GERMAIN-DES-PRÉS) Probably the oldest church in Paris, it once belonged to an abbey of the same name. The original basilica (AD 558) was destroyed and rebuilt many times. The Romanesque steeple and its massive tower date from 1014. Inside, the choir and sanctuary are as they were in the 12th century, and the marble shafts used in the slender columns are 14 centuries old. Pl. St-Germain-des-Prés, 6e (phone: 43-25-41-71).

Surrounding the church is the *quartier* of Paris's "fashionable" intellectuals and artists, with art galleries, boutiques, and renowned cafés for people watching such as the *Flore* (Sartre's favorite) and *Les Deux Magots* (once a Hemingway haunt).

MUSÉE DE CLUNY (CLUNY MUSEUM) One of the last remaining examples of medieval domestic architecture in Paris. The 15th-century residence of the abbots of Cluny later became the home of Mary Tudor and now is a museum of medieval arts and crafts, including the celebrated *Lady and the Unicorn* tapestry. Open daily, except Tuesdays, from 9:30 AM to 5:15 PM in summer; 9:30 AM to 12:30 PM and 2 to 5:15 PM in winter. Admission charge. 6 Pl. Paul-Painlevé, 5e (phone: 43-25-62-00).

EGLISE ST-SÉVERIN (CHURCH OF ST. SÉVERIN) This church still retains its beautiful Flamboyant Gothic ambulatory, considered a masterpiece of its kind, and lovely old stained glass windows dating from the 15th and 16th centuries. The small garden and the restored charnel house also are of interest. 3 Rue des Prêtres, 5e (phone: 43-25-96-63).

EGLISE ST-JULIEN-LE-PAUVRE (CHURCH OF ST. JULIAN THE POOR) One of the smallest and oldest churches (12th to 13th century) in Paris offers a superb view of Notre-Dame from its charming Place René-Viviani. 1 Rue St-Julien-le-Pauvre, 5e (no phone).

THE ISLANDS

ILE DE LA CITÉ The birthplace of Paris, settled by Gallic fishermen about 250 BC, this island in the Seine is so rich in historical monuments that an entire day could be spent here and on the neighboring Ile St-Louis. A walk all around the islands, along the lovely, tree-shaded quays on both banks of the Seine, opens up one breathtaking view (of Notre-Dame Cathedral, the *Louvre*, and the Pont Neuf) after another.

Cathédrale de Notre-Dame de Paris (Cathedral of Our Lady) It is said that the Druids once worshiped on this consecrated ground. The Romans built their temple, and many Christian churches followed. In 1163, the foundations were laid for the present cathedral, one of the world's finest examples of Gothic architecture, grand in size and proportion. It took more than 200 years to build, working from the plans of a single anonymous architect. Henri IV and Napoleon were crowned here. Take a guided tour (offered in English at noon Tuesdays and Wednesdays and in French at noon other weekdays, 2:30 PM Saturdays, and 2 PM Sundays) or quietly explore on your own, but be sure to climb the 225-foot towers (open 9:30 AM to noon and 2 to 6 PM in summer; 10 AM to 5 PM in winter) for a marvelous view of the city and try to see the splendid 13th-century stained glass rose windows at sunset. Pl. du Parvis de Notre-Dame, 4e (phone: 43-26-07-39).

Palais de Justice and La Sainte-Chapelle This monumental complex recalls centuries of history; it was the first seat of the Roman military government, then the headquarters of the early kings of the Capetian dynasty, and finally the law courts. In the 13th century, St-Louis (Louis IX) built a new palace and added Sainte-Chapelle to house the Sacred Crown of Thorns and other holy relics. Its 15 soaring stained glass windows (plus a later rose window), with more than 1,100 brilliantly colored and exquisitely detailed miniature scenes of biblical life, are among the unquestioned masterpieces of medieval French art, and the graceful, gleaming 247-foot spire is one of the city's most beautiful and understated landmarks — particularly stunning on a sunny day. Open daily from 10 AM to 5 PM in winter, 9:30 AM to 6:30 PM in summer. Admission charge. 4 Bd. du Palais, 1er (phone: 43-54-30-09).

Conciergerie This remnant of the Old Royal Palace sits like a fairy-tale castle on the Ile de la Cité. Used as a prison during the Revolution, it was here that Marie-Antoinette, the Duke of Orléans, Mme. du Barry, and others of lesser fame awaited the guillotine. For the bicentennial of the French Revolution in 1989, its prisons were restored and "peopled" with mannequins representing former prisoners. Upstairs are the cells — straw in the cells for those who slept on the floor and the *pistole* cells for those with enough influence and power to merit a bed — and sometimes even a desk, chair, and lantern. There are documents and engravings dating from the time of Ravaillac, the 17th-century royal assassin, illustrating the past of this sinister palace. Don't miss Marie-Antoinette's cell, and the Girondins' chapel where the moderate Girondin deputies shared their last meal. Open daily 9:30 AM to 6:30 PM in summer; 9:30 AM to 6 PM in September, April and May; 10 AM to 4:30 PM from October to April. Closed holidays. Admission charge. 4 Bd. du Palais, 1er (phone: 43-54-30-06).

ILE ST-LOUIS Walk across the footbridge at the back of Notre-Dame and you're in a charming, tranquil village. This "enchanted isle" has managed to keep its provincial charm despite its central location. Follow the main street, Rue St-Louis-en-l'Ile, down the middle of the island, past courtyards, balconies, old doors, curious stairways, the Eglise St-Louis, and discreet plaques bearing the names of illustrious former residents (Mme. Curie, Voltaire, Baudelaire, Gautier, and Daumier, for example); then take the quay back along the edge.

Sources and Resources

TOURIST INFORMATION

For information in the US, contact the French Government Tourist Office (610 Fifth Ave., New York, NY 10020; phone: 212-757-1125). In Paris, the

Office du Tourisme de Paris (127 Champs-Elysées, 8e; phone: 49-52-53-56), open daily from 9 AM to 8 PM, is the place to go for information, brochures, maps, or hotel reservations. If you call the office, be prepared for a 4- to 5-minute wait before someone answers. Other offices are found at major train stations, such as the Gare du Nord (phone: 45-26-94-82) and the Gare de Lyon (phone: 43-43-33-24).

LOCAL COVERAGE *Paris Selection* is the official tourist office magazine in French and English. It lists events, sights, "Paris by Night" tours, places to hear jazz, some hotels, restaurants, shopping, and other information. Far more complete are three weekly guides, *L'Officiel des Spectacles, Paris 7,* and *Pariscope.* All are in simple French and are available at newsstands.

For insights on eating out and finding the best of French food and wine, consult *The Food Lover's Guide to Paris* (Workman, $12.95) by American-in-Paris Patricia Wells. She also contributes a weekly column on restaurants to the *International Herald Tribune.* English-language magazines are *Boulevard* (sold at newsstands) and *WHERE* (as we went to press, distributed in hotels).

TELEPHONE The area code for Paris is 1. For more information, see GETTING READY TO GO.

GETTING AROUND

BOAT See Paris from the Seine by day and by night. Prices are reasonable for a ride on one of these modern, glass-enclosed river ramblers, which provide a constantly changing picture of the city. Contact *Bateaux-Mouches* (Pont d'Alma, 7e; phone: 42-25-96-10), *Les Bateaux Parisiens* (Pont d'Iéna, 7e; phone: 47-05-50-00), or *Vedettes Pont-Neuf* (Pl. Vert-Galant, 1er; phone: 46-33-98-38). *Paris Canal* (phone: 42-40-96-97) and *Canauxrama* (13 Quai de la Loire; phone: 42-39-15-00) offer 3-hour barge trips starting on the Seine, then navigating through some of the city's old canals, locks, and a subterranean water route under the Bastille. An interesting commentary is given in both English and French. *Paris Canal* also has two trips daily between the *Musée d'Orsay* and the Parc de la Villette — one leaves from the *Musée d'Orsay* at 9:30 AM and the other departs from the Parc de la Villette at 2:30 PM. *Canauxrama* boats leave from the Bassin de la Villette at 9:15 AM and 2:45 PM, and also from the Port de l'Arsenal at 9:45 AM and 2:30 PM. The *Batobus* carries passengers to stops along the Seine from April to September; stops (watch for the signs on the *quais*) are near the Eiffel Tower, the *Musée d'Orsay,* the *Passarelle des Arts,* the *Louvre,* Notre-Dame, and the Hôtel de Ville.

BUS They generally operate from 6:30 AM to 9:30 PM, although some run later. Slow, but good for sightseeing. Métro tickets are valid on all city-run buses, but you will need a new ticket if you change buses. Unlike the métro, buses charge by distance; two or more tickets are usually needed for a ride across town. Lines are numbered, and both stops and buses have signs indicating routes. The Paris *Regional Rapid Transit Authority* (*RATP*), which operates both the métro and bus system, also has designated certain lines as being of particular interest to tourists. A panel on the front of the bus indicates in English and German "This bus is good for sightseeing." *RATP* has a tourist office at Place de la Madeleine, next to the flower market (phone: 43-46-14-14), which organizes bus trips in Paris and the region.

CAR RENTAL For information about renting a car in Paris, see GETTING READY TO GO.

MÉTRO Operating from 5:30 AM to about 1 AM, it is generally safe (although pickpockets abound in certain areas), clean, quiet, easy to use, and since the *RATP* began to sponsor cultural events and art exhibits in some subway stops in an effort to cut down on crime and make commuting more enjoyable, entertaining as well. The events have been so popular that so far they've been offered in about 200 of Paris's 368 métro stations.

The different lines are identified by the names of their terminals at either end. Every station has clear directional maps, some with push-button devices that light up the proper route after a destination button is pushed. Keep your ticket (you may need to show it to one of the controllers who regularly patrol the métro) and don't cheat; there are spot checks. The *RATP* recently abolished the métro's long-standing first and second class system. There is now only one class of ticket.

A 10-ticket book (*carnet*) is available at a reduced rate; the same tickets can be used on buses, but on the métro you will need only one ticket per ride. The Paris-Visite card, a tourist ticket that entitles the bearer to 1, 3, or 5 consecutive days of unlimited travel on the métro and on city-run buses, may be purchased in France upon presentation of your passport at 44 subway stations and 4 regional express stations, or at any of the 6 *French National Railroad* stations. In the US, the card is available by money order from *Marketing Challengers International* (10 E. 21st St., New York, NY 10010; phone: 212-529-8484). The *carte orange*, a 1-month, unlimited travel pass for métro or bus, is available at all métro stations; you need a small (passport-size) photo to attach to the card. Ask for a 2-zone (metropolitan Paris) ticket.

MOTORCYCLE For those traveling with less than the requisite four suitcases, this is the fastest (and most unusual) method of getting to Orly airport. *Omega Transport* (phone: 42-42-11-11) offers a 30-minute ride on BMW motorcycles from the center of Paris out to the airport.

> **NOTE** Handy streetside bus and subway directions are now available in some métro stations from *SITU* (*Système d'Information des Trajets Urbains*), a computer that prints out the fastest routing onto a wallet-size piece of paper, complete with the estimated length of the trip. The *RATP*

service is free and augments the lighted wall maps that guide métro riders. High-traffic spots such as the Châtelet métro station, outside the Gare Montparnasse, and on the Boulevard St-Germain, now sport *SITU* machines.

TAXI Taxis can be found at stands at main intersections, outside railway stations and official buildings, and in the streets. A taxi is available if the entire "TAXI" sign is illuminated (with a white light); the small light *beside* the roof light signifies availability after dark; no light means the driver is off duty. But be aware that Parisian cab drivers are notoriously selective about where they will go, and how many passengers they will allow in their cab — a foursome inevitably has trouble: by law, no one may ride in the front seat. Also by law, a cab at a taxi stand must take you wherever you want to go. (Good news for those who don't appreciate being snubbed by cabbies: The Paris taxi drivers' association has instituted a new program to teach potential drivers good manners, along with a soupçon of English.) You also can call *Taxi Bleu* (phone: 49-36-10-10) or *Radio Taxi* (phone: 47-39-33-33). The meter starts running from the time the cab is dispatched, and a tip of about 15% is customary. Fares increase at night and on Sundays and holidays.

TRAIN Paris has six main train stations, each one serving a different area of the country. The general information number is 45-82-50-50; for telephone reservations, 45-65-60-60. For additional information, in English, contact a branch of the tourist office within each station. North: Gare du Nord (18 Rue de Dunkerque; phone: 45-26-94-82); East: Gare de l'Est (Pl. du 11-Novembre; phone: 46-07-17-73); Southeast: Gare de Lyon (20 Bd. Diderot; phone: 43-43-33-24); Southwest: Gare d'Austerlitz (51 Quai d'Austerlitz; phone: 45-84-91-70); West: Gare Montparnasse (17 Bd. de Vaugirard; phone: 43-22-19-19); West and Northwest: Gare St-Lazare (20 Rue de Rome; phone: 42-85-88-00). The *TGV* (*train à grande vitesse*), the world's fastest train, has cut 2 hours off the usual 4-hour ride between Paris and Lyons; it similarly shortens traveling time to Marseilles, the Côte d'Azur, the Atlantic Coast, the English Channel at Calais, and Switzerland. Most *TGVs* leave from the Gare de Lyon, except for the Atlantic Coast run, which departs from the Gare Montparnasse, and the Lille-Calais run which leaves from the recently renovated Gare du Nord and connects at Calais to the "Chunnel," the trans-Channel tunnel connecting France and Great Britain. Reservations (including seats) are necessary on all *TGVs*; tickets can be purchased from machines in all main train stations. A *TGV* station in Massy, 16 miles (25 km) south of Paris, is right near Orly; a 15-minute ride on the *RER* (suburban train), it's ideal for those who are traveling to other parts of France and want to avoid going into Paris. There also is a train (called the *Orlyval*) that travels between Orly Airport and Paris in less than half an hour.

LOCAL SERVICES

BABY-SITTING One of the many agencies in Paris is *Kid's Service* (17 Rue Molière, 1er; phone: 42-96-04-16). Whether the sitter is hired directly or through an agency, ask for and check references.

DRY CLEANER/TAILOR Dry cleaners are available throughout the city. Note that many have two different price schedules (*pressings*), one for "economic" service, another for faster, more expensive service. The less expensive prices may be posted outside, but unless you specify, your clothes will be given the expensive treatment. *John Baillie, Real Scotch Tailor* (1 Rue Auber at Pl. de l'Opéra, 2e; phone: 47-42-49-24 or 47-42-49-17) is a reputable firm that does tailoring French-style, despite its name.

LIMOUSINE SERVICE *Compagnie des Limousines* (37 Rue Acacias, 17e; phone: 43-80-79-41); *Executive Car/Carey Limousine* (25 Rue d'Astorg, 8e; phone: 42-65-54-20; fax: 42-65-25-93).

MEDICAL EMERGENCY For information on local medical services and pharmacies, see GETTING READY TO GO.

MESSENGER SERVICE Most hotels will arrange for pickups and deliveries.

OFFICE EQUIPMENT RENTAL *Office Equipment* (43 Rue Beaubourg, 3e; phone: 42-72-07-00) offers rental of Macintosh computers.

PHOTOCOPIES In addition to the numerous small outlets specializing in photocopies, facilities are available in many stationery stores and post offices.

TELECONFERENCE FACILITIES *Hôtel Méridien,* 81 Bd. Gouvion-St-Cyr, 17e (phone: 40-68-34-34) and other hotels.

TELEX AND FAX SERVICES *PTT* (Postes et Télécommunications), open daily, including Sundays, from 8 AM to 7:30 PM, at 7 Rue Feydeau, 2e (phone: 42-33-20-12), and from 8 to 10:30 PM at 5 Rue Feydeau, just next door; any post office will send a fax for you, but prices are astronomical (at press time, around $40 for 2 pages to the US).

TRANSLATOR For a list of accredited translators, contact the Consulate of the American Embassy (phone: 42-96-14-88), or *Berlitz* (29 Rue de la Michodière, 2e; phone: 47-42-88-37).

TUXEDO RENTAL *Au Cor de Chasse,* 40 Rue de Buci, 6e (phone: 43-26-51-89).

SPECIAL EVENTS

After the *Christmas* season, Paris prepares for the January fashion shows, when press and buyers come to town to pass judgment on the spring and summer haute couture collections. (The general public can see what the designers have wrought after the professionals leave. Most stores hold big semi-annual sales at this time.) More buyers come to town in February and March for the ready-to-wear shows (fall and winter clothes), open to the trade only. March is the month of the first *Foire Nationale à la Brocante et aux Jambons* of the year. This fair of regional food products held concurrently with an antiques flea market (not items of the best quality, but not junk, either) is repeated in September. The running of the *Prix du Président de la République,* the first big horse race of the year, takes place at *Auteuil* in April. From late April to early May is the *Foire de Paris,* the capital's big international trade fair. In late April or May there's the *Paris Marathon;* in late May (through early June), it's the illustrious *French Open* tennis championship, popularly known as the *Roland Garros,* after the stadium in which it's held. Horse races crowd the calendar in June — there's not only the *Prix de Diane* at *Chantilly,* but also the *Grande Semaine* at *Longchamp,* the *Grande Steeplechase de Paris* at *Auteuil,* and *St-Cloud.* And in the middle of June, the *Festival du Marais* begins a month's worth of music and dance performances in the courtyards of the Marais district's old townhouses. June is also when most Paris stores hold their second big semi-annual sale. *Bastille Day,* July 14, is celebrated with music and fireworks, parades, and dancing till dawn in every neighborhood. Meanwhile, the *Tour de France* is under way; the cyclists arrive in Paris for the finish of the 3-week race later in July. Also in July, press and buyers arrive to view the fall and winter haute couture collections, but the ready-to-wear shows (spring and summer clothes) wait until September and October, because August for Parisians is vacation time. Practically the whole country takes a holiday then, and in the capital the classical concerts of the *Festival Estival* (in July and August) are among the few distractions. When they finish, the *Festival d'Automne,* a celebration of the contemporary in music, dance, and theater, takes over (from mid-September through December). The *Foire Nationale à la Brocante et aux Jambons* returns in September, but in even-numbered years it's eclipsed by the *Biennale des Antiquaires,* a major antiques event from late September to early October. Also in even years, usually in November, is the *Paris Motor Show.* Every year on the first Sunday of October, the last big horse race of the season, the *Prix de l'Arc de Triomphe,* is run at *Longchamp;* and every year in early October, Paris holds the *Fête des Vendanges à Montmartre* to celebrate the harvest of the city's last remaining vineyard. On November 11, ceremonies at the Arc de Triomphe and a parade mark *Armistice Day;* the *Open de Paris* tennis tournament is also played this month. An *International Cat Show* and a *Horse and Pony Show* come in early December; then comes *Christmas,* which is celebrated most movingly with a *Christmas Eve* midnight mass at Notre-Dame. At midnight a week later, the *New Year* bows in to spontaneous street revelry in the Latin Quarter and along the Champs-Elysées.

MUSEUMS

Many museums (*musées*) in Paris charge an admission fee, unless otherwise indicated below. In addition to those described in *Special Places,* museums and sites of interest include the following:

ARCHAEOLOGICAL CRYPT OF NOTRE-DAME Exhibits in this ancient crypt on which the cathedral was built include floor plans that show the evolution of the cathedral and earlier religious structures built on this spot. Open daily from 10 AM to 5:30 PM in summer; to 5 PM in winter. Under the square in front of Notre-Dame, at Parvis de Notre-Dame, 4e (phone: 43-29-83-51).

BIBLIOTHÈQUE-MUSÉE DE L'OPÉRA PARIS/GARNIER This new museum and library traces the history of opera in Paris from its beginnings in the 17th century. Open daily 10 AM to 6 PM in summer; 10 AM to 5 PM in winter. Palais Garnier, Pl. de L'Opera, 9e (phone: 47-42-07-02).

CATACOMBS Dating from the Gallo-Roman era and also containing the remains of Danton, Robespierre, and many others. Filled with thousands of skeletons and skulls, the site is macabre, fascinating, and definitely not for the claustrophobic. Bring a flashlight. Open 9 to 11 AM and 2 to 4 PM weekdays; 2 to 6 PM weekends. Closed Mondays and holidays. 1 Pl. Denfert-Rochereau, 14e (phone: 43-22-47-63).

EGOUTS (SEWERS OF PARIS) The tour of this dark, rank underground city of tunnels has become an incredibly popular attraction; lines sometimes stretch for an hour. Open from 11 AM to 5 PM; closed Thursdays and Fridays, and holidays and the days preceding and following them. Pl. de la Résistance, in front of 93 Quai d'Orsay, 7e (phone: 47-05-10-29).

MAISON DE BALZAC The house where the writer lived, with a garden leading to one of the prettiest little alleys in Paris. Open 10 AM to 5:30 PM; closed Mondays. 47 Rue Raynouard, 16e (phone: 42-24-56-38).

MANUFACTURE DES GOBELINS The famous tapestry factory, in operation since the 15th century. Guided tours of the workshops take place Tuesdays, Wednesdays, and Thursdays from 2:15 to 3:15 PM. 42 Av. des Gobelins, 13e (phone: 43-37-12-60).

MÉMORIAL DE LA DÉPORTATION Set in a tranquil garden in the shadow of Notre-Dame at the tip of Ile de la Cité, this monument is dedicated to 200,000 French women and men of all religions and races who died in Nazi concentration camps during World War II. Pl. de l'Ile-de-France, 4e.

MÉMORIAL DU MARTYR JUIF INCONNU A moving tribute to Jews killed during the Holocaust, this 37-year-old, renovated memorial includes World War II documents and photographs. Open daily from 10 AM to noon and 2 to 5:30 PM, except Saturday mornings, Sundays, holidays, and Jewish religious holidays. 17 Rue Geoffroy L'Asniers, 4e (phone: 42-77-44-72). The French Government Tourist Office has published a booklet, *France for the Jewish Traveler,* that describes these two memorials, as well as other places of interest to Jews visiting France.

MUSÉE DES ANTIQUITÉS NATIONALES Archaeological specimens from prehistoric through Merovingian times, including an impressive Gallo-Roman collection. Open daily, except Tuesdays, from 9:30 AM to noon and 1:30 to 5:15 PM. Pl. du Château, St-Germain-en-Laye (phone: 34-51-53-65).

MUSÉE DES ARTS AFRICAINS ET OCÉANIENS One of the world's finest collections of African and Polynesian art. Open 10 AM to noon and 1:30 to 5:30 PM; closed Tuesdays. Bois de Vicennes, 293 Av. Daumesnil, 12e (phone: 43-43-14-54).

MUSÉE DES ARTS DE LA MODE ET DU TEXTILE Chronicles the history of the fashion and textile industries with opulent exhibits. Adjacent to the *Musée National des Arts Décoratifs*. Open Wednesdays through Saturdays 12:30 to 6 PM; Sundays 11 AM to 6 PM. 109 Rue de Rivoli, 1er (phone: 42-60-32-14).

MUSÉE DES ARTS ET TRADITIONS POPULAIRES Traditional arts and crafts from rural France. Open daily from 9:45 AM to 5:15 PM. Closed Tuesdays. 6 Av. du Mahatma-Gandhi, 16e (phone: 40-67-90-00).

MUSÉE CERNUSCHI Art of China. Open 10 AM to 5:30 PM; closed Mondays and holidays. 7 Av. Vélasquez, 8e (phone: 45-63-50-75).

MUSÉE DE LA CHASSE ET DE LA NATURE Art, weapons, and tapestries relating to the hunt. Of particular interest is the courtyard where horses once were kept — it is decorated with sculpture. Open daily except Tuesdays from 10 AM to 12:30 PM and 1:30 to 5:30 PM. 60 Rue des Archives, 3e (phone: 42-72-86-43).

MUSÉE COGNACQ-JAY Art, snuffboxes, and watches from the 17th and 18th centuries. Located in a stunningly beautiful mansion in the Marais. Open 10 AM to 5:40 PM; closed Mondays. 8 Rue Elzévir, 3e (phone: 40-27-07-21).

MUSÉE DES COLLECTIONS HISTORIQUES DE LA PRÉFECTURE DE POLICE On the second floor of this modern police precinct are historic arrest orders (for Charlotte Corday, among others), collections of contemporary engravings, and guillotine blades. Open Mondays through Saturdays from 9 AM to 5 PM. 1 *bis* Rue des Carmes, 5e (phone: 43-29-21-57).

MUSÉE DAPPER/ARTS AFRICAINS This splendid collection of African art is housed in a charming private house near l'Etoile. Open daily 11 AM to 7 PM. 50 Av. Victor Hugo, 16e (phone: 45-00-01-50).

MUSÉE EUGÈNE-DELACROIX Studio and garden of the great painter; exhibits change yearly. Open 9:45 AM to 12:30 PM and 2 to 5:15 PM; closed Tuesdays. 6 Rue de Furstenberg, 6e (phone: 43-54-04-87).

MUSÉE GRÉVIN Waxworks of French history from Charlemagne to the present day. Open Mondays through Fridays from 10:30 AM to 6:45 PM; weekends from 1 to 7 PM. 10 Bd. Montmartre, 9e (phone: 47-70-85-05). A branch devoted to La Belle Epoque is in the *Forum des Halles* shopping complex. Open daily (same hours as above). Pl. Carrée, 1er (phone: 40-26-28-50).

MUSÉE GUIMET The *Louvre*'s Far East collection. The museum's boutique, with reproductions inspired by the collection, including dishes and objects, is also well worth a visit. Open 9:45 AM to 8 PM. Closed Tuesdays. 6 Pl. d'Iéna, 16e (phone: 47-23-61-65).

MUSÉE GUSTAVE-MOREAU A collection of the works of the early symbolist. Open Thursdays through Sundays from 10 AM to 12:45 PM and 2 to 5:15 PM; Mondays and Wednesdays from 11 AM to 5:15 PM; closed Tuesdays. 14 Rue de la Rochefoucauld, 9e (phone: 48-74-38-50).

MUSÉE DE L'INSTITUT DU MONDE ARABE Arab and Islamic arts from the 9th to the 19th centuries. Open from 1 to 8 PM. Closed Mondays. 23 Quai St-Bernard, 5e (phone: 40-51-38-38).

MUSÉE JACQUEMART-ANDRÉ Eighteenth-century French decorative art and European Renaissance treasures, as well as frequent special exhibitions. Closed Mondays and Tuesdays. 158 Bd. Haussmann, 8e (phone: 42-89-04-91).

MUSÉE MARMOTTAN Superb Monets, including the nine masterpieces that were stolen in a daring 1985 robbery. Happily, however, all were recovered in a villa in Corsica and have been cleaned — some for the first time — before being rehung. Open daily 10 AM to 5:30 PM; closed Mondays. 2 Rue Louis-Boilly, 16e (phone: 42-24-07-02).

MUSÉE DE LA MODE ET DU COSTUME A panorama of French contributions to fashion in the elegant Palais Galliera. Open Tuesdays 2:30 to 5:45 PM; Wednesdays through Sundays 10 AM to 5:45 PM. Closed Mondays. 10 Av. Pierre-Ier de Serbie, 16e (phone: 47-20-85-23).

MUSÉE DE LA MONNAIE More than 2,000 coins and 450 medallions, plus historic coinage machines. Open daily, except Mondays, from 1 to 6 PM. 11 Quai de Conti, 6e (phone: 40-46-55-35).

MUSÉE MONTMARTRE A rich collection of paintings, drawings, and documents depicting life in this quarter. Open 2 to 6 PM in summer; 2:30 to 6 PM in winter; closed Mondays. 12 Rue Cortot, 18e (phone: 46-06-61-11).

MUSÉE DE LA MUSIQUE Set to open later this year, this museum will house a collection of 700 rare instruments. It is part of the vast Cité de la Musique project, comprising concert halls, a school, and other music-related activities, as well as the Conservatoire National Supérieur de la Musique, also set for completion later this year. 211 Av. Jean Jaurès, 19e (phone: 42-40-27-28).

MUSÉE NATIONAL DES ARTS DÉCORATIFS Furniture and applied arts from the Middle Ages to the present, Oriental carpets, and Dubuffet paintings and drawings. Galerie Art Nouveau–Art Deco features Lanvin's bedroom and bath. It also houses 3 centuries of French posters. Open 12:30 PM to 6 PM; closed Mondays and Tuesdays. Admission charge. 107 Rue de Rivoli, 1er (phone: 42-60-32-14).

MUSÉE NISSIM DE CAMONDO A former manor house filled with beautiful furnishings and art objects from the 18th century. Open 10 AM to noon and 2 to 5 PM; closed Mondays, Tuesdays, and holidays. 63 Rue de Monceau, 8e (phone: 45-63-26-32).

MUSÉE DU ROCK Forty years of legend, myth, and music are on display, with wax figures of more than 30 rock stars. Open daily 10:30 AM to 6 PM. *Forum des Halles,* Porte du Louvre, 1er (phone: 40-28-08-13).

MUSÉE DE SÈVRES Just outside Paris, next door to the Sèvres factory, is one of the world's finest collections of porcelain. Open 10 AM to 5 PM; closed Tuesdays. 4 Grand-Rue, Sèvres (phone: 45-34-99-05).

MUSÉE DU VIN Housed in a 13th-century abbey whose interior was destroyed during the Revolution, the museum was restored in 1981. The history and making of wine are traced through displays, artifacts, and a series of wax figure tableaux. Open daily, except Mondays, from noon to 6 PM; Saturdays and Sundays to 5:30 PM. Admission charge includes a glass of wine. 5-7 Pl. Charles-Dickens, 16e (phone: 45-25-63-26).

PARISTORIC This 45-minute film on Paris, past and present, with an English soundtrack available on headsets, is a well-done capsule portrait of the city's 2,000-year history. Open daily, 9 AM to 9 PM April to November; 9 AM to 6 PM November to April. Admission charge. Espace Hébertot, 78 *bis* Bd. des Batignolles, 17e (phone: 42-93-93-46).

PAVILLON DES ARTS An exhibition space in the mushroom-shape buildings overlooking the *Forum des Halles* complex. Presentations range from ancient to modern, paintings to sculpture. Open 10:30 AM to 5:30 PM; closed Mondays and holidays. 101 Rue Rambuteau, 1er (phone: 42-33-82-50).

VIDÉOTHÈQUE DE PARIS A veritable treasure trove of information about the City of Light, this extensive computerized video archive contains thousands of films, documentaries, and videos on Paris dating from the turn of the century to today. Open Tuesdays through Sundays from 12:30 to 8:30 PM. 2 Grand Galerie, 1er (phone: 40-26-34-30 or 40-26-30-60).

GALLERIES

Few artists live in Montparnasse nowadays; Paris's finest galleries are clustered on the Right Bank around the *Centre Georges-Pompidou* and the Place de la Concorde, and on the Left Bank on or near the Rue de Seine — although fine galleries can be found all over the city.

ADRIEN MAEGHT A prestigious list of artists that includes Miró, Matisse, Calder, and Chagall are displayed in this Left Bank gallery. 42 and 46 Rue du Bac, 7e (phone: 45-48-45-15).

AGATHE GAILLARD Contemporary photography, including Cartier-Bresson and the like. 3 Rue du Pont-Louis-Philippe, 4e (phone: 42-77-38-24).

ARTCURIAL Early moderns, such as Braque and Sonia Delaunay, as well as sculpture and prints, with an extensive, multilingual collection of art books in its bookshop. 9 Av. Matignon, 8e (phone: 42-99-16-16).

BEAUBOURG Well-known names in the Paris art scene, including Niki de Saint-Phalle, César, Tinguely, Klossowski. 23 Rue du Renard, 4e (phone: 42-71-20-50).

CAROLINE CORRE Exhibitions by contemporary artists, specializing in unique artists' books. 14 Rue Guénégaud, 6e (phone: 43-54-57-67).

CLAUDE BERNARD Francis Bacon, David Hockney, and Raymond Mason are among the artists exhibited here. 5 Rue des Beaux-Arts, 6e (phone: 43-26-97-07).

DANIEL MALINGUE Works by the Impressionists, as well as notable Parisian artists from the 1930s to the 1950s — Foujita, Fautrier, and so forth. 26 Av. Matignon, 8e (phone: 42-66-60-33).

DANIEL TEMPLON Major contemporary American and Italian artists are featured. 30 Rue Beaubourg, 3e (phone: 42-72-14-10).

DARTHEA SPEYER Run by a former American embassy attaché, now an art dealer. Contemporary painting. 6 Rue Jacques-Callot, 6e (phone: 43-54-78-41).

GALERIE DE FRANCE A prestigious gallery located in a majestic space features the works of historical avant-garde artists such as Brancusi and Gabo, as well as contemporary artists such as Matta, Aillaud, and Arroyo. 52 Rue de la Verrerie, 4e (phone: 42-74-38-00).

HERVÉ ODERMATT CAZEAU Early moderns — among them Picasso, Léger, Pissarro — and antiques. 85 *bis* Rue du Faubourg-St-Honoré, 8e (phone: 42-66-92-58).

ISY BRACHOT Master surrealists, American hyper-realists, and new realists. 35 Rue Guénégaud, 6e (phone: 43-54-22-40).

JEAN FOURNIER This dealer defended abstract expressionism in 1955 and remains faithful to the cause in his main gallery, where he also exhibits the works of promising young artists. 44 Rue Quincampoix, 4e (phone: 42-77-32-31).

LELONG The great moderns on view include Tàpies, Bacon, Alechinsky, Donald Judd, and Voss. 13-14 Rue de Téhéran, 8e (phone: 45-63-13-19).

MARWAN HOSS In an elegant, recently remodeled space near the Tuileries, are displayed Hartung, Henri Hayden, Gozalez, and Zao Wou-Ki. 12 Rue d'Alger, 1er (phone: 42-96-37-96).

NIKKI DIANA MARQUARDT Spacious gallery of contemporary work opened by an enterprising dealer from the Bronx. 9 Pl. des Vosges, 4e (phone: 42-78-21-00).

VIRGINIA ZABRISKIE Early and contemporary photography by Atget, Brassaï, Diane Arbus. Also painting and, occasionally, sculpture. 37 Rue Quincampoix, 4e (phone: 42-72-35-47).

YVON LAMBERT A dealer with an eye for the avant-avant-garde, he also exhibits the works of major artists from the 1970s and 1980s, including Jammes, Lewitt, Serra, and Schnabel. 108 Rue Vieille-du-Temple, 3e (phone: 42-71-09-33).

SHOPPING

From new-wave fashions to classic haute couture, Paris starts the trends and sets the styles the world copies. Prices are generally high, but more than a few people are willing to pay for the quality of the merchandise, not to mention the cachet of a Paris label, which enhances the appeal of many things besides clothing.

The big department stores are excellent places to get an idea of what's available. They include *Galeries Lafayette* (40 Bd. Haussmann, 9e; phone: 42-82-34-56; and other locations); *Au Printemps* (64 Bd. Haussmann, 9e; phone: 42-82-50-00); *La Samaritaine* (19 Rue de la Monnaie, 1er; phone: 40-41-20-20); *Le Bazar de l'Hôtel de Ville* (52 Rue de Rivoli, 4e; phone: 42-74-90-00); and *Au Bon Marché* (22 Rue de Sèvres, 7e; phone: 45-49-21-22).

Both *Galeries Lafayette* and *Au Printemps* hold excellent fashion shows that are open to the public at no charge. The former has shows on Wednesdays at 11 AM from April through October; there also are shows on Fridays. Reservations are necessary, and you should make them as early as possible by contacting the store (see telephone number, above). *Au Printemps* holds shows every Tuesday at 10 AM. They also take place on Fridays from March through October, and on Mondays from May through September. Admittance to these shows can be arranged through the store's US representative, *Au Printemps* (10 E. 21st St., Suite 600, New York, NY 10010; phone: 212-529-8484). In addition to receiving an invitation card that will get you into fashion shows for a full calendar year, you will receive a discount card that's good for 10% off any *Au Printemps* purchase over $20. The *Anne-Marie Victory Organization* (136 E. 64th St., New York, NY 10021; phone: 212-486-0353) sponsors trips that include viewing collections from such designers as Chanel, Givenchy, Nina Ricci, Ungaro, and Vicky Tiel.

Three major shopping centers — *Porte Maillot* (Pl. de la Porte Maillot), *Maine Montparnasse* (at the intersection of Bd. Montparnasse and Rue de Rennes), and *Le Forum des Halles* (see *Special Places*) — also are worth a visit, as is the lovely *Galerie Vivienne,* one of Paris's glass-roofed *galeries,* the 19th-century precursors of the modern-day shopping mall (main entrance at 4 Rue des Petits-Champs, 2e).

A FEW TIPS Sales (*soldes*) take place during the first weeks in January and in late June and July. Any shop labeled *dégriffé* (the word means, literally, "without the label") offers year-round discounts on brand-name clothing, often last season's styles. Discount shops also are known as "stock" shops. The French Value Added Tax (VAT; typically 18.6% and as high as 33.33% on luxury articles) can be refunded on most purchases made by foreigners, provided a minimum of 2,000F (about $370 at press time) is spent in one store. For more information, see "How to Get a Tax Refund" in *Shopping Spree* in DIVERSIONS.

In addition to elegant fashion, chic shoes, and leather goods, the best and most expensive antiques dealers are along the Faubourg-St-Honoré on the Right Bank. For antique hunters on the Left Bank, there's *Le Carré Rive Gauche,* an association of more than 100 antiques shops in the area bordered by Quai Voltaire, Rue de l'Université, Rue des Sts-Pères, and Rue du Bac. Antiques and curio collectors should explore Paris's several flea markets, which include the *Montreuil,* near the Porte de Montreuil, especially good for secondhand clothing; *Vanves,* near the Porte de Vanves, for furniture and fine bric-a-brac that is often snapped up by antiques dealers (it's best to arrive early on Saturday morning); and the largest and best-known, *Puces de St-Ouen,* near the Porte de Clignancourt, which offers an admirable array of antiques. For more information see *An Odyssey of the Old: Antiques Hunting in Paris* in DIVERSIONS.

What follows is a sampling of the wealth of shops in Paris; many have more than one location in the city. For a list of the variety of vendibles for which Paris is famous—and the best areas to purchase them—see *Shopping Spree* in DIVERSIONS. And for a detailed description of the gastronomic emporium that is *Fauchon,* see *Quintessential Paris* in DIVERSIONS.

ABSINTHE Chic is the word here — everything from one-of-a-kind silk hats to satin-covered settees — in this elegant little shop near the Place des Victoires. 74 Rue Jean-Jacques Rousseau, 1er (phone: 42-33-54-44).

ACCESSOIRE Very feminine footwear, often seen on the pages of *Elle* magazine. 6 Rue du Cherche-Midi, 6e, and other locations around the city (phone: 45-48-36-08).

AGNÈS B Supremely wearable, trendy, casual clothes. Four stores on the block-long Rue du Jour, 1er: men at No. 3 (phone: 42-33-04-13); young children and infants at No. 4 (phone: 40-39-96-88); women at No. 6 (phone: 45-08-56-56); and *Lolita,* for little girls, at No. 10 (phone: 40-26-36-87). Also at 17 Av. Pierre-I-de-Serbie, 16e (phone: 47-20-22-44); and 81 Rue d'Assas, 6e (phone: 46-33-70-20).

APRÈS-MIDI DE CHIEN Women's and children's formfitting togs in what the French dub "Anglo-Saxon"–style — tweedy jackets, jodhpurs, and print skirts. 10 Rue du Jour, 1er (phone: 40-26-92-78) and other locations.

ARNYS Conservative and elegant men's clothing. 14 Rue de Sèvres, 6e (phone: 45-48-76-99).

AZZEDINE ALAÏA The Tunisian designer who brought the body back. 7 Rue de Moussy, 4e (phone: 42-72-19-19).

BACCARAT High-quality porcelain and crystal. 30 *bis* Rue du Paradis, 10e (phone: 47-70-64-30); and 11 Pl. de la Madeleine, 8e (phone: 42-65-36-26).

LA BAGAGERIE Perhaps the best bag and belt boutique in the world. 12 Rue Tronchet, 8e (phone: 42-65-03-40), and other locations.

AU BAIN MARIE The most beautiful kitchenware and tabletop accessories, with an emphasis on Art Deco designs. 8 Rue Boissy-d'Anglas, 8e (phone: 42-66-59-74).

BALENCIAGA Ready-to-wear and designer haute couture. 10 Av. George-V, 8e (phone: 47-20-21-11).

BARTHÉLÉMY In a city of great cheese stores, this is at the top of almost everyone's *fromagerie* list. Platters of assorted cheeses are available. 51 Rue de Grenelle, 7e (phone: 45-48-56-75).

BERTHILLON Heavenly ice cream; Parisians often line up outside for a small carton for a special party. Flavors, which change with the season, include wild strawberry, calvados crunch, and candied chestnut. 31 Rue St-Louis-en-l'Ile, 4e (phone: 43-54-31-61). Several cafés on the Ile St-Louis also serve scoops of Berthillon.

BIBA Many styles of designer-label women's clothes such as Gaultier and Junko Shimada. 18 Rue de Sèvres, 6e (phone: 45-48-89-18).

BOUCHERON One of several fine jewelers clustered around the elegant Place Vendôme. 26 Pl. Vendôme, 1er (phone: 42-61-58-16).

BOUTIQUE LE FLORE You'll find silver-plated eggcups and other bistro accoutrements in this annex of the celebrated *Café Le Flore.* 26 Rue St-Benoît, 6e (phone: 45-44-33-40).

BRENTANO'S British and American novels, critiques on the American arts, and a variety of travel, technical, and business books — in English. 37 Av. de l'Opéra, 2e (phone: 42-61-52-50).

CACHAREL Fashionable ready-to-wear in great prints, for children and adults. 34 Rue Tronchet, 8e (phone: 47-42-12-61), and other locations.

CAREL Beautiful shoes. 12 Rond-Point des Champs-Elysées, 8e (phone: 45-62-30-62), and other locations.

CARITA Paris's most extensive — and friendliest — beauty/hair salon. 11 Rue du Faubourg-St-Honoré, 8e (phone: 42-68-13-40).

CARTIER Fabulous jewelry. 11-13 Rue de la Paix, 2e (phone: 42-61-58-56), and other locations.

CASTELBAJAC Trendy designer togs for men and women. 31 Pl. du Marché St-Honoré, 1er (phone: 42-60-78-40), and other locations.

CAVES TAILLEVENT One of Paris's best and most fairly priced wine shops, run by the owners of the three-star restaurant of the same name. 199 Rue du Faubourg-St-Honoré, 8e (phone: 45-61-14-09).

CÉLINE A popular women's boutique for clothing and accessories. 24 Rue François-Ier, 8e (phone: 47-20-22-83); 3 Av. Victor-Hugo, 16e (phone: 45-01-70-48); and other locations.

CERRUTI For women's clothing, 15 Pl. de la Madeleine, 8e (phone: 47-42-10-78); for men's, 27 Rue Royale, 8e (phone: 42-65-68-72).

CHANEL Classic women's fashions, inspired by the late, legendary Coco Chanel, now under the direction of Karl Lagerfeld. 42 Av. Montaigne, 8e (phone: 47-23-74-12) — this address covers three individual buildings: one for shoes, another for clothing and cosmetics, and the third for watches; and 29-31 Rue Cambon, 1er (phone: 42-86-28-00), headquarters for haute couture as well as ready-to-wear and accessories. The newest branch at 5 Pl. Vendôme, 1er (phone: 42-86-28-00) sells nothing but Chanel-designed watches.

CHANTAL THOMASS Ultra-feminine fashions and sexy lingerie in a new boutique near the Palais-Royal. 1 Rue Vivienne, 1er (phone: 40-15-02-36), and other locations.

CHARLES JOURDAN Sleek, high-fashion footwear. 86 Av. des Champs-Elysées, 8e (phone: 45-62-29-28); 5 Pl. de la Madeleine, 1er (phone: 42-61-50-07); and other locations.

CHARLEY An excellent selection of lingerie, plus personal attention, and relatively low prices. 14 Rue du Faubourg-St-Honoré, 8e (phone: 47-42-17-70).

CHARVET Paris's answer to Savile Row. An all-in-one men's shop, where shirts are the house specialty — they stock more than 4,000. Ties, too. 28 Pl. Vendôme, 1er (phone: 42-60-30-70).

LA CHÂTELAINE Where all of Paris shops for exquisite (and costly) toys and clothing for children and grandchildren. 170 Av. Victor-Hugo, 16e (phone: 47-27-44-07).

CHAUMET Crownmakers for most of Europe's royalty. Expensive jewels, including antique watches covered with semi-precious stones. 12 Pl. Vendôme, 1er (phone: 42-60-32-82); and 46 Av. George-V, 8e (phone: 49-52-08-25).

CHLOÉ Designs for women. 60 Rue du Faubourg-St-Honoré, 8e (phone: 42-66-01-39).

CHRISTIAN DIOR One of the most famous couture names in the world. 28-30 Av. Montaigne, 8e; *Miss Dior* and *Baby Dior* for children also are at this location (phone: 40-73-54-44).

CHRISTIAN LACROIX This designer offers the "hautest" of haute couture. 26 Av. Montaigne, 8e (phone: 47-23-44-40) and 8 Av. George-V, 8e (phone 47-20-81-31).

CHRISTOFLE The internationally famous silversmith. 9 Rue Royale, 8e (phone: 49-33-43-00).

CLAUDE MONTANA Ready-to-wear and haute couture from this au courant designer. 3 Rue des Petits-Champs, 1er (phone: 40-20-02-14).

COESNON Arguably one of Paris's finest *charcuteries,* in spite of its diminutive size. The terrines, pâtés, *boudin blanc aux truffles,* and other temptations are the best of their kind. 30 Rue Dauphine, 6e (phone: 43-54-35-80).

COMMES DES GARÇONS Asymmetrical-style clothing for *des filles* and *des garçons.* 40-42 Rue Etienne-Marcel, 1er (phone: 42-33-05-21).

COMPTOIRS DE LA TOUR D'ARGENT Glassware, napkins, silver items, and other objects bearing the celebrated restaurant's logo. 2 Rue de Cardinal-Lemoine, 5e (phone: 46-33-45-58).

COURRÈGES Another bastion of haute couture. 40 Rue François-Ier, 8e (phone: 47-20-70-44) and 46 Rue du Faubourg-St-Honoré, 8e (phone: 42-65-37-75).

CRISTALLERIES DE SAINT LOUIS Handmade lead crystal at good prices. They will pack and ship purchases. 13 Rue Royale, 8e (phone: 40-17-01-74).

DALLOYAU Fine purveyor of pastries and inventor of the sinful (and incredibly delicious) *gâteau opéra,* a confection of coffee and chocolate cream frosted with the darkest of chocolate and topped with an edible gold leaf. 99-101 Rue du Faubourg-St-Honoré, 8e (phone: 43-59-18-10); 2 Pl. Edmond-Rostand, 6e (phone: 43-29-31-10); and other locations.

DEBAUVE ET GALLAIS The decor of the building dating from 1800 is as fine as the delicious chocolates sold here. 30 Rue des Sts-Pères, 7e (phone: 45-48-54-67).

DIDIER LAMARTHE Elegant handbags and accessories. 219 Rue du Faubou⌐
St-Honoré, 1er (phone: 42-97-44-46).

DINERS EN VILLE Irresistible antique glassware, dishes, and tablecloths. 27 Rue
de Varenne, 7e (phone: 42-22-78-33).

DOMINIQUE MORLOTTI A current favorite of Paris's best-dressed men. 25 Rue
St-Sulpice, 6e (phone: 43-54-89-89).

DOROTHÉE BIS Colorful women's knit sportswear. 33 Rue de Sèvres, 6e (phone:
42-22-02-90).

LES DRUGSTORES PUBLICIS A uniquely French version of the American drugstore, with an amazing variety of goods — perfume, books, records, foreign newspapers, magazines, film, cigarettes, food, and more, all wildly
overpriced. 149 Bd. St-Germain, 6e (phone: 42-22-92-50); 133 Av. des
Champs-Elysées, 8e (phone: 47-23-54-34); and 1 Av. Matignon, 8e (phone:
43-59-38-70).

E. DEHILLERIN An enormous selection of professional cookware. 18-20 Rue
Coquillière, 1er (phone: 42-36-53-13).

ELLE The magazine that sums up Parisian feminine style has a clothes and home
furnishings boutique. 30 Rue St-Sulpice, 6e (phone: 43-26-46-10).

EMANUEL UNGARO Couturier boutique for women. 2 Av. Montaigne, 8e (phone:
47-23-61-94).

EMILIANO ZAPATA An eclectic collection of women's fashions in brightly colored
fabrics and stylish cuts. 35 Rue de Sèvres, 6e (phone: 45-48-92-71).

EMMANUELLE KHANH Feminine clothes in lovely fabrics, including embroidered
linen. 2 Rue de Tournon, 6e (phone: 46-33-41-03).

ERÈS Avant-garde sportswear for men and women. 2 Rue Tronchet, 8e (phone:
47-42-24-55).

FABRICE Trendy, fine costume jewelry. 33 and 54 Rue Bonaparte, 6e (phone:
43-26-57-95).

FLORIANE Smart and well made clothes for infants and children. 45 Rue de
Sèvres, 6e (phone: 45-49-97-61), and other locations.

FRANCK ET FILS A department store for women's designer clothes ranging from
Yves Saint Laurent to Thierry Mugler. 80 Rue de Passy, 16e (phone:
46-47-86-00).

FRATELLI ROSSETTI All kinds of shoes, made from buttery-soft leather, for men
and women. 54 Rue du Faubourg-St-Honoré, 8e (phone: 42-65-26-60).

GALIGNANI This shop sells books in English and French. It has been run by the
same family since the beginning of the 19th century. 224 Rue de Rivoli, 1er
(phone: 42-60-76-07).

GEORGES RECH One of the most popular makers of classy, very Parisian styles, and at more affordable prices than other manufacturers of similarly styled goods. 273 Rue du Faubourg St-Honoré, 1er (phone: 42-61-41-14); 54 Rue Bonaparte, 6e (phone: 43-26-84-11); and other locations.

GIANNI VERSACE A 3-story mega-store adorned with Empire antiques (across from the Elysée Palace at 62 Rue du Faubourg-St-Honoré, 8e; phone: 47-42-88-02), it sells the designer's men's, women's, and children's lines. A smaller Left Bank outlet featuring only women's clothing is at 67 Rue des Sts-Pères, 6e (phone: 45-44-09-52).

GIORGIO ARMANI The legendary Italian designer has two shops on the elegant Place Vendôme: No. 6 (phone: 42-61-55-09), for his top-of-the-line clothes; and *Emporio Armani*, No. 25 (phone 42-61-02-34), for his less expensive line.

GIVENCHY Beautifully tailored clothing by the master couturier. 8 Av. George-V, 8e (phone: 47-20-81-31); and 8 Av. Montaigne, 8e (phone: 47-23-44-40).

GUERLAIN For fine perfume and cosmetics. 2 Pl. Vendôme, 1er; 68 Champs-Elysées, 8e (phone: 45-62-52-57); 29 Rue de Sèvres, 6e (phone: 42-22-46-60); and 93 Rue de Passy, 16e (phone: 42-91-60-02).

GUY LAROCHE Classic and conservative couture. 30 Rue du Faubourg-St-Honoré, 8e (phone: 42-65-62-74); and 29 Av. Montaigne, 8e (phone: 40-69-69-50).

HANAE MORI The grande dame of Japanese designers in Paris. 9 Rue du Faubourg-St-Honoré, 8e (phone: 47-42-78-78).

HÉDIARD Pricey but choice food shop, notable for its assortment of coffees and teas. Chic tearoom upstairs. 21 Pl. de la Madeleine, 8e (phone: 42-66-44-36).

HERMÈS For very high quality ties, scarves, classic clothes, handbags, shoes, saddles, and accessories. 24 Rue du Faubourg-St-Honoré, 8e (phone: 40-17-47-17).

HÔTEL DROUOT Paris's huge auction house operates daily except Sundays. Good buys. 9 Rue Drouot, 9e (phone: 48-00-20-20).

IGN (FRENCH NATIONAL GEOGRAPHIC INSTITUTE) All manner of maps — ancient and modern, foreign and domestic, esoteric and mundane — are sold here. 136 *bis* Rue Grenelle, 7e (phone: 42-25-87-90); and 107 Rue La Boëtie, 8e.

INÈS DE LA FRESSANGE The former Chanel model has opened this very chic shop, which sells everything from classic white silk shirts to furniture gilded with her signature oak leaf. 14 Av. de Montaigne, 8e (phone: 47-23-08-94).

ISSEY MIYAKE "In" shop, selling women's clothing made by the Japanese artist-designer. Classic, more expensive line at 201 Bd. St-Germain, 7e (phone: 45-44-60-88); latest collections at 3 Pl. des Vosges, 4e (phone: 48-87-01-86).

JEAN-PAUL GAULTIER Designer clothes for men and women. 6 Rue Vivienne, 2e (phone: 42-86-05-05).

JIL SANDER The leading German designer of womenswear's first boutique in Paris. 52 Av. Montaigne, 8e (phone: 44-95-06-70).

JUNKO SHIMADA Formfitting clothes from the chic Japanese designer. 54 Rue Etienne Marcel, 2e (phone: 42-36-36-97).

JULE DES PRÉS Bouquets of dried flowers and herbs, as well as dried aromatic plants made into potpourri. 19 Rue du Cherche-Midi, 6e (phone: 45-48-26-84); 46 Rue du Roi-de-Sicile, 4e (phone: 45-48-26-84).

KARL LAGERFELD Women's clothing in a more adventurous spirit than those he designs for Chanel. 19 Rue du Faubourg-St-Honoré, 8e (phone: 42-66-64-64).

KENZO Avant-garde fashions by the Japanese designer. A *Kenzo* children's shop is located in the passageway next to the store. 3 Pl. des Victoires, 1er (phone: 40-39-72-03).

KITCHEN BAZAAR Specializes in everything imaginable for the smart kitchen. 11 Av. du Maine, 15e (phone: 42-22-91-17). A second store, *Kitchen Bazaar Autrement,* features ethnic kitchen utensils from all over the world. 6 Av. du Maine, 15e (phone: 45-48-89-00).

LALIQUE The famous crystal. 11 Rue Royale, 8e (phone: 42-66-52-40).

LANVIN Another fabulous designer, with several spacious, colorful boutiques under one roof. 15 and 22 Rue du Faubourg-St-Honoré, 8e (phone: 42-65-14-40); and 2 Rue Cambon, 1er (phone: 42-60-38-83).

LEGRAND FILLE ET FILS Fine wines and spirits and articles for the *cave* and table, such as *rattes* (wrought-iron candle holders used in real wine cellars), plus excellent maps of French wine regions. 1 Rue Banque, 2e (phone: 42-60-07-12).

LENÔTRE Specializes in pastries and other desserts — from exquisite éclairs and fruit mousses to charlottes and chocolates. 44 Rue d'Auteuil, 16e (phone: 45-24-52-52), and several other locations.

LESCÊNE-DURA Everything for the wine lover or maker, except wine. 63 Rue de la Verrerie, 4e (phone: 42-72-08-74).

LIMOGES-UNIC Two stores on the same street, the first selling rather expensive items, the second offering many varieties of Limoges china as well as a good selection of typically French Porcelaine de Paris. 12 and 58 Rue de Paradis, 10e (phone: 47-70-54-49 and 47-70-61-49).

LOLITA LEMPICKA Iconoclastic, formfitting women's wear. 3 *bis* Rue de Rosiers, 4e (phone: 42-74-42-94), and other locations.

LOUIS FÉRAUD Couturier fashions for women at 88 Rue du Faubourg-St-Honoré, 8e, and for men at No. 62 (phone: 40-07-01-16), and other locations.

LOUIS VUITTON High-quality luggage and handbags. The agreeable, efficient, and well-mannered staff at the modern Avenue Montaigne branch are a pleasure after the chilly reception at the original Avenue Marceau shop. 54 Av. Montaigne, 8e (phone: 45-62-47-00) and 78 *bis* Av. Marceau, 8e (phone: 47-20-47-00).

LUMICRYSTAL Located in the building where Corot lived and died, this fine china and crystal store carries Baccarat, Daum, Limoges, and items from Puiforcat. 22 Rue de Paradis, 10e (phone: 47-70-27-97).

LA MAISON DU CHOCOLAT Robert Linxe, perhaps the most talented chocolate maker in the French capital, produces delicate, meltingly delicious confections. 225 Rue de Faubourg-St-Honoré, 8e (phone: 42-27-39-44), and 6 Rue Pierre-Charron, 8e (phone: 47-23-38-25).

LA MAISON DE L'ESCARGOT Prepares and sells more than 10 tons of snails annually, following a secret recipe that is 75 years old. 68 Rue Fondary, 15e (phone: 45-77-93-82).

MAISON DE LA TRUFFE The world's largest truffles retailer. (They're fresh, not preserved, from November to March.) 19 Pl. de la Madeleine, 8e (phone: 42-65-53-22).

MARCHÉ AUX PUCES Paris's famous *Flea Market,* with 3,000 dealers in antiques and secondhand items, who are clustered in various smaller markets. The *Marché Biron* for fine bric-a-brac is one of the best. Open Saturdays, Sundays, and Mondays. Bargaining is a must. Porte de Clignancourt, 18e.

MARIA LUISA The hautest of haute couture and daring new looks from Paris's top designers are the stock in trade here. 2 Rue Cambon, 1er (phone: 47-03-96-15).

MARIE MERCIÉ Fashionable hats, including turbans and velvet berêts. 56 Rue Tiquetonne, 2e (phone: 40-26-60-68); and 23 Rue St-Sulpice, 6e (phone: 43-26-45-83).

MARITHÉE & FRANÇOIS GIRBAUD Not just jeans at this shop for men and women. 38 Rue Etienne-Marcel, 2e (phone: 42-33-54-69).

MAUD FRIZON Sophisticated, imaginative shoes and handbags. 83 Rue des Sts-Pères, 6e (phone: 42-22-06-93).

MAX MARA Carries a line of Italian ready-to-wear that expresses many different moods (in six distinct collections) — from classic chic to trendy — and all at surprisingly affordable prices: Among several locations: 37 Rue du Four, 6e (phone: 43-29-91-10); and 265 Rue du Faubourg-St-Honoré, 1er (phone: 40-20-04-58).

MICHEL SWISS The best place to buy perfume in the city, offering a voluminous selection, cheerful service, discounts of 25% for payment with cash or traveler's checks (20% for credit cards), and, in addition, a 25% tax refund on the balance to American visitors who spend more than 1,200F (about $220). That brings the total discount to almost 44%. 16 Rue de la Paix, 2e (phone: 42-61-71-71).

MISS MAUD High-style shoes for young folks' feet. At several locations, including 90 Rue du Faubourg-St-Honoré, 8e (phone: 42-65-27-96).

MISSONI Innovative, original Italian knitwear. 43 Rue du Bac, 7e (phone: 45-48-38-02).

M.O.R.A. One of Paris's "professional" cookware shops, though it sells to individuals as well. Just about any piece of equipment you can imagine, and an interesting selection of cookbooks — in French. 13 Rue Montmartre, 1er (phone: 45-08-19-24).

MORABITO Magnificent handbags and luggage at steep prices. 1 Pl. Vendôme, 1er (phone: 42-60-30-76).

MOTSCH ET FILS Fine hatmaker for men and women since 1887 — Jean Gabin was a customer. 42 Av. George-V, 8e (phone: 47-23-79-22).

MURIEL GRATEAU An eclectic shop, with silk blouses and fine table linen. Jardin du Palais-Royal, under the arcade, 1er (phone: 40-20-90-30).

LE MUST DE CARTIER Actually two boutiques, on either side of the *Ritz* hotel, offering such Cartier items as lighters and watches at prices that, though not low, are almost bearable when you deduct the 25% VAT tax. 7-23 Pl. Vendôme, 1er (phone: 42-61-55-55).

AU NAIN BLEU The city's greatest toy store. 408 Rue du Faubourg-St-Honoré, 8e (phone: 42-60-39-01).

NINA RICCI Women's fashions, as well as the famous perfume. 17 Rue François-Ier, 8e (phone: 47-23-78-88); and 39 Av. Montaigne, 8e (phone: 47-23-78-88).

L'OLIVIER The finest cooking oils, from several varieties of olive oil to walnut, hazelnut, and more. 23 Rue de Rivoli, 4e (phone: 48-04-56-59).

PACO RABANNE A very French designer famous for dresses mixing fabric and metals. 7 Rue du Cherche-Midi, 6e (phone: 42-22-87-80).

PALOMA PICASSO Perfume, clothing, and jewelry from one of France's preeminent designers and you-know-who's daughter. 5 Rue de la Paix, 2e (phone: 42-86-02-21).

PAPIER PLUS One of Paris's finest *papeteries* (stationery stores). 9 Rue du Pont Louis Philippe, 4e (phone: 42-77-70-49).

PER SPOOK One of the city's best younger designers. 18 Av. George-V, 8e (phone: 47-23-00-19), and elsewhere.

AU PETIT MATELOT Classic sportswear, outdoor togs, and nautical accessories for men, women, and children. Especially terrific are their Tyrolean-style olive or navy loden coats. 27 Av. de la Grande-Armée, 16e (phone: 45-00-15-51).

PIERRE BALMAIN Couturier boutique for women's fashions. 44 Rue François-Ier, 8e (phone: 47-20-98-79), and other locations.

PIERRE CARDIN A famous designer's own boutique. 83 Rue du Faubourg-St-Honoré, 8e (phone: 42-66-62-94); 27 Av. Victor-Hugo, 16e (phone: 45-01-88-13); 14 Pl. François-Ier, 8e (phone: 45-63-29-13); and other locations.

POILÂNE Considered by many French to sell the best bread in the country; the large and crusty round country-style loaves dubbed *pain Poilâne,* taste delicious with soup, pâté, cheese, or cassoulet. 8 Rue du Cherche-Midi, 6e (phone: 45-48-42-59).

POPY MORENI Unusually designed unisex clothes inspired by the commedia dell'arte, located in one of the loveliest squares in the city. 13 Pl. des Vosges, 4e (phone: 42-77-09-96).

PORTHAULT Expensive, but elegantly exquisite bed and table linen. 18 Av. Montaigne, 8e (phone: 47-20-75-25).

PUIFORCAT Art Deco tableware in a beautiful setting. 22 Rue François-Ier, 8e (phone: 47-20-74-27).

ROBERT CLERGERIE Among Paris's finest footwear, these slightly chunky, thick-soled shoes and boots will actually stand up to the perils of cobblestone streets. 5 Rue du Cherche-Midi, 6e (phone: 45-48-75-47), and other locations.

ROMEO GIGLI Men's and women's arty ready-to-wear and haute couture. 46 Rue de Sévigné, 3e (phone: 48-04-57-05).

SHAKESPEARE AND COMPANY This legendary English-language bookstore, opposite Notre-Dame, is something of a tourist attraction in itself. 37 Rue de la Bûcherie, 5e (no phone).

SIDONIE LARIZZI Heavenly handmade women's shoes. 8 Rue Marignan, 8e (phone: 43-59-38-87).

SONIA RYKIEL Stunning sportswear and knits. 175 Bd. St-Germain, 6e (phone: 49-54-60-60); and 70 Rue du Faubourg-St-Honoré, 8e (phone: 42-65-20-81).

SOULEIADO Vibrant, traditional Provençal fabrics made into scarves, shawls, totes, and tableware. 78 Rue de Seine, 6e (phone: 43-54-62-25); and 83 Av. Paul-Doumer, 16e (phone: 42-24-99-34).

STÉPHANE KÉLIAN High-fashion, high-quality, and high-priced (but not completely unreasonable) men's and women's shoes, in several locations, including 4 Pl. des Victoires, 1er (phone: 42-61-60-74).

TARTINE ET CHOCOLAT Clothing for children, from infancy to 12 years old, and dresses for moms-to-be. Their trademark item: striped unisex overalls. 90 Rue de Rennes, 6e (phone: 42-22-67-34).

TED LAPIDUS A compromise between haute couture and excellent ready-to-wear. 23 Rue du Faubourg-St-Honoré, 8e (phone: 44-60-89-91); 35 Rue François-Ier, 8e (phone: 47-20-56-14); and other locations.

THIERRY MUGLER Dramatic ready-to-wear for women. 10 Pl. des Victoires, 2e (phone: 42-60-06-37); and other locations.

TRUSSARDI Italian ready-to-wear from a designer whose leather goods and canvas carryalls are much appreciated by the French and Japanese. 21 Rue du Faubourg-St-Honoré, 8e (phone: 42-65-11-40).

LA TUILE À LOUP Crafts from France's provinces, including Burgundy pottery and Normandy lace. 35 Rue Daubenton, 5e (phone: 47-07-28-90).

VALENTINO Ready-to-wear and haute couture fashions for men and women from the Italian designer. 17-19 Av. Montaigne, 8e (phone: 47-23-64-61).

VAN CLEEF & ARPELS One of the world's great jewelers. 22 Pl. Vendôme, 1er (phone: 42-61-58-58).

VICKY TIEL Strapless evening gowns decorated with beads and bows, as well as contemporary sweaters and baseball-style jackets. 21 Rue Bonaparte, 6e (phone: 46-33-53-58).

VICTOIRE Ready-to-wear from up-and-coming designers such as André Walker, with attractive accessories and jewelry. 10 and 12 Pl. des Victoires, 2e (phone: 42-60-96-21 and 42-61-09-02), and other locations.

VIRGIN MEGASTORE The British have taken over the Parisian market in CDs, records, and video cassettes. Though the selection is staggering, the store is usually so crowded that browsing is impossible. 56-60 Champs-Elysées, 8e (phone: 40-74-06-48).

WALTER STEIGER Some of the capital's most expensive and exclusive footwear for men and women. The flagship shop displays satin slippers like precious jewels — and with prices to match. 83 Rue du Faubourg-St-Honoré, 8e (phone: 42-66-65-08).

W. H. SMITH AND SONS The largest bookstore in Paris (with more space now that the upstairs tearoom has been converted into additional book displays) for reading material in English. It sells the Sunday *New York Times,* in addition to many British and American magazines and books. 248 Rue de Rivoli, 1er (phone: 42-60-37-97).

YOHJI YAMAMOTO This Japanese designer presents highly unusual outerwear, which may make timid souls think twice before donning an outfit. For women, 25 Rue du Louvre, 1er (phone: 42-21-42-93); and for men, 47 Rue Etienne Marcel, 1er (phone: 45-08-82-45).

YVES SAINT LAURENT The world-renowned designer, considered one of the most famous names in high fashion. The Right Bank location on the Rue du Faubourg-St-Honoré has been redesigned and serves as the prototype for the remodeling of all the couturier's shops around the world. 38 Rue du Faubourg-St-Honoré, 8e (phone: 42-65-01-15); 5 Av. Marceau, 8e (phone: 47-23-72-71); 6 Pl. St-Sulpice, 6e (phone: 43-29-43-00); and other locations.

BEST DISCOUNT SHOPS

If you're one of those — like us — who believes that the eighth deadly sin is buying retail, you'll treasure these inexpensive outlets.

ANNA LOWE Saint Laurent's styling, among others, at a discount. 35 Av. Matignon, 8e (phone: 43-59-96-61).

ANNE PARÉE Great buys on French perfume, Dior scarves, men's ties, Limoges china, and Vuarnet sunglasses. A 40% discount (including VAT) is given on purchases totaling 1,500F (about $275) or more. Mail order, too. 10 Rue Duphot, 1er (phone: 42-60-03-26).

BAB'S High fashion at low — or at least reasonable — prices. 29 Av. Marceau, 16e (phone: 47-20-84-74) and 89 *bis* Av. des Ternes, 17e (phone: 45-74-02-74).

BIDERMANN Menswear from Saint Laurent, Kenzo, and Courrèges, in a warehouse of a store in the Marais. 114 Rue de Turenne, 3e (phone: 44-61-17-00).

BOËTIE 104 Good buys on men's and women's shoes. 104 Rue La Boëtie, 8e (phone: 43-59-72-38).

CACHAREL STOCK Surprisingly current Cacharel fashions at about a 40% discount. 114 Rue d'Alésia, 14e (phone: 45-42-53-04).

CATHERINE BARIL Women's ready-to-wear by designers such as Yves Saint Laurent and Jean-Louis Scherrer. 14 Rue de la Tour, 16e (phone: 45-20-95-21) and 25 Rue de la Tour, 16e (phone: 45-27-11-46).

CHERCHEMINIPPES One of the best Parisian *dépôt-vente* shops for high-quality children's clothes. The adult clothing *dépôt-vente* collections just down the street are also worth a visit. 160 Rue du Cherche-Midi, 6e (phone: 92-22-33-89).

DENTS DE LAIT Marked-down, first-quality designer children's clothes. 15 Rue Vavin, 6e (phone: 46-33-90-92).

DÉPÔT DES GRANDES MARQUES A third-floor shop near the stock market, featuring up to 50% markdowns on Louis Féraud, Cerruti, Renoma, and similar labels. 15 Rue de la Banque, 2e (phone: 42-96-99-04).

DIDIER LUDOT Designer fashions at down-to-earth prices at this thrift shop across from the Jardin du Palais Royal. 19 Galerie Montpensier, 1er (phone: 42-96-06-56).

DOROTHÉE BIS STOCK Ms. Bis's well-known designs at about 40% off. 74 Rue d'Alésia, 14e (phone: 45-42-17-11).

EIFFEL SHOPPING Another bastion of fine French perfumes at discounted prices, which also stocks Lalique crystal, watches, and upscale costume jewelry. 9 Av. de Suffren, 7e (phone: 45-66-55-30).

HALLE BYS High fashions at discount prices. 60 Rue de Richelieu, 2e (phone: 42-96-65-42).

JEAN-LOUIS SCHERRER Haute couture labels by Scherrer and others at about half their original prices. 29 Av. Ledru-Rollin, 12e (phone: 46-28-39-27).

LANVIN SOLDES TROIS Lanvin fashions at about half their normal retail cost. 3 Rue de Vienne, 8e (no phone).

MENDÈS Less-than-wholesale prices on haute couture, especially Saint Laurent and Lanvin. 65 Rue Montmartre, 2e (phone: 45-08-52-62 or 42-36-83-32).

MISS GRIFFES The very best of haute couture in small sizes (up to size 10) at small prices. Alterations, too. Open Mondays through Fridays from 11 AM to 6 PM. 19 Rue de Penthièvre, 8e (phone: 42-65-10-00).

MOUTON À CINQ PATTES Ready-to-wear clothing for men, women, and children at 50% off original prices. 8 and 18 Rue St-Placide, 6e (phone: 45-48-86-26); and other locations.

RÉCIPROQUE Billed as the largest *dépôt-vente* in Paris, this outlet features names like Chanel, Alaïa, Lanvin, and Scherrer, as well as fine objets d'art. Several hundred square yards of display area are arranged by designer and by size. Five locations on the Rue de la Pompe, 16e: No. 89 for artworks; No. 93 for women's evening wear; No. 95 for women's sportswear; No. 103 for men's clothing and accessories (phone: 47-04-30-28 for these four); and No. 123 for women's coats and accessories (phone: 47-27-30-28).

STÉPHANE Men's designer suits by Pierre Balmain, Ted Lapidus, and André Courrèges at a 25% to 45% discount. 130 Bd. St-Germain, 6e (phone: 46-33-94-55).

STOCK GRIFFES Women's ready-to-wear apparel at 40% off their original prices. 7 Rue St-Merri, 4e (phone: 48-04-93-89).

STOCK SYSTEM Prêt-à-porter clothing for men and women at a 30% discount. 112 Rue d'Alésia, 14e (phone: 45-43-80-86).

Also, Rue du Paradis (10e) is the best area to shop for crystal and porcelain — Baccarat, Saint-Louis, Haviland, Bernardaud, and Villeroy & Boch — at amazing priçes. Try *Boutique Paradis*, No. 1 *bis*; *L'Art et La Table*, No. 3; *Porcelain Savary*, No. 9; *Arts Céramiques*, No. 15; and *Cristallerie Paradis*, at No. 17.

SECOND BESTS	If haute couture prices paralyze your pocket-

book, several shops in the city offer pre-owned, high-style clothes with down-to-earth price tags. *L'Astucerie* (105 Rue de Javel, 15e; phone: 45-57-94-74) offers designerwear and accessories — from Hermès scarves and Kelly bags to Vuitton luggage; *La Marette* (25 Galerie Vivienne, 2e; phone: 42-60-08-19) carries designer items including a selection of stylish children's outfits and accessories; and *Troc'Eve* (25 Rue Violet, 15e; phone: 45-79-38-36) has an impressive stock of pre-owned designer clothes in perfect condition.

SPORTS AND FITNESS

BIKING Rentals are available in the Bois de Boulogne and the Bois de Vincennes, or contact the *Fédération Française de Cyclo-Tourisme* (*FFCT;* 8 Rue Jean-Marie-Jégo, 13e; phone: 45-80-30-21) for bike rentals and bike shops throughout France; *Bicyclub* (8 Pl. de la Porte-Champerrat, 17e; phone: 47-66-55-92); or *Paris-Vélo* (2 Rue du Fer-à-Moulin, 5e; phone: 43-37-59-22). In addition to renting bicycles, *Paris by Cycle* (99 Rue de la Jonquière, 17e; phone: 42-63-36-63) arranges guided group tours of the city and of Versailles, as well as bike trips alternating with horseback rides. The world-famous *Tour de France* bicycle race takes place in July and ends in Paris.

Three organizations that also arrange group rides for different levels in and around Paris during spring and fall are *CIMH* (a government-sponsored clearinghouse for sports activities; 15 Rue Gay-Lussac, 5e; phone: 43-25-70-90); *Mountain Bike Trip* (6 Pl. Etienne Pernet, 15e; phone: 48-42-57-87); and the *Movement for Defense of the Bicycle* (32 Rue Raymond-Losserand; phone: 45-82-84-76 or 43-20-26-02).

FITNESS CENTERS The *Gymnase Club* (208 Rue de Vaugirard, 15e; phone: 47-83-99-45; and many other locations); *Club Quartier Latin* (19 Rue de Pontoise, 5e; phone: 43-54-82-45); *Club Jean de Beauvais* (5 Rue de Jean-de-Beauvais, 5e; phone: 46-33-16-80); *Espace Beaujon* (208 Rue du Faubourg-St-Honoré, 8e; phone: 42-89-12-32); and *Espace Vit'Halles* (48

Rue Rambuteau; phone: 42-77-21-71) are open daily to non-members for a fee.

GOLF Although there are no 18-hole courses within the city, several major lay-outs are close by. The *Fédération Française de Golf* (69 Av. Victor-Hugo, 16e; phone: 45-02-13-55) and the French Ministry of Tourism set up a system whereby travelers and others who are not members of a local golf club can play. Greens fees vary according to the day and season, but average about $40 (at press time), except during weekends, when prices rise. Call ahead to reserve. For information on golf courses just beyond Paris, see *Great Golf Nearby* in DIVERSIONS.

In addition, there is a 9-hole municipal course at the *St-Cloud* race-course (1 Rue du Camp Canadien, St-Cloud; phone: 47-71-39-22) just west of the city.

HORSE RACING If Paris has a sporting passion, it's horses. The French invented the pari-mutuel betting system (based on equally distributed winnings) and there are eight tracks in and around the city, a half-dozen racing sheets, and several hundred places to bet during a season that runs year-round. Here are our odds-on favorites for a great day at the races.

WINNING TRACKS

Auteuil Opened in 1870 for steeplechase only, *Auteuil* is not like any other park; there are over 40 permanent obstacles spread across 30 acres. More than 60,000 Parisians turn out for the fashion stroll on the third Sunday in June, the *Grand Steeplechase de Paris* (this is where Hemingway took Ezra Pound to the races!). Best tip for this track is a reservation at the *Panoramique de l'Hippodrome* restaurant (phone: 42-88-91-38), or take your winnings over to the neighboring *Pré Catelan* (phone: 45-24-55-58), a singular, if pricey, dining experience. Bois de Boulogne (phone: 45-27-12-24).

Longchamp The temple of flat racing since 1855, *Longchamp* is the center of the country's thoroughbred racing, the most prestigious site and the one for which hopeful entries train at nearby Maisons-Laffitte, Enghien, Chan-tilly, Evry, and St-Cloud. The track's two highlight events are the *Grand Prix de Paris* in late June, which carries a purse of 1 million francs in prize money for the winner, and the *Prix de l'Arc de Triomphe* in early October, one of Europe's richest races at 5 million francs. Bois de Boulogne (phone: 42-24-13-29).

Saint Cloud This course in a chic suburb just west of Paris offers flat racing from spring to fall, with the prestigious *Grand Prix de St-Cloud* held the first Sunday in July. St-Cloud (phone: 47-71-39-22).

From late April until early September, a number of historic tracks around Paris open for selected racing dates. In late spring, races are scheduled in Fountainebleu, and the French equivalent of *Ascot,* the *Prix de Diane/Hermès,* is held at *Chantilly* (phone: 42-66-92-O2), about 25 miles (40 km) north of Paris, as part of the *Grande Semaine.* Chantilly, which many consider the most beautiful racetrack in the world, also has inaugurated a magnificent horse racing museum. Legend has it that a duke of the 17th century was reincarnated as a horse and had stables fit for a king — or, at least, a duke — built for him. Though never used, the stables have now been converted into the *Musée Vivant du Cheval* (phone: 44-57-13-13). After these events, the Parisian racing crowd moves on to summer racing at Deauville (about 2 hours from Paris). The best way to find out times, dates, and racing tips is by reading *Paris-Turf, Tiercé* magazine, *France-Soir,* or *L'Equipe,* all available at newsstands.

Vincennes A taxi ride into the woods, the *Champs de Courses de Vincennes* is the scene of Paris night racing, particularly trotting. Popular with die-hard bettors, the track has a rough reputation and is, in fact, a center of blue-collar values: red wine at the bar, corn yellow cigarettes, and spicy *merguez* (sausage) sandwiches. The major highlight of the Vincennes season is the *Prix d'Amérique* for trotters, in the dead cold of January. Reservations are advised for the track restaurant, *Le Paddock* (phone: 43-68-64-94). Bois de Vincennes (phone: 47-42-07-70).

OFF-TRACK BETTING The words win, place, and show are as dear to a Frenchman's heart as liberty, fraternity, and equality. Identifiable by their bright green and red logos, there are over 7,000 PMU (Pari-Mutuel Urbaine) outlets in French cafés and tobacco shops for off-track betting. The overall system is the third-largest public service industry in France, and is easier to play than the lottery. First, the traditional system involves marking an entry card for the next day's feature race. A minimum bet is 6F (about $1.10). Inaugurated last year, a more modern — and costlier — system involves course cafés. Carrying a stiff admission charge, these neighborhood betting parlors offer satellite broadcasts of a full slate of day or night racing direct from trackside; payouts are immediate. The food is often good, and the ambience convivial. There are presently about 2 dozen of these cafés in Paris, and their numbers are growing rapidly. Try the *Boul' Mich* (Pl. St-André-des-Arts; métro: St-Michel), where the barman usually has a winning tip.

JOGGING The streets and sidewalks of Paris may be ideal for lovers, but they're not meant for runners. There are, however, a number of places where you can jog happily; one of the most pleasant is the 2,500-acre Bois de Boulogne. Four more central parks are the Jardin du Luxembourg (reachable by métro: Luxembourg), the Champ-de-Mars gardens (just behind the Eiffel Tower; métro: Iéna), Parc Monceau (métro: Monceau), the Jardin des Tuileries (métro: Tuileries, Louvre, or Concorde), and the Jardin des Plantes (métro: Gare d'Austerlitz).

SOCCER There are matches from early August to mid-June at Parc des Princes. Av. du Parc-des-Princes, 16e (phone: 42-88-02-76).

SQUASH *Squash Rennes Raspail* (149 Rue de Rennes, 6e; phone: 45-44-24-35) has seven courts, a golf-practice center, and saunas. *Stadium Squash Club* (44 Av. d'Ivry, 13e; phone: 45-85-39-06) has 14 air conditioned courts.

SWIMMING Paris boasts a large number of pools for visitors who like to combine sidestrokes with sightseeing. Among them: *Piscine des Halles* (10 Pl. de la Rotonde, 1er; phone: 42-36-98-44); *Piscine du Quartier Latin* (19 Rue de Pontoise, 5e; phone: 43-54-82-45); *Butte-aux-Cailles* (5 Pl. Paul-Verlaine, 13e; phone: 45-89-60-05); *Keller* (14 Rue de l'Ingénieur-Robert-Keller, 15e; phone: 45-77-12-12); *Jean-Taris* (16 Rue Thouin, 5e; phone: 43-25-54-03); *Tour Montparnasse* (beneath the tower at 66 Bd. de Montparnasse, 15e; phone: 45-38-65-19); *Piscine Georges-Vallerey* (148 Av. Gambetta, 20e; phone: 40-31-15-20); *Aquaboulevard* (5 Rue Louis-Armand, 15e; phone: 40-60-10-00); and *Roger La Gall* (34 Bd. Carnot, 12e; phone: 46-28-77-03).

TENNIS Courts are available in the Jardins du Luxembourg for a nominal fee, but be certain to arrive early, as this is a popular spot. For general information on courts in Paris, call *Ligue Régionale de Paris* (74 Rue de Rome, 17e; phone: 45-22-22-08), or the *Fédération Française de Tennis* (*Roland Garros Stadium*, 16e; phone: 47-43-48-00). For information on courts outside of Paris, and on obtaining tickets for the *French Open*, see *Game, Set, and Match: Tennis Around Paris*, in DIVERSIONS.

THEATER AND OPERA

The most complete listings of theaters, operas, concerts, and movies are found in *L'Officiel des Spectacles* and *Pariscope* (see *Tourist Information*, above). The season generally is from September to June. Tickets are less expensive than in New York and are obtained at each box office, through brokers (*American Express* and *Thomas Cook* act in that capacity and are good), at any of the large *FNAC* stores (136 Rue de Rennes, 6e; phone: 49-54-30-00; and in the *Forum des Halles*, 1er; phone: 40-41-40-00); at the *Virgin Megastore* (52-60 Champs-Elysées, 8e; phone: 42-56-52-60), via your hotel's trusty concierge, or with the high-tech Billetels at the *Galeries Lafayette*, the *Centre Georges-Pompidou*, and other locations. Insert a credit card into a slot in the Billetel and choose from over 100 upcoming theater events and concerts. The device will spew out a display of dates, seats, and prices, from which you can order your tickets — they will be printed on the spot and charged to your account. Theater tickets can also be reserved through *SOS-Théâtre* (73 Champs-Elysées, 8e; phone: 42-25-67-07). Half-price, day-of-performance theater tickets are available at the kiosks at 15 Place de la Madeleine, 8e (Tuesdays through Saturdays from 12:30 to 8 PM, Sundays from 12:30 to 6 PM). The curtain usually goes up at 8:30 PM.

The theatrical and operatic map of France has undergone some startling changes in the past decade, and the country literally bristles with first-rate repertory groups and opera companies. The lively arts here are, in fact, livelier than ever.

Don't bypass an evening at the theater just because your French is a high school relic; it's a fine way to become a part of local life. In your favor is the current style of splashy, highly visual productions where spectacle trumps text. Where classics are concerned, English copies generally can be found — and at any rate, Paris's most-performed playwright is the *formidable* Guillaume Shakespeare.

What follows is a selection of our favorite theaters and opera houses.

CENTER STAGE

La Comédie-Française The undisputed dowager queen of French theater, as much a national monument as the Eiffel Tower, this dramatic doyenne presents a steady diet of lavish productions of great classics by Corneille, Racine, Molière, Rostand, and the happy few 20th-century playwrights like Anouilh, Giraudoux, and Sartre who have been received into the inner circle of French culture. The *CF* is streamlining its fin de siècle image, but even at its stodgiest, it's well worth seeing. The company also presents productions in the renovated 350-seat *Théâtre du Vieux-Colombier* next door. 2 Rue de Richelieu, 1er (phone: 40-15-00-15).

L'Odéon–Théâtre de L'Europe The chameleon-like *Odéon* has, for years, been the joker in the French theatrical pack. After the turbulent period when it housed the fabled company under Jean-Louis Barrault and Madeleine Renaud and ranked among the most popular houses in the city, it became an annex of the *Comédie-Française.* Now it can be seen in yet another incarnation, as the *Théâtre de l'Europe.* Under the direction of one of Europe's foremost men of the theater, Giorgio Strehler of Milan's *Piccolo Teatro,* it became a kind of theatrical Common Market, with original-language productions from all over Europe. Pl. Paul-Claudel, 6e (phone: 43-25-70-32).

Opéra de Paris In a futuristic opera house on the Place de la Bastille, the *Opéra de La Bastille* (120 Rue de Lyon, 12e; phone: 43-43-96-96 for information; 44-73-13-00 for reservations) began regular performances in 1990 under the baton of Myung-Whun Chung, and the former home of grand opera, the *Palais Garnier,* at the melodramatic end of Av. de l'Opéra is the site of the best in ballet (*Théâtre National de l'Opéra,* 8 Rue Scribe, 9e; phone: 40-17-35-35). The other mainstays of Paris opera are the *Théâtre National de l'Opéra Comique,* at the *Salle Favart* (5 Rue Favart,

2e; phone: 42-86-88-83), and the *Théâtre Musical de Paris/Châtelet* (1 Pl. du Châtelet, 4e; phone: 40-28-28-40), in the old *Châtelet* theater. The latter, once the stronghold of the frothy operetta, now does everything from early Offenbach to late Verdi, importing productions from other European operas as well. The touch is light and stylish, the accent utterly French. The *Opéra Comique* isn't especially comic. The theater is smaller, the performers, as a rule, less well-known; but the administration is the same, and the repertory is comparably vast.

Known for its continually evolving and inventive style, the *Théâtre Des Amandiers* (7 Av. Pablo-Picasso; phone: 46-14-70-00) is in Nanterre, a working class suburb of Paris. Recent presentations have included such time-honored classics as the Oedipus trilogy by Sophocles, but a trip to the box office can turn up any number of theatrical surprises. The theater is about 20 minutes by the *RER* city-rail from downtown Paris. New formats, odd curtain times, and a constant redefining of theater and its audience are the watchwords of the *Théâtre National de Chaillot* (Pl. du Trocadéro et du 11-Novembre, 6e; phone: 47-27-81-15), whose repertory ranges from *Hamlet* and *The Three Sisters* to *Faust* for children — performed by marionettes — to new texts by Algerian workers, and contemporary musical happenings. And *Théâtre du Soleil* (La Cartoucherie de Vincennes, Rte. du Champ de Manoeuvres, Bois de Vincennes, 12e; phone: 43-74-24-08 or 43-74-87-63), housed in an old cartridge factory, always has had a colorful, sweeping style with a popular mood and political overtones. That was true in the dazzling production *1789,* which made the troupe's international reputation during that other year of French upheaval, 1968, and in the more recent Shakespeare series as well.

Paris's many café-theaters offer amusing songs, sketches, satires, and takeoffs on topical trends and events. Among them are *Café de la Gare* (41 Rue du Temple, 4e; phone: 42-78-52-51) and *Café d'Edgar* (58 Bd. Edgar-Quinet, 14e; phone: 42-79-97-97). In addition, several vessels moored along the quays offer theatrical performances, ranging from classical French plays to magic shows. The *Péniche Opéra* boat (phone: 42-45-18-20) is berthed on a Right Bank canal; nearby is the *Metamorphosis* (phone: 42-61-33-70). At the Quai Malaquais, on the Left Bank, are *L'Ouragan* (phone: 40-46-01-24) and the *Mare au Diable* (phone: 40-46-90-67). Prices for the shows are comparable to those at land-based venues.

CINEMA

With no fewer than 200 movie houses, Paris is a real treat for film buffs. No other metropolis offers such a cinematographic feast — current French chic, recent imports from across the Atlantic, grainy 1930s classics, and the latest and most select of Third World and Eastern European offerings. In any given week, there are up to 200 different movies shown, the foreign films generally in their original versions with French subtitles.

Film distribution is erratic, to say the least, so the French often get their favorite American flicks up to 6 months late. But the system works both ways: Many of the front-runners at Cannes first hit the screens here, which gives you a jump on friends back home.

Both *Pariscope* and *L'Officiel de Spectacles,* which come out on Wednesday, the day the programs change, contain the full selection each week. *Pariscope* has thought of almost every possible way to classify films, sorting them into new releases and revivals, broad categories (for instance, the *drame psychologique* label means it will be heavier than a *comédie dramatique*), location by *arrondissement,* late-night showings, and so on.

Films shown with their original-language soundtracks are called VO (*version originale*); it's worth watching out for that crucial "VO" tag, or you may find yourself wincing at a French-dubbed version of an English-language film, called VF (*version française*). Broadly speaking, the un-dubbed variety of film flourishes on the Champs-Elysées and on the Left Bank, and it's also a safe bet to avoid the mostly French-patronized houses of Les Grands Boulevards.

The timetables aren't always reliable, so it's worth checking by telephone — if you can decipher the recorded messages that spell out exactly when the five or so showings a day begin. A *séance* (sitting) generally begins with advertisements, and the movie proper begins 15 to 20 minutes later.

There's more room in the big movie houses on the Champs-Elysées, but the cozier Latin Quarter establishments tend to specialize in the unusual and avant-garde — often the only showing such films will ever get. The ultimate in high-tech, the *Géode,* offers a B-Max hemispherical screen, cupped inside a reflecting geodesic dome, at La Villette Sciences and Industry complex. The program is, however, limited to a single scientifically oriented film at any given time, whereas the *Forum Horizon,* in the underground section of the *Forum des Halles,* offers a choice of four first-run movies and claims to have one of the city's best sound systems. The remodeled *Max Linder Panorama* (24 Bd. Poissonnière, 9e; phone: 48-24-00-47 or, for a recording of screening times, 48-24-88-88) has a spacious lobby where you can purchase tickets on arrival and wait in comfort. The *Kinopanorama* (60 Av. de la Motte-Picquet, 15e; phone: 43-06-50-50) boasts the widest screen in Paris, and another big screen is the *Grand Rex* (1 Bd. Poissonnière, 9e; phone: 42-36-83-93). Some more out-of-the-way venues like the *Olympique Entrepôt* and the *Lucernaire* in Montparnasse are social centers in themselves, incorporating restaurants and/or other theaters.

Paris's *Cinémathèque* — at the Palais de Chaillot, which also has an interesting *Cinema Museum* — runs a packed schedule of reruns at rates lower than those of the commercial cinemas. Daily afternoon and evening programs from the museum's eclectic archives of over 20,000 films often include several running concurrently, so that a James Cagney gangster epic can share billing with a 1950s British comedy and a Brazilian thriller; come early as seating is limited (phone: 47-04-24-24). The *Cinémathèque* also operates theaters in the *Centre Georges-Pompidou*'s Salle Garance (phone: 42-78-37-29) and in the *Palais de Tokyo* (13 Av. President-Wilson, 16e; phone: 47-04-24-24). The *Vidéothèque de Paris,* in the *Forum des Halles,* is the world's first public video library. Visitors can select individual showings or attend regularly scheduled theater screenings of films and television programs chronicling Paris's history (phone: 40-26-34-30).

Then there are two period pieces almost worth a visit in themselves. *Le Ranelagh* (5 Rue des Vignes, 16e; phone: 42-88-64-44) has an exquisite 19th-century interior where films are screened and live theater performed. *La Pagode* (57 *bis* Rue de Babylone, 7e; phone: 47-05-12-15), with flying cranes, cherry blossoms, and a tearoom, is built around a Japanese temple that was shipped over to Paris by the proprietor of a department store in the 1920s.

MUSIC

The *Orchestre de Paris,* under the direction of Semyon Bychkov, is based at the *Salle Pleyel* — the *Carnegie Hall* of Paris (252 Rue du Faubourg-St-Honoré, 8e; phone: 45-61-06-30). Other classical recitals are held at the *Salle Gaveau* (45 Rue La Boëtie, 8e; phone: 49-53-05-07), at the *Théâtre des Champs-Elysées* (15 Av. Montaigne, 8e; phone: 47-20-36-37), and at the *Palais des Congrès* (Porte Maillot, 17e; phone: 40-68-00-72). The *Nouvelle Orchestre Philharmonic* performs at a variety of places, including the *Grand Auditorium* at *Maison de Radio France* (116 Av. du Président-Kennedy, 16e; phone: 42-30-15-16 or 42-30-18-18). Special concerts frequently are held in Paris's many places of worship, with moving music at high mass on Sundays. The *Palais des Congrès* and the *Olympia* (28 Bd. des Capucines, 9e; phone: 47-42-25-49) are the places to see well-known international pop and rock artists. Innovative contemporary music — much of it created by computer — is the province of the *Institut de Recherche et de Coopération Acoustique Musique* (IRCAM), whose musicians can be heard in various auditoriums of the *Centre Georges-Pompidou* (31 Rue St-Merri, 4e; phone: 42-77-12-33).

In Paris, during summer and fall, festival translates into a musical orgy — from classical to pop rock — it's all here for the listening.

Festival Estival and Festival d'Automne The former, in July and August, brings a musical kaleidoscope of Gregorian chants, Bartók string quartets, Rameau opera, and more to the city's most picturesque and acoustically delightful churches. The *Festival d'Automne* takes up where the *Estival* leaves off and concentrates on the musically contemporary, generally focusing on one or two main themes or composers and including a certain number of brand-new works. Its moving spirit is Pierre Boulez, France's top musical talent. Information: *Festival Estival de Paris,* 20 Rue Geoffroy

l'Asnier, Paris 75004 (phone: 48-04-98-01); and *Festival d'Automne,* 156
Rue de Rivoli, Paris 75001 (phone: 42-96-12-27).

NIGHTCLUBS AND NIGHTLIFE

Organized "Paris by Night" group tours (*Cityrama, Paris Vision,* and
other operators offer them; see *Special Places*) include at least one *"Spectacle"* — beautiful women in minimal, yet elaborate, costumes, with lavish
sets and effects and sophisticated striptease. Most music halls offer a
package (starting as high as $120 per person), with dinner, dancing, and
a half bottle of champagne. It is possible to go to these places on your own,
save money by skipping dinner and the champagne (both usually way
below par), and take a seat at the bar to see the show. The most famous
extravaganzas occur nightly at *Crazy Horse* (12 Av. George-V, 8e; phone:
47-23-32-32), *Lido* (116 *bis* Champs-Elysées, 8e; phone: 40-76-56-10),
Moulin Rouge (Pl. Blanche, 18e; phone: 46-06-00-19), and *Paradis Latin*
(28 Rue du Cardinal-Lemoine, 5e; phone: 43-29-07-07). An amusing evening can also be spent at such smaller cabarets as *René Cousinier* (*La
Branlette;* 4 Impasse Marie-Blanche, 18e; phone: 46-06-49-46), *Au Lapin
Agile* (22 Rue des Saules, 18e; phone: 46-06-85-87), and *Michou* (80 Rue
des Martyrs, 18e; phone: 46-06-16-04). Reserve all a few days in advance.

There's one big difference between discotheques and private clubs.
Fashionable "in" spots like *Le Palace* (8 Rue Faubourg-Montmartre, 9e;
phone: 42-46-10-87), *Régine's* (49 Rue de Ponthieu, 8e; phone: 43-59-21-
60), *Chez Castel* (15 Rue Princesse, 6e, members only; phone: 43-26-90-
22), *Olivia Valère* (40 Rue de Colisée, 8e, members only; phone: 42-25-11-
68), and *Les Bains* (7 Rue du Bourg-l'Abbé, 3e; phone: 48-87-01-80)
superscreen potential guests. No reason is given for accepting some and
turning others away; go with a regular or look as if you'd fit in with the
crowd. Go early and on a weeknight — when your chances of getting past
the gatekeeper are at least 50-50. (One expensive way to get into *Régine's,
Chez Castel,* or *Les Bains:* Have your hotel make dinner reservations for
you there.) Don't despair if you're refused; the following places are just as
much fun and usually more hospitable: *La Ménagerie* (72 Rue Marbeuf,
8e; phone: 42-71-18-48), where you might run into Thierry Mugler or
Madonna; *Keur Samba* (73 Rue de la Boétie, 8e; phone: 43-59-03-10) for
an African mood; *Shéhérazade* (3 Rue de Liège, 9e; phone: 48-74-85-26)
for jazz-rap in a former Russian cabaret; *Chapelle des Lombards* (19 Rue
de Lappe, 11e; phone: 43-57-24-24) for a Brazilian beat; *Le Cirque* (49 Rue
de Ponthieu, 8e; phone: 42-25-12-13), a mainly gay nightclub; *Niel's* (27
Av. des Ternes, 17e; phone: 47-66-45-00), chic and popular with the film
crowd; and *L'Ecume des Nuits* (*Hôtel Méridien,* 81 Bd. Gouvion-St-Cyr,
17e; phone: 40-68-34-34).

Some pleasant, popular bars for a nightcap include *Bar de la Closerie
des Lilas* (171 Bd. Montparnasse, 6e; phone: 43-26-70-50), *Harry's New
York Bar* (see *Wine Bars,* below), *Fouquet's* (99 Champs-Elysées, 8e;

phone: 47-23-70-60), *Ascot Bar* (66 Rue Pierre-Charron, 8e; phone: 43-59-28-15), *Bar Anglais* (*Plaza-Athénée Hôtel,* 25 Av. Montaigne, 8e; phone: 47-23-92-36), and *Pub Winston Churchill* (5 Rue de Presbourg, 16e; phone: 40-67-17-37).

Jazz buffs have a large choice including *Caveau de la Huchette* (5 Rue de la Huchette, 5e; phone: 43-26-65-05), *Le Bilboquet* (13 Rue St-Benoît, 6e; phone: 45-48-81-84), *New Morning* (7-9 Rue des Petites-Ecuries, 10e; phone: 45-23-51-41), *La Villa* (29 Rue Jacob, 6e; phone: 43-26-60-00), and *Le Petit Journal* (71 Bd. St-Michel, 6e; phone: 43-26-28-59), and *Arbuci* (25 Rue de Buci, 6e; phone: 45-23-51-41).

Enghien-les-Bains, 8 miles (13 km) away, is the only casino in the Paris vicinity (3 Av. de Ceinture, Enghien-les-Bains; phone: 34-12-90-00). For more information, see *Casinos Royale* in DIVERSIONS.

Best in Town

CHECKING IN

Paris offers a broad choice of accommodations, from luxurious palaces with every service to more humble budget hotels. However, they all are strictly controlled by the government and must post their rates, so you can be sure that the price you are being charged is correct.

Below is our selection from all categories; in general, expect to spend (gulp!) at least $500 and way up per night for a double room in the "palace" hotels, which we've listed as very expensive; from $250 to $500 in the expensive range; $150 to $250 is considered moderate; less than $150 is inexpensive.

Except for July, August, and December, the least crowded months, hotel rooms usually are at a premium in Paris. To reserve your first choice, we advise making reservations at least a month in advance, even farther ahead for the smaller, less expensive places listed. Watch for the dates of special events, when hotels are even more crowded than usual. The apartment rentals offered by *Paris Accueil/Paris Séjour* are an alternative to the hotel options listed here. For further information see CITY ACCOMMODATIONS.

Street addresses of the hotels below are followed by the number of their *arrondissement* (neighborhood).

For an unforgettable experience in the City of Light, we begin with our favorites, followed by our cost and quality choices, listed by price category.

GRAND HOTELS

In an increasingly homogeneous and anonymous world, the fine Parisian hotel remains one of the last bastions of charm and luxury. From the first warm, flaky croissant to the last turned-down eiderdown, a stay in one of them is a study in perpetual pampering that makes for an experience that is not to be missed on any account. Such a hotel may have a sleek, urbane lobby throbbing with the pulse of Paris. Or it may be a small, exclusive, little-known retreat on a cobbled Left Bank street whose stone walls have welcomed weary travelers for centuries. All offer complete business services and accept major credit cards. They are what we call the grand hotels.

Bristol Headquarters to dignitaries visiting the Elysées Palace (the French White House), located just a few steps down the street, this elegant establishment boasts 152 rooms and 45 suites, all beautifully decorated, and 2 restaurants — one for summer and another for winter; the first is a light and airy glassed-in room overlooking the garden; the second is a richly wood-paneled room, a reassuring reminder of Old World craftsmanship. The open and exquisite elevator bespeaks an earlier age, the enlargement of the marvelously designed marble bathrooms have transformed them into veritable oases of comfort, and the hotel service is merely superb. An elegant and comfortable lobby and cocktail lounge add to the charm; there's also a heated swimming pool on the sixth-floor terrace, an amenity seldom found in Paris hotels. 112 Rue du Faubourg-St-Honoré, 8e (phone: 42-66-91-45; fax: 42-66-68-68).

Crillon Today's heavy traffic gives the Place de la Concorde a frenetic atmosphere far at odds with its spirit in the 18th century. But here, within the Sienese marble foyers and the 163 elegant rooms and suites of this Relais & Châteaux member, guests are largely insulated from the world outside. Diplomats from nearby Embassy Row, observed by ever-present journalists, buy and sell countries in the bar (considered one of the city's most sophisticated meeting places), or dine in the 2 restaurants, *L'Obélisque* and the two-Michelin-star *Les Ambassadeurs.* Rooms facing the street, though rather noisy, have a view *sans pareil;* those on the courtyards are just as nice and rather more tranquil. An elegant boutique to the left of the entrance carries plush terry cloth robes, signature silk scarves, china, and other gift items. 10 Pl. de la Concorde, 8e (phone: 42-65-24-24; fax: 44-71-15-02).

George V The lobby is a League of Nations of private enterprise; it also seems to be where the *Cannes Film Festival* crowd spends the other 11 months of the year, so numerous are the stars and starlets, directors, producers, and other movie folk who congregate here, staying in the 298 rooms and 53 suites. The Eiffel Tower is just across the river, the Champs-Elysées just down the block, and the Arc de Triomphe around the corner; most of the rest of Paris can be seen from the panoramic windows of rooms higher up in the hotel. Even those who can't afford one of them — or the tranquil chambers facing the gracious courtyard — should be sure to stop for one of the establishment's utterly lyrical croissants, enjoy a mean martini in the lively and chic bar, or dine in the 2 restaurants. 31 Av. George-V, 8e (phone: 47-23-54-00; fax: 47-20-40-00).

Lancaster If location is almost everything, this charming 19th-century townhouse qualifies: steps from the Champs-Elysées and 2 blocks from the Faubourg-St-Honoré. Admired by the literati, dignitaries, socialites, Americans in the know, and even the haughtiest of Parisians, this Savoy Group establishment exudes an air of gentility and calm, and above all, coziness. Aside from its handsome 18th-century antiques and objets d'art, every one of its only 52 rooms and 7 suites (and there are no more than 10 on each floor) offers its own charm. Try to book accommodations on the sixth — the top — floor, where a view of the Eiffel Tower or Sacré-Coeur or the hotel's garden is sure to be had from either a balcony or a terrace. There's an old-fashioned bar with garden murals, a delightful spot for taking mid-morning coffee, afternoon tea, or a post-prandial liqueur, and a relaxed and refined restaurant, with alfresco dining when the weather permits. If the pleasure of truly personal service, gracious surroundings with nary a glimmer of glitz are your preference, you've come to the right place. 7 Rue de Berri, 8e (phone: 43-59-90-43; in the US, 800-223-6800; fax: 42-89-22-71).

Lutétia With 286 rooms and 21 suites, and the only real palace hotel on the Left Bank, this aristocrat of elegantly ornamented quarry stone has reigned at the corner of Rue de Sèvres and Boulevard Raspail since 1910. Lovers of the Belle Epoque and Art Deco periods find their element here. From outrageous gray-striped balloon awnings and bowers of sculptured stone flowers framing its graceful arched windows to the regal red lobby appointed with crystal chandeliers, Art Deco skylights, and intricately carved wrought iron, this is a quintessentially Parisian place (owned by the Taillevent family, it's one of the city's few grand hotels still in French hands); it also offers some of the most fantastic views in Paris from its upper floors. Best perspective in the house is from Room 71, a seventh-floor corner room from whose balcony nearly all of Paris's most famous monuments can be seen. 45 Bd. Raspail, 6e (phone: 49-54-46-46; fax: 49-54-46-00).

Montalembert Also on the Left Bank, this intimate and exquisite little place is known for its privacy. The 56 rooms and suites are now available in two styles — traditional yellow- and mustard-stripe schemes with restored period armoires and sleigh beds, or in contemporary style with straight geometric lines and fireplaces. (If you're over 6 feet tall, ask for one of the modern rooms — the beds are longer.) Bathrooms are small, but high-tech. The hotel's *Le Montalembert* restaurant, which replaced *L'Arpège,* serves delicious fare. 3 Rue Montalembert, 7e (phone: 45-48-68-11; in the US, 800-628-8929; fax: 42-22-58-19).

Plaza-Athénée Careful renovations have preserved the charm of this ever elegant European hotel — from the 215 rooms and 41 suites done in Louis XV and XVI to the *Relais* grill, where *tout Paris* seems to be eternally lunching, and the idyllic *Régence* restaurant, which is like a set for some Parisian *Mikado,* with its chirping birds, pools, and a bridge. On the elegant Avenue Montaigne, this hotel is a little more sedate and a little more French than the *George V* (above). It is an haute bastion that takes its dignity very seriously (a discreet note in each bathroom offers an unobtrusive route in and out of the hotel for those in jogging togs). 25 Av. Montaigne, 8e (phone: 47-23-78-33; fax: 47-20-20-70).

Résidence Maxim's Pierre Cardin's luxurious venture is located a few steps from the Champs-Elysées and the Elysées Palace. No expense has been spared here to create sybaritic splendor; this distinguished favorite of the rich and famous (it was Bette Davis's Paris hideaway) caters to those who can afford the best. (The Presidential Suite rents for $4,000 a night!) From its classic lobby, secluded bar (*Le Maximin,* open late), and *L'Atmosphere,* its world class restaurant, to its 37 suites and 4 rooms, it cleverly combines modern statuary in 19th-century Belle Epoque surroundings. 42 Av. Gabriel, 8e (phone: 45-61-96-33; fax: 42-89-06-07).

Ritz The Right Bank establishment that César Ritz created and made synonymous with all the finer things in life is so much a part of French tradition and literature that every year an occasional perambulator, coming upon it suddenly, is startled to find that it still exists, much less reigns as majestically as ever over the Place Vendôme. Marcel Proust wrote most of *Remembrance of Things Past* in a cork-lined room here; Georges-Auguste Escoffier put France at the top of the culinary Olympus from its kitchen. The *Ritz Club,* a nightclub and discotheque built about the same time as its new super spa, is open to guests and club members only. But even if you can't afford to stay in one of the 142 rooms or 45 suites, have a glass of champagne in the elegant bar. 15 Pl. Vendôme, 1er (phone: 42-60-38-30; fax: 42-60-23-71).

St. James's Club Like an English club or a private mansion, it's something out of an Evelyn Waugh novel. Located in a residential section within a stroll of the Bois de Boulogne, this secluded 19th-century château — with 17 rooms and 31 suites (including 4 penthouse suites with a winter garden), its own walled courtyard and regal fountain, library bar, health club, and elegant restaurant overlooking a rose garden, plus a more relaxed grill (the *Club Room*) — gives one a sense of a weekend in the English countryside. Though billed as a private club, hotel guests are welcome to stay after paying a temporary membership fee of about $10. (Non-members not staying at the hotel, however, cannot dine or sip cocktails here.) 5 Pl. Chancelier-Adenauer, Av. Bugeaud, 16e (phone: 47-04-29-29; in the US, 800-641-0300; fax: 45-53-00-61).

VERY EXPENSIVE

Balzac Very private, this luxurious, charming hotel with 70 rooms and suites is ideally located off the Champs-Elysées. Another plus is that the Paris branch of the *Bice* restaurant is right here. Those who enjoy nocturnal pleasures can dance until dawn in the discotheque. Business facilities include 24-hour room service, an English-speaking concierge, foreign currency exchange, and photocopiers. Major credit cards accepted. 6 Rue Balzac, 8e (phone: 45-61-97-22; fax: 45-25-24-82).

Grand This completely renovated property, part of the Inter-Continental chain, has long been a favorite of Americans abroad, with its "meeting place of the world," the *Café de la Paix*. It has 545 rooms and luxurious suites, plus cheerful bars and restaurants — and a prime location (next to the *Opéra*). For exercise enthusiasts, there is a health spa on the fifth floor. Business facilities include 24-hour room service, meeting rooms for up to 1,200, an English-speaking concierge, foreign currency exchange, secretarial services in English, A/V equipment, photocopiers, cable television news, and express checkout. Major credit cards accepted. 2 Rue Scribe, 9e (phone: 40-07-32-32; in the US, 800-327-0200; fax: 42-66-12-51).

L'Hôtel Small, but chic, this Left Bank hostelry is favored by experienced international travelers (Oscar Wilde died here). The 24 rooms and 3 suites are tiny, but beautifully appointed (antiques, fresh flowers, marble baths). The attractive restaurant serves first-rate fare. Business facilities include meeting rooms for up to 50, an English-speaking concierge, foreign currency exchange, secretarial services in English, photocopiers, translation services, and express checkout. Major credit cards accepted. 13 Rue des Beaux-Arts, 6e (phone: 43-25-27-22; fax: 43-25-64-81).

Inter-Continental The 452 rooms and suites have been meticulously restored to re-create turn-of-the-century elegance with modern conveniences. The top-floor Louis XVI "garret" rooms are cozy and look out over the Tuileries. There's an American-style coffee shop, a grill, and a popular bar. Business facilities include 24-hour room service, meeting rooms for up to 1,000, an English-speaking concierge, foreign currency exchange, secretarial services in English, A/V equipment, photocopiers, translation services, and express checkout. Major credit cards accepted. 3 Rue de Castiglione, 1er (phone: 44-77-11-11; fax: 44-77-14-60).

Méridien *Air France*'s well-run, 1,025-room, modern American-style property has all the expected French flair. Rooms are on the small side, but tastefully decorated, quiet, and with good views. There are 4 attractive restaurants (one of which serves Japanese fare), a shopping arcade, lively bars, and a chic nightclub, *L'Ecume des Nuits*. Business facilities include 24-hour room service, meeting rooms for up to 2,000, an English-speaking concierge, foreign currency exchange, secretarial services in English, A/V equipment, photocopiers, translation services, and express checkout. Major credit cards accepted. 81 Bd. Gouvion-St-Cyr, 17e (phone: 40-68-34-34; fax: 40-68-31-31).

Méridien Montparnasse With 952 rooms, this ultramodern giant is in the heart of Montparnasse. It has a futuristic lobby, efficient service, a coffee shop, bars, and the *Montparnasse 25* restaurant, with a view, and in summer, a garden restaurant. There is also an ample brunch served in the restaurant on Sunday mornings. Business facilities include 24-hour room service, meeting rooms for up to 2,000, an English-speaking concierge, foreign currency exchange, secretarial services in English, A/V equipment, photocopiers, computers, translation services, and express checkout. Major credit cards accepted. 19 Rue du Commandant-René-Mouchotte, 14e (phone: 44-36-44-36; fax: 44-36-49-00).

Meurice Refined Louis XV and XVI elegance and a wide range of services are offered for a franc or two less than those of the other "palaces." The ideally located hotel, a member of the CIGA chain, has 179 rooms and 35 especially nice suites, a popular bar, *Le Meurice* (a restaurant overlooking the Rue de Rivoli), and the chandeliered *Pompadour* tearoom. Business facilities include 24-hour room service, meeting rooms for up to 150, an English-speaking concierge, foreign currency exchange, secretarial services in English, A/V equipment, photocopiers, computers, cable television news, and translation services. Major credit cards accepted. 228 Rue de Rivoli, 1er (phone: 44-58-10-10; fax: 44-58-10-15).

Paris Hilton International Its 455 modern rooms are only a few steps from the Eiffel Tower. Those facing the river have the best view. *Le Western* serves T-bone steaks, apple pie à la mode, and brownies (mostly to French diners). The coffee shop is a magnet for homesick Americans. Business facilities include 24-hour room service, meeting rooms for up to 1,000, an English-speaking concierge, foreign currency exchange, secretarial services in English, A/V equipment, photocopiers, translation services, and express checkout. Major credit cards accepted. 18 Av. de Suffren, 15e (phone: 42-73-92-00; fax: 47-83-62-66).

Pavillon de la Reine Supreme location for the Marais's only luxury hotel, owned by the management of the *Relais Christine* (see below) and similarly appointed. Its 55 rooms (most are on the small side) look out on a garden or courtyard. Business facilities include 24-hour room service, foreign currency exchange, and photocopiers. Major credit cards accepted. 28 Pl. des Vosges, 3e (phone: 42-77-96-40; fax: 42-77-63-06).

Pont Royal Right in the midst of Paris's most exclusive antiques and shopping district, this former 18th-century *hôtel particulier* (private home) has been a well-kept secret. Each of the spacious rooms (there are 73, plus 5 suites) is tastefully appointed with fine French antiques and sumptuous fabrics. The formal dining room, *Les Antiquaires,* serves first-rate fare. Business facilities include an English-speaking concierge, foreign currency exchange, secretarial services in English, and computers. Restaurant closed Sundays. Major credit cards accepted. 7 Rue Montalembert, 7e (phone: 45-44-38-27; fax: 45-44-92-07).

Raphaël A very spacious, stately place, with a Turner in the lobby downstairs and paneling painted with sphinxes in the generous rooms. Less well-known among the top Paris hotels, its 87 rooms and 23 suites attract film folk and the like. And for those who savor strolling down the Champs-Elysées, it's only a short walk away. Business facilities include 24-hour room service, meeting rooms for up to 150, an English-speaking concierge, foreign currency exchange, secretarial services in English, A/V equipment, photocopiers, computers, translation services, and express checkout. Major credit cards accepted. 17 Av. Kléber, 16e (phone: 44-28-00-28; fax: 45-01-21-50).

Relais Carré d'Or For those visitors who are in Paris for a long stay, this hostelry (with all the amenities of a luxury hotel) provides a variety of accommodations — from studios to multi-room apartments — all with modern kitchens, marble bathrooms, and lovely, understated furnishings. Most have balconies overlooking the hotel's garden or Avenue George-V. Business facilities include 24-hour room service, meeting rooms for up to 30, an English-speaking concierge, foreign currency exchange, secretarial services in English, A/V equipment, photocopiers, computers, cable television, translation services, and express checkout. Major credit cards accepted. 46 Av. George-V, 8e (phone: 40-70-05-05; fax: 47-23-30-90).

Relais Christine Formerly a 16th-century cloister, this lovely place boasts modern fixtures, 34 rooms, 17 suites — and lots of old-fashioned charm. Ask for a room with a courtyard or garden view; the suites and the ground-floor room with a private *terrasse* are particularly luxurious. Business facilities include meeting rooms for up to 20, foreign currency exchange, and photocopiers. Major credit cards accepted. 3 Rue Christine, 6e (phone: 43-26-71-80; fax: 43-26-89-38).

Royal Monceau This elegant, impeccably decorated 180-room, 39-suite property, not far from the Arc de Triomphe, has 3 restaurants — including one with an attractive garden setting — as well as 2 bars, a fitness center, pool, Jacuzzi, and beauty salon. The Sunday brunch is a delight. Business facilities include 24-hour room service, meeting rooms for up to 250, an English-speaking concierge, foreign currency exchange, secretarial services in English, A/V equipment, photocopiers, computers, translation services, and express checkout. Major credit cards accepted. 37 Av. Hoche, 8e (phone: 45-61-98-00; fax: 45-63-28-93).

San Régis This is an elegant place to feel at home in comfortable surroundings. There are 34 rooms and 10 suites, all beautifully appointed, as well as a restaurant. Business facilities include an English-speaking concierge, foreign currency exchange, photocopiers, computers, and cable television news. Major credit cards accepted. 12 Rue Jean-Goujon, 8e (phone: 43-59-41-90; fax: 45-61-05-48).

La Trémoille Built in 1886, this former *hôtel particulier* (private home) is a true gem. Each of the 110 spacious rooms in this charming historic landmark building is beautifully appointed. The atmosphere is understated elegance, and the location, just off Avenue Montaigne, a bonus. Business facilities include a meeting room for up to 10, an English-speaking concierge, secretarial services in English, and A/V equipment. Major credit cards accepted. 14 Rue de la Trémoille, 8e (phone: 47-23-34-20; fax: 40-70-01-08).

Le Vernet This sister hotel to the elegant *Royal Monceau* has 60 modern rooms and 3 suites and is located just a few steps from the Arc de Triomphe. Guests have complimentary access to the health club at the *Royal Monceau*. Business facilities include 24-hour room service, meeting rooms for up to 15, an English-speaking concierge, foreign currency exchange, A/V equipment, photocopiers, computers, translation services, and express checkout. Major credit cards accepted. 25 Rue Vernet, 8e (phone: 47-23-43-10; fax: 40-70-10-14).

de Vigny A small and elegant 25-room, 12-suite hotel with lots of mahogany and chintz. Suite 504 has its own stairway leading to a glass-roofed *salon* with a spectacular view. No restaurant, but nonsmoking rooms and parking are available. 9 Rue Balzac, 8e (phone: 40-75-04-39; fax: 40-75-05-81).

Westminster Between the *Opéra* and the *Ritz,* this establishment has regained some of its lost luster. The paneling, marble fireplaces, and parquet floors of its traditional decor remain; air conditioning has been installed in most rooms. There's also a restaurant, *Le Céladon,* and a cocktail lounge. Some of the 101 rooms and 18 apartments overlook the street, some an inner courtyard. Business facilities include 24-hour room service, meeting rooms for up to 70, an English-speaking concierge, foreign currency exchange, secretarial services in English, A/V equipment, photocopiers, and translation services. Major credit cards accepted. 13 Rue de la Paix, 2e (phone: 42-61-57-46; fax: 42-60-30-66).

EXPENSIVE

Abbaye St-Germain On a quiet street, this small, delightful place once was a convent. The lobby has exposed stone arches, and the elegant rooms (we especially admire No. 4, whose doors open onto the charming courtyard) are furnished with antiques, tastefully selected fabrics, and marble baths. Unfortunately, there continue to be some complaints about the service. Business facilities include an English-speaking concierge, foreign currency exchange, and photocopiers. Major credit cards accepted. 10 Rue Cassette, 6e (phone: 45-44-38-11; fax: 45-48-07-86).

Colbert Each of the 40 rooms and 2 suites in this Left Bank hostelry has a glass door leading onto a balcony. Decorated in pastel tones, there is a mini-bar and television set in each room. No restaurant, but breakfast is included. Major credit cards accepted. 7 Rue de l'Hôtel-Colbert, 5e (phone: 43-25-85-65; in the US, 800-366-1510; fax: 43-25-80-19).

Duc de St-Simon In two big townhouses in a beautiful, quiet backwater off the Boulevard St-Germain, this elegant 29-room, 5-suite establishment veritably reeks of the Proust era. No restaurant. Business facilities include foreign currency exchange and photocopiers. No credit cards accepted. A 5-minute walk from the spectacular *Musée d'Orsay,* at 14 Rue de St-Simon, 7e (phone: 45-48-35-66; fax: 45-48-68-25).

Jeu de Paume The architect-owner of this former *jeu de paume* (tennis court) has artfully married old and new in this addition to the exclusive Ile St-Louis hotels. High-tech lighting, modern artwork, and a sleek glass elevator are set against ancient ceiling beams and limestone brick hearths. The 30 rooms and 2 suites are comfortable and not unreasonably priced, and each one overlooks the lovely garden. There is also a music salon with a piano. Business facilities include 24-hour room service, meeting rooms for up to 30, foreign currency exchange, secretarial services in English, and photocopiers. Major credit cards accepted. 54 Rue St-Louis-en-l'Ile, 4e (phone: 43-26-14-18; fax: 40-46-02-76).

Montaigne This unpretentious establishment is a true find. Each of its 29 rooms is comfortable, clean, and chicly decorated. There's a bar and a breakfast room, but no restaurant. Major credit cards accepted. 6 Av. Montaigne, 8e (phone: 47-20-30-50; fax: 47-20-94-12).

Le Parc Victor Hugo A sumptuous 115-room hotel, it features a large interior garden; its restaurant, *Le Relais du Parc,* was set up by superchef Joël Robuchon, whose own three-star establishment, *Jamin,* is nearby. Major credit cards accepted. 57 Av. Raymond-Poincaré, 16e (phone: 45-53-44-60; fax: 47-27-53-04).

Prince de Galles An excellent location (a next-door neighbor of the pricier *George V*) and impeccable style make this hostelry a good choice. All 173 rooms and suites are individually decorated. This Marriott member offers a restaurant and an oak-paneled bar; parking is available. Business facilities include 24-hour room service, meeting rooms for up to 150, English-speaking concierge, foreign currency exchange, secretarial services in English, A/V equipment, photocopiers, computers, translation services, and express checkout. Major credit cards accepted. 33 Av. George-V, 8e (phone: 47-23-55-11; fax: 47-20-96-92).

Le Relais Médicis With the same owners as the *Saint-Germain,* this elegant 16-room establishment boasts marble bathrooms and beamed ceilings. Major credit cards accepted. There is no restaurant. 23 Rue Racine, 6e (phone: 43-26-00-60; fax: 40-46-83-39).

Le Relais Saint-Germain In a 17th-century building, this hostelry with 10 guestrooms and 1 suite is ideally situated on the Left Bank just steps from the Boulevard St-Germain and the area's best shops, eateries, and galleries. It is attractively decorated, and charming down to its massive ceiling beams and huge flower bouquets. A rare find. No restaurant. Major credit cards accepted. 9 Carrefour de l'Odéon, 6e (phone: 43-29-12-05; fax: 46-33-45-30).

Résidence du Roy Within easy reach of the Champs-Elysées, this establishment offers self-contained studios, suites, and duplexes, complete with kitchen facilities. No restaurant. Business facilities include meeting rooms for up to 20, English-speaking concierge, A/V equipment, photocopiers, and express checkout. Major credit cards accepted. 8 Rue François-Ier, 8e (phone: 42-89-59-59; fax: 40-74-07-92).

Tuileries With a good location in a "real" neighborhood in the heart of the city, this 26-room, 4-suite hotel has a well-tended look and attractive carved wood bedsteads. It is also one of the few *"Relais de Silence"* (especially quiet hotels) in Paris. Major credit cards accepted. 10 Rue St-Hyacinthe, 1er (phone: 42-61-04-17 or 42-61-06-94; fax: 49-27-91-56).

L'Université The 27 charming, antiques-decorated rooms of all shapes and sizes are in a former 18th-century mansion. No restaurant. No credit cards accepted. 22 Rue de l'Université, 7e (phone: 42-61-09-39; fax: 42-60-40-84).

MODERATE

Angleterre Its 29 classic, unpretentious rooms and 1 suite are in what once was the British Embassy, now a national monument. No dining room. Business facilities include an English-speaking concierge, foreign currency exchange, and photocopiers. Major credit cards accepted. 44 Rue Jacob, 6e (phone: 42-60-34-72; fax: 42-60-16-93).

Bretonnerie This restored 17th-century townhouse takes itself seriously, with petit point, dark wood furnishings, and several beamed attic rooms that overlook the narrow streets of the fashionable Marais area. No restaurant. MasterCard and Visa accepted. 22 Rue Ste-Croix-de-la-Bretonnerie, 4e (phone: 48-87-77-63; fax: 42-77-26-78).

Britannique Within minutes of the *Louvre* and Notre-Dame, this hotel was a Quaker mission house during World War I. All 40 rooms are equipped with mini-bars, hair dryers, and satellite TV. No restaurant. Major credit cards accepted. 20 Av. Victoria, 1er (phone: 42-33-74-59; in the US, 800-366-1510; fax: 42-33-82-65).

Chomel Sprucely decorated, this 23-room establishment is near the *Au Bon Marché* department store. There is no restaurant. Major credit cards accepted. 15 Rue Chomel, 7e (phone: 45-48-55-52; fax: 45-48-89-76).

Danube St-Germain The 45 rooms and 6 elegant suites, all with four-poster bamboo beds, are comfortable, and some of them overlook an attractive courtyard typical of the Left Bank. No restaurant. Business facilities include foreign currency exchange and photocopiers. American Express accepted. 58 Rue Jacob, 6e (phone: 42-60-34-70; fax: 42-60-81-18).

Deux Continents A cozy red sitting room looks invitingly onto the street here, in this 40-room establishment on the Left Bank. No restaurant. Major credit cards accepted. 25 Rue Jacob, 6e (phone: 43-26-72-46).

Deux Iles On the historic Ile St-Louis, this beautifully redecorated 17th-century house has a garden with a Portuguese fountain, but no restaurant. Though small, the 17 rooms boast French provincial fabrics and Louis XIV ceramic tiles in the bathrooms. Business facilities include foreign currency exchange. No credit cards accepted. 59 Rue St-Louis-en-l'Ile, 4e (phone: 43-26-13-35; fax: 43-29-60-25).

Duminy-Vendôme This 19th-century building near the Place Vendôme has been completely renovated and decorated in 1920s style. The rooms are comfortable, and the neighborhood could not be more central. No restaurant. Major credit cards accepted. 3 Rue du Mont Tabor, 1er (phone: 42-60-32-80; fax: 42-96-07-63).

Ferrandi Popular with international businessmen, this no-frills hostelry is done up in browns and blues, with a winding wood staircase and a quiet lounge. The 41 rooms and 1 suite have antique furnishings. No dining room. Major credit cards accepted. 92 Rue du Cherche-Midi, 6e (phone: 42-22-97-40; fax: 45-44-89-97).

Fleurie This lovely, 29-room family-run hotel in a former 18th-century townhouse offers friendly service and some air conditioned rooms, but no restaurant. MasterCard and Visa accepted. 32-34 Rue Grégoire de Tours, 6e (phone: 43-29-59-81; fax: 43-29-68-44).

Grand Hôtel de l'Univers Modern and tucked away on a quiet street, it's also only 2 steps away from St-Germain-des-Prés and the Latin Quarter. No restaurant. Major credit cards accepted. 6 Rue Grégoire-de-Tours, 6e (phone: 43-29-37-00; fax: 40-51-06-45).

Grandes Ecoles Just the sort of place that people recommend only to the right friends (even the proprietress wants to keep it a secret). Insulated from the street by a delightful courtyard and its garden, it is a simple 48-room 19th-century private house with plain comforts, but it's long on atmosphere. There aren't many like it in Paris, but beware that booking is difficult and the owner has been known to give away reserved rooms. No restaurant. Major credit cards accepted. 75 Rue Cardinal-Lemoine, 5e (phone: 43-26-79-23; fax: 43-25-28-15).

Le Jardin des Plantes In addition to a magnificent setting across from the Parisian Botanical Gardens, near the Sorbonne, it offers 33 airy, rooms with mini-bars, TV sets, and hair dryers; some have alcoves large enough for extra beds for children. A sauna is available in the basement. Art exhibits and classical music concerts are held on Sundays in the vaulted cellar. No restaurant. Major credit cards accepted. 5 Rue Linné, 5e (phone: 47-07-06-20; fax: 47-07-62-74).

Lenox St-Germain Between the busy St-Germain area and the boutiques nearby, it's small (32 rooms) and very tastefully done, with a small bar but no dining room. Popular with the fashion crowd. Major credit cards accepted. 9 Rue de l'Université, 7e (phone: 42-96-10-95; fax: 42-61-52-83).

Lord Byron On a quiet street off the Champs-Elysées, it has a pleasant courtyard and 30 comfortable, homey rooms. The staff is friendly and speaks good English. No restaurant. Major credit cards accepted. 5 Rue de Chateaubriand, 8e (phone: 43-59-89-98; fax: 42-89-46-04).

Lutèce Here are 23 smallish but luxurious rooms (one split-level) on the charming Ile St-Louis. Positively ravishing, with exquisite toile fabric and wallpaper and raw wood beams; no restaurant, though. No credit cards accepted. 65 Rue St-Louis-en-l'Ile, 4e (phone: 43-26-23-52; fax: 43-29-60-25).

Madison Offers 55 large, bright rooms, some with balconies, and all with air conditioning. No restaurant. Major credit cards accepted. 143 Bd. St-Germain, 6e (phone: 40-51-60-00; fax: 40-51-60-01).

Des Marroniers Good rates and an excellent location, in the heart of the Left Bank, make this 37-room hotel a real bargain. It has a garden courtyard and pretty breakfast room. No credit cards accepted. 21 Rue Jacob, 6e (phone: 43-25-30-60; fax: 40-46-83-56).

Novanox This ultramodern hotel with high-tech furniture has old-fashioned amenities, like brioche for breakfast. Service is exceptionally friendly. MasterCard and Visa accepted. 155 Bd. du Montparnasse, 6e (phone: 46-33-63-60; fax: 43-26-61-72).

Odéon Small (34 rooms), modernized, and charming, it's in the heart of the St-Germain area on the Left Bank. No restaurant. Major credit cards accepted. 3 Rue de l'Odéon, 6e (phone: 43-25-90-67; fax: 43-25-55-98).

Parc St-Séverin An interesting property in the heart of the 5th *arrondissement* on the Left Bank, it has a total of 27 rooms, including a top-floor penthouse with a wraparound balcony. The decor is modern but understated, and the overall ambience is appealing, even though the neighborhood is less than the quietest in Paris. No restaurant. Major credit cards accepted. 22 Rue de la Parcheminerie, 5e (phone: 43-54-32-17; fax: 43-54-70-71).

Pavillon Bastille A small 19th-century *hôtel particulier* with a 17th-century fountain in its courtyard, conveniently located near the Place de la Bastille. All 24 smallish rooms and 1 suite are cheerfully decorated in blues and yellows, and are equipped with mini-bars. No restaurant. Major credit cards accepted. 65 Rue de Lyon, 12e (phone: 43-43-65-65; fax: 43-43-96-52).

Récamier An amazing bargain for those who manage to reserve a room in this simple 30-room hotel right on the elegant Place St-Sulpice. A very peaceful place. No restaurant. No credit cards accepted. 3 *bis* Pl. St-Sulpice, 6e (phone: 43-26-04-89).

Regent's Garden On a quiet street near l'Etoile, it has 39 spacious rooms, some with large marble fireplaces, and 3 suites. The property is run by young hoteliers who make you feel as if you are in your own home. A country atmosphere pervades. There's also a garden and parking, but no dining room. Major credit cards accepted. 6 Rue Pierre-Demours, 17e (phone: 45-74-07-30; fax: 40-55-01-42).

Résidence Charles-Dullin In a sleepy corner of Montmartre, near the leafy square of the *Théâtre de l'Atelier,* this residential hotel charges nightly, weekly, and monthly rates. The apartments have kitchens, and some overlook a peaceful garden. Major credit cards accepted. 10 Pl. Charles-Dullin, 18e (phone: 42-57-14-55; fax: 42-54-48-87).

St-André-des-Arts A rambling old favorite among the chic and hip whose purses are slim but whose tastes are discerning. There are 34 rooms but no restaurant. No credit cards accepted. 66 Rue St-André-des-Arts, 6e (phone: 43-26-96-16).

St-Germain-des-Prés In the heart of one of Paris's loveliest districts, this comfortable hotel is a good bargain. Of the 30 rooms, request one on the courtyard, as the street can be noisy. No restaurant. MasterCard and Visa accepted. 36 Rue Bonaparte, 6e (phone: 43-26-00-19; fax: 40-46-83-63).

Le St-Grégoire A small 18th-century mansion on the Left Bank, this hostelry has an intimate cozy atmosphere, a warm fire in the hearth, a restaurant, and 19 tastefully furnished rooms and 1 suite; 2 of the rooms have terraces overlooking a garden. Major credit cards accepted. 43 Rue de l'Abbé-Grégoire, 6e (phone: 45-48-23-23; fax: 45-48-33-95).

St-Louis Marais On a quiet residential street on the edge of the chic Marais, this tiny hotel is a short walk from the Place des Vosges, the *Louvre,* the quays along the Seine, and the Bastille nightclubs. Dating from the 18th century, when it belonged to the Celestins Convent, it has 15 small rooms but no restaurant. Historical status has barred the installation of an elevator, however. No credit cards accepted. 1 Rue Charles-V, 4e (phone: 48-87-87-04; fax: 48-87-33-26).

St-Thomas-d'Aquin Built in the 1880s, this unpretentious hotel is a simple, functional base from which to explore a shopper's paradise of new wave designer boutiques and tiny restaurants. The 21 rooms are clean and neat, and baths are modern (though tubs are half-size). Breakfast is included. Major credit cards accepted. 3 Rue du Pré-aux-Clercs, 7e (phone: 42-61-01-22; fax: 42-61-41-43).

Solférino A cozy place with Oriental rugs scattered about. The 34 tiny rooms have floral wallpaper, and there's a plant-filled breakfast and sitting room. Major credit cards accepted. 91 Rue de Lille, 7e (phone: 47-05-85-54).

Le Stendahl A luxurious 42-room hostelry at non-luxury prices near the Place Vendôme, featuring antiques, air conditioning, and Jacuzzis, but no dining room. The suites are particularly charming — try either No. 52 or No. 53. Major credit cards accepted. 22 Rue Danielle Casanova, 2e (phone: 44-58-52-52; fax: 44-58-52-00).

Suède A delightful hotel situated in the quiet seventh *arrondissement,* just around the corner from the prime minister's residence. All 40 rooms and 1 suite are beautifully appointed; those overlooking the garden are smaller but much prettier. Breakfast is served in a simple salon or, in good weather, in a beautiful courtyard. Major credit cards accepted. 31 Rue Vaneau, 7e (phone: 47-05-00-08; fax: 47-05-69-27).

Villa des Artistes Quiet luxury is the drawing card of this popular Latin Quarter hotel with 59 rooms and its own patio-garden. No restaurant. 9 Rue de la Grande-Chaumière, 6e (phone: 43-26-60-86; fax: 43-54-73-70).

West End Friendly, with 47 rooms, it's on the Right Bank. The front desk keeps a close, concerned watch on comings and goings, which some may find reassuring. No restaurant. Major credit cards accepted. 7 Rue Clément-Marot, 8e (phone: 47-20-30-78; fax: 47-20-34-42).

INEXPENSIVE

Chancelier Boucherat A plain, friendly 39-room establishment with no airs and with a clientele that returns. Near the Place de la République. Room rates include breakfast. Major credit cards accepted. 110 Rue de Turenne, 3e (phone: 42-72-86-83).

Delavigne Good value and location (just down the street from the *Odéon* theater), it has an enlightened manager who says he isn't interested in simply handing out keys, but enjoys introducing foreigners to Paris. Thirty-four rooms; no restaurant. Major credit cards accepted. 1 Rue Casimir-Delavigne, 6e (phone: 43-29-31-50; fax: 43-29-78-56).

Deux Avenues A quiet 32-room hotel offering friendly service, near a lively street market. No restaurant. MasterCard and Visa accepted. 38 Rue Poncelet, 17e (phone: 42-27-44-35; fax: 47-63-95-48).

Esmeralda Some of the rooms look directly at Notre-Dame over the gardens of St-Julien-le-Pauvre, one of Paris's most ancient churches. The oak beams and furniture round out the medieval atmosphere. Small and friendly, especially popular with the theatrical crowd. No restaurant. No credit cards accepted. 4 Rue St-Julien-le-Pauvre, 5e (phone: 43-54-19-20; fax: 40-51-00-68).

Jeanne d'Arc This little place on a quiet street in the Marais doesn't get top marks for decor and its facilities are simple, but somehow its appeal has spread from Minnesota to Melbourne. It's well placed, near the Place des Vosges, and the management is friendly and speaks English. No restaurant. Major credit cards accepted. 3 Rue de Jarente, 4e (phone: 48-87-62-11).

Oriental A simple but comfortable 32-room hotel near Notre-Dame. No restaurant. MasterCard and Visa accepted. 2 Rue d'Arras, 5e (phone: 43-54-38-12; fax: 40-51-86-78).

Prima-Lepic A 38-room hotel in Montmartre, a busy neighborhood of winding little streets that evoke the romance of *la vie bohème,* Utrillo, Picasso, Toulouse-Lautrec and the *Moulin Rouge.* Decorated by cheerful young owners, rooms sport pretty floral wallpapers and one-of-a-kind furnishings — a wicker chair, a mirrored armoire, a 1930s lamp. No. 56, on the top floor, looks out over Paris, and travelers with a child should make special note of room No. 2, which connects to another room. No restaurant, but there's an elevator, and the public spaces are charming. MasterCard and Visa accepted. 29 Rue Lepic, 18e (phone: 46-06-44-64; fax: 46-06-66-11).

Le Vieux Marais Near the *Centre Georges-Pompidou,* this agreeable hostelry has brightly sprigged walls in the 30 cheerful, if not very large, rooms. The breakfast room has an impressive wall-size engraving of the Place des Vosges, not far away. Major credit cards accepted. In the Marais area, at 8 Rue du Plâtre, 4e (phone: 42-78-47-22; fax: 42-78-34-32).

Welcome Overlooking the Boulevard St-Germain, it's simple but comfortable. Of the 30 rooms, those on the street are noisy. No restaurant. No credit cards accepted. 66 Rue de Seine, 6e (phone: 46-34-24-80; fax: 40-46-81-59).

EATING OUT

Paris considers itself the culinary capital of the world, and you will never forget food for long here. Whether you grab a freshly baked croissant and café au lait for breakfast or splurge on an epicurean fantasy for dinner, this is the city in which to indulge all your gastronomic dreams. Remember, too, that there is no such thing as "French" food; rather, Paris provides the perfect mosaic in which to try regional delights from Provence, Alsace, Normandy, Brittany, and other places.

Restaurants classed as very expensive charge $250 and way up for two; expensive is $150 to $200; moderate, $100 to $150; inexpensive, less than $100; and very inexpensive, $50 or less. A service charge of 15% is added to the bill, but most people leave a small additional tip for good service; wine is not included in the price. Street addresses of the restaurants below are followed by their *arrondissement* number.

Nonsmokers needs have been met with the passage of a law requiring that all restaurants in Paris provide smoke-free areas. Compliance with this ruling has been somewhat erratic, however. Those places with several dining rooms have no problem offering smoke-free rooms; bustling brasseries seem to be on an "on demand" system. There is widespread resentment of this legislation *à l'Américaine,* so legislation aside, don't expect totally smoke-free dining in Paris!

> **NOTE** To save frustration and embarrassment, always *reconfirm* dinner reservations before noon on the appointed day. (For information about making written dinner reservations, see USEFUL WORDS AND PHRASES.) Also remember that some of the better restaurants do not accept credit cards; it's a good idea to check when making your reservations. It may come as a surprise to discover that many of the elite Paris restaurants close over the weekend; also note that many Paris restaurants are closed for part or all of July or August. It's best to check ahead in order to avoid disappointment at the restaurant of your choice, and it's also worth remembering that many offer special lunch menus at considerably lower prices. Here are our favorites, followed by our cost and quality choices, listed by price category. *Bon appétit!*

For an unforgettable dining experience, we begin with our culinary favorites in and around Paris, followed by our cost and quality choices, listed by price category.

HAUTE GASTRONOMIE

L'Ambroisie Promoted to three-star status by Michelin in 1988, this elegant establishment is the showcase for chef Bernard Pacaud's equally elegant cuisine. The menu is limited to only a few sublime entrées, many with a southern French accent, such as *escargots aux herbs niçoises* (snails in an herb sauce), crayfish with morel mushrooms, and grilled mullet with tiny purple artichokes. But the quality more than compensates for the limited number of choices. Closed Sundays, Monday lunch, August, and 2 weeks in February. Reservations necessary. Major credit cards accepted. 9 Pl. des Vosges, 4e (phone: 42-78-51-45).

Amphyclès Chef Philippe Groult has earned two Michelin stars for his restaurant near the Place des Ternes. Protégé and former sous chef of Paris's superchef Joël Robuchon (see *Jamin*), Groult turns out a fine, well-tempered, and contemporary cuisine with a Provençal flair. If the brightly lit modern decor of his small establishment is forgettably neutral, the food is certainly memorable. There are splendid creamy soups, lamb stew with rosemary, lobster salad with sweet red peppers, and a rock lobster risotto. Closed Saturday lunch, Sundays, and most of July. Reservations necessary. Major credit cards accepted. 78 Av. des Ternes, 17e (phone: 40-68-01-01).

L'Arpège The minimalist decor of this much-lauded establishment belies the succulent, generous cuisine prepared by two-star chef Alain Passard, such as veal sweetbreads with truffles and chestnuts, lobster and turnips in a sweet-and-sour vinaigrette sauce, and lemon soufflé flavored with cloves. The prix fixe lunch menu is a relative bargain. Closed Saturdays, Sunday lunch, and August. Reservations necessary. Major credit cards accepted. 84 Rue de Varenne, 7e (phone: 45-51-47-33).

Le Grand Véfour Established in 1760 in the stately courtyard of the Palais-Royal, this is a place of thick carpets and frescoed mirrors, where the choice dishes (two Michelin stars) have been named for dignitaries who have discussed affairs of state here since the time of Robespierre. The delectable dishes, such as crayfish with olive oil and spices, or potato-truffle terrine, are every bit as enthralling as the history. In honor of both, gentlemen still are required to wear jacket and tie. Closed Saturday lunch, Sundays, and all of August. Reservations necessary. Major credit cards accepted. 17 Rue de Beaujolais, 1er (phone: 42-96-56-27).

Jamin This small (40-seat) restaurant offers what many believe is Paris's finest cuisine (Michelin gives it three stars). Chef Joël Robuchon calls his cooking *"moderne,"* similar to but not always as light as nouvelle. Outstanding dishes on the constantly evolving menu have included a cream of sea urchins and fennel, and an ethereal glazed cabbage with veal sweetbreads, morel mushrooms, and grilled asparagus. Reserve at least 2 months in advance. Closed weekends and most of July. Reservations necessary. Major credit cards accepted. 32 Rue de Longchamp, 16e (phone: 47-27-12-27).

Lasserre The waiters are in tails, the ceiling glides open to reveal the stars, the decanted burgundy is poured over the flame of a candle to detect sediment, and the impeccable service makes diners feel that somehow they deserve all this. The cuisine — heavy on foie gras, caviar, truffles, and rich sauces — is traditional French at its most heavenly (two Michelin stars), and the wine cellar is a virtual museum of French oenology. Not surprisingly, making dinner reservations is akin to booking seats for a sold-out Broadway musical, so think ahead. Way ahead. Closed Sundays, Monday lunch, and August. Reservations necessary. Major credit cards accepted. 17 Av. Franklin-Roosevelt, 8e (phone: 43-59-53-43).

Lucas-Carton The lush, plush Belle Epoque premises, under the chef/owner's hat of Alain Senderens, are the perfect place to sample a few bites of truffle salad, lobster with vanilla, or anything else on the ever-changing menu. This quirky and innovative cooking combines many tenets of nouvelle cuisine with Oriental influences, and Michelin lost no time in awarding it three stars. The utensils and serving pieces are almost as alluring as the food. Closed Saturdays and Sundays, most of August, and December 24 to January 3. Reservations necessary. Major credit cards accepted. 9 Pl. de la Madeleine, 8e (phone: 42-65-22-90).

Maxim's Paris's most celebrated Belle Epoque restaurant was a century old in
1991; happily, more than just a memory of its glory endures. There are
Parisians who say it's too crowded with Japanese high school girls pretend-
ing they're Gigi; many feel it's highly overrated. (In fact, at owner Pierre
Cardin's request, it is completely unrated by Michelin.) And yet, for the
experience, the gentle rustle of silk, the sparkle of silver, and the soft
strains of a string quartet, there's none like it. The service is impeccable;
you'll find twice as many waiters at your table as at any comparable
restaurant (and trying to keep track of them can be as dizzying as champagne). The food is surprisingly good; try the *Challans canard aux cerises*
(Challans duck with cherries). The wine list is extensive and intelligent;
sommeliers, delightfully helpful; and the scenes at tables around its elegant
salons are tableaux from Colette. Careful, though: Fridays remain a
strictly black-tie-only tradition (they don't always mention this on the
phone) with an orchestra for dancing from 9:30 PM to 2 AM. Closed
Sundays in July and August. Reservations necessary. Major credit cards
accepted. 3 Rue Royale, 8e (phone: 42-65-27-94).

Pré Catelan Gaston Lenôtre's dreamy dinner palace in the Bois de Boulogne is
another one of those wonderful special occasion spots — particularly in
summer. Dining on the flower-decked terrace here is a memorable experience in itself and the food — which has earned two Michelin stars — is
equal to the ambience. Offerings include lobster served with geranium-
flavored vegetables or Dublin Bay prawns grilled in walnut oil. Desserts
here are to die for, not surprising since owner Lenôtre is, above all, a
pastry chef, his main claim to fame being the string of glittering pastry
shops around the capital bearing his name. Closed Sunday evenings, Mondays, and 2 weeks in February. Reservations necessary. Major credit cards
accepted. Rte. de Suresnes, Bois de Boulogne, 16e (phone: 45-24-55-58).

Taillevent Named after the famed medieval chef Taillevent, this three-star dining
room occupies a distinguished 19th-century mansion complete with fine
paintings, porcelain dinnerware, and aristocratic decor that make it look
as if the French Revolution was really just a bad dream. Long-time chef
Claude Deligne has retired, but the traditions and many of the recipes he
established are being maintained by Philippe Legendre, who is also adding
new items to the menu. The salad of warm sweetbreads, the succulent duck
dishes, and the rainbow assortment of soufflés are among the pillars of the
Parisian gastronomic community. The wine list is one of the city's best and
most reasonably priced. One of the most difficult restaurant reservations
in France — but we insist you try. Closed Saturdays, Sundays, part of
February, and most of August. Reservations necessary. Major credit cards
accepted. 15 Rue Lamennais, 8e (phone: 45-61-12-90).

La Tour d'Argent For many, this place is too trendy, too touristy, overrated, and
overpriced, but Paris's senior three-star restaurant continues to amaze and
entertain with its cuisine and the most romantic view of any restaurant in

the city. The gold-toned room brings to mind Cole Porter's "elegant, swellegant party." In fact, Porter occasionally dined here, as did a host of other luminaries, from Franklin Roosevelt to Paul McCartney, Greta Garbo to the Aga Khan. The specialty here is a Charente duck pressed at tableside just as it was a century ago (each duck is assigned a number); also not to be missed are the classic quenelles in mornay sauce with fresh black truffles. Because it has a reservations book thicker than the Manhattan telephone directory, it's often impossible to book for evenings at certain times of the year. Best tip: Book a windowside table for lunch when there's a fixed price menu. The view of Notre-Dame and the Seine is just as splendid by daylight. Ask to see the spectacular wine list, one of France's best. Closed Mondays. Reservations necessary. Major credit cards accepted. 15 Quai de la Tournelle, 5e (phone: 43-54-23-31).

BEST BISTROS

L'Ami Louis The archetypal Parisian bistro, small and scruffy but with huge portions of food that we rate as marvelous (and pricey). Specialties include formidable servings of foie gras, roast chicken, spring lamb, ham, and burgundy wines. A favorite among Americans, this is the place to sample authentic French fries. Closed Mondays, Tuesdays, and most of July and August. Reservations necessary. Major credit cards accepted. 32 Rue de Vertbois, 3e (phone: 48-87-77-48).

L'Assiette The chef, Lulu, is very much present in her slightly scruffy bistro that attracts a fashionable clientele for delicious and generous servings of roast duck, potato salad with fresh truffles, and *coquilles St-Jacques* (sea scallops) in cream. The wine list is sublime, the prices astronomical. Closed Mondays, Tuesdays, and August. Reservations necessary. MasterCard and Visa accepted. 181 Rue du Château, 14e (phone: 43-22-64-86).

Astier An honest-to-goodness neighborhood spot that always is packed, it offers the staples of bourgeois cooking, lovingly prepared and remarkably inexpensive. Closed Saturdays, Sundays, and August. Reservations advised. Major credit cards accepted. 44 Rue Jean-Pierre-Timbaud, 11e (phone: 43-57-16-35).

Le Bistrot d'à Côté Chef Michel Rostang offers *cuisine de terroir* (uncomplicated, back-to-basics regional fare) in a turn-of-the-century bistro. Closed Saturday lunch, Sundays, and the first 2 weeks of August. Reservations advised. Major credit cards accepted. 10 Rue Gustave-Flaubert, 17e (phone: 42-67-05-81).

Le Caméleon A true bistro, with marble tables, moleskin banquettes, and the spirit of 1920s Montparnasse. The casserole-roasted veal and *morue provençale* (salt cod in tomato sauce with garlic mayonnaise) are guaranteed to please. Closed Sundays, Mondays, and August. Reservations advised. No credit cards accepted. 6 Rue de Chevreuse, 6e (phone: 43-20-63-43).

Cartet This friendly place serves Lyonnais specialties with a focus on charcuterie and meats, such as *côtes de veau* (veal chops with morel mushrooms). Closed weekends and August. Reservations advised. Major credit cards accepted. 62 Rue de Malte, 11e (phone: 48-05-17-65).

Chez Benoît A pretty but unpretentious bistro with wonderful old-fashioned Lyonnaise cooking and exquisite wines. Just about at the top of the bistro list (in prices as well as food and atmosphere), it's rated one Michelin star. Closed weekends and August. Reservations necessary. No credit cards accepted. 20 Rue St-Martin, 4e (phone: 42-72-25-76).

Chez Georges This narrow, old-fashioned bistro is a bastion of traditional French cooking. Closed Sundays and holidays. Reservations advised. Major credit cards accepted. 1 Rue du Mail, 2e (phone: 42-60-07-11).

Chez Pauline The perfect bistro. The tiny, wood-paneled downstairs room (ask to be seated there) is brightened by large mirrors and fresh flowers. Try the oysters in a watercress sauce or the assortment of seafood with a saffron sauce, and save room for dessert — *mille-feuille* of orange with raspberry sauce is sublime. Closed Saturday evenings, Sundays, July, from August 1 to 17, and from December 24 to January 2. Reservations advised (and should be made well in advance). Major credit cards accepted. 5 Rue Villedo, 1er (phone: 42-96-20-70).

Le Grizzli One of Paris's best bistros, the food here is southwestern France in accent, featuring duck and garlic. Closed Sundays, and Monday lunch. Major credit cards accepted. 7 Rue St-Martin, 4e (phone: 48-87-77-56).

Le Petit Marquery A true, family-run bistro on the Left Bank. Although the prices run rather high, the old-fashioned cuisine and *petit crus* wines are excellent. Closed Sundays, Mondays, December 25 through January 1, and late July to early September. Reservations advised. Major credit cards accepted. 9 Bd. du Port Royal, 13e (phone: 43-31-58-59).

Robert et Louise Family bistro, with warm paneled decor and a very high standard for ingredients and cooking. Try the *boeuf bourguignon* or the open-fire–grilled *côte de boeuf.* Also good are the *fromage blanc* and the *vin en pichet.* Closed Sundays, holidays, and August. Reservations unnecessary. No credit cards accepted. 64 Rue Vieille-du-Temple, 3e (phone: 42-78-55-89).

La Rôtisserie d'en Face Comfortably low-key decor, tiled floors, and an open, uncluttered atmosphere provide the backdrop for superchef Jacques Cagna's bistro fare, such as grilled chicken, roast leg of lamb, and thick steaks. Closed Saturday for lunch and Sundays. Reservations advised. MasterCard and Visa accepted. 2 Rue Christine, 6e (phone: 43-26-40-98).

Le Trumilou The formidable proprietress sets the tone of this robust establishment on the Seine, which serves huge, steaming portions of game in season, *truite aux amandes* (trout with almonds), and chicken under a frieze of some excruciatingly bad rustic oils. Amazingly cheerful service. Closed Mondays. Reservations unnecessary. Major credit cards accepted. 84 Quai de l'Hôtel-de-Ville, 4e (phone: 42-77-63-98).

VERY EXPENSIVE

Les Ambassadeurs A two-Michelin-star dining establishment that offers a soul-satisfying meal gracefully presented in elegant surroundings — from the 20-foot-high ceilings to the massive crystal chandeliers to the stunning views of the Place de la Concorde. Delicious dishes such as *gratin dauphinois de homard avec crème au caviar* (potato gratin with lobster in caviar sauce) and veal sweetbreads in a light wine sauce are perfectly complemented by one of the exceptional wines from the *cave* (wine cellar). Open daily. Major credit cards accepted. 10 Pl. de la Concorde, in the *Crillon*, 8e (phone: 44-71-16-16; fax: 44-71-15-02).

Beauvilliers With its intimate dining rooms and hydrangea-rimmed summer terraces, this one-Michelin-star restaurant on the northern slope of the Butte of Montmartre is one of the most romantic spots in Paris. The food — a rich, generous cuisine prepared in the best bourgeois tradition — complements the setting. Try the rabbit and parsley terrine, *turbot au jus de jarret,* and a remarkable praline chocolate cake. Closed the first 2 weeks in September, Monday lunch, and Sundays. Reservations necessary. Major credit cards accepted. 52 Rue Lamarck, 18e (phone: 42-54-54-42).

Laurent This *grande luxe* restaurant near the Champs-Elysées has been brought back to its former glory by chef Philippe Braun who was trained by superchef Joël Robuchon. You'll find the finest products cooked to perfection (the freshest fish served with rare morel mushrooms, and game in season), one of the city's best wine lists, all at appropriately elevated prices. Closed Saturday lunch, Sundays, and part of August. Reservations necessary. Major credit cards accepted. 41 Av. Gabriel, 8e (phone: 42-25-00-39).

Vivarois Claude Peyrot is one of France's finest chefs. Specialties in his small, elegant eating place feature *la cuisine du marché,* so offerings may vary according to what is available when the chef goes to market, but a splendid grilled turbot with capers is usually on the menu. Michelin has awarded it two stars. Closed weekends and August. Reservations necessary. Major credit cards accepted. 192 Av. Victor-Hugo, 16e (phone: 45-04-04-31).

EXPENSIVE

Apicius Jean-Pierre Vigato's highly original recipes have earned him two Michelin stars. Favorites include *tourte de canard* (duck in pastry), potato purée with truffles, and *crème brûlée* made with cherries. Closed weekends and August. Reservations necessary. Major credit cards accepted. 122 Av. de Villiers, 17e (phone: 43-80-19-66).

Auberge des Deux Signes This place was once the cellars of the priory of St-Julien-le-Pauvre; try to get an upstairs table overlooking the gardens. Auvergnat cooking (ham, charcuterie, cabbage, and potato dishes) is prepared with a lighter (less fat) touch. Closed Saturday lunch, Sundays, and August. Reservations necessary. Major credit cards accepted. 46 Rue Galande, 5e (phone: 43-25-46-56).

Bistro 121 A hearty menu and excellent wines are offered in a modern setting that's always chic and crowded. Try the *canard au fruit de la passion* (duck with passion fruit) or one of the many first-rate fish dishes. One Michelin star. Open daily; service until midnight. Reservations advised. Major credit cards accepted. 121 Rue de la Convention, 15e (phone: 45-57-52-90).

Le Carré des Feuillants Alain Dutournier of *Le Trou Gascon* has set up shop right in midtown, offering such creations as *perdreau sauvage* (wild partridge) with cumin, apricots, and fresh coriander. Michelin has awarded him two stars. Closed Saturdays for lunch (and dinner in July), Sundays, and August. Reservations necessary. Major credit cards accepted. 14 Rue de Castiglione, 1er (phone: 42-86-82-82).

Chiberta Elegant and modern, and boasting the acclaimed (two Michelin stars) nouvelle cuisine of Philippe da Silva. Try the goat cheese ravioli, or the fish with ginger and mango in puff pastry. Closed weekends, August, and December 24 to January 3. Reservations necessary. Major credit cards accepted. 3 Rue Arsène-Houssaye, 8e (phone: 45-63-77-90).

La Coquille A classic bistro, where the service is unpretentious and warm, and the food consistent, although the seafood (except the scallops) is usually overcooked. From October to May, the house specialty is *coquilles St-Jacques,* a version that consists of scallops roasted with butter, shallots, and parsley. Closed Sundays, Mondays, late July to early September, and December 23 to January 3. Reservations advised. Major credit cards accepted. 6 Rue du Débarcadère, 17e (phone: 45-72-10-73).

Le Divellec This bright and airy, two-Michelin-star place serves exquisitely fresh seafood. Try the sea bass, the *rouget,* and the sautéed turbot. The latter is served with "black pasta" — thick strips of pasta flavored with squid ink — an unusual and delicious concoction. Closed Sundays, Mondays, August, and December 24 to January 3. Reservations necessary. Major credit cards accepted. 107 Rue de l'Université, 7e (phone: 45-51-91-96).

Drouant Founded in 1880, this classic favorite reopened after an extensive facelift, with an ambitious chef who favors classic French recipes. Michelin has awarded it one star. Open daily. Reservations necessary. Major credit cards accepted. 18 Rue Gaillon, 2e (phone: 42-65-15-16).

Duquesnoy Jean-Paul Duquesnoy, one of Paris's most promising young chefs, is in his element in enchanting quarters. Warm carved woods and tasteful decor set the stage for specialties that include cabbage stuffed with duck; *crème brûlée* with walnuts is a delight. Two Michelin stars. Closed Saturday lunch and Sundays. Reservations necessary. Major credit cards accepted. 6 Av. Bosquet, 7e (phone: 47-05-96-78).

Faucher Chef-owner Gerard Faucher has drawn praise (and one Michelin star) for his light touch with fish dishes and desserts. Closed Saturday lunch, Sundays, and 1 week in August. Reservations necessary. Major credit cards accepted. 123 Av. Wagram, 17e (phone: 42-27-61-50).

Faugeron Among the finest nouvelle restaurants, awarded two stars by Michelin, its menu includes simple but exquisitely prepared dishes such as soft-boiled eggs with truffle purée. Lovely service, a first-rate wine list, and one of Paris's prettiest table settings in what once was an old school. Closed weekends and August. Reservations necessary. Major credit cards accepted. 52 Rue de Longchamp, 16e (phone: 47-04-24-53).

La Ferme St-Simon Among our favorites for wholesome *cuisine d'autrefois* (old-fashioned cooking). Nothing very chichi here, just well-prepared, authentic dishes — the kinds you'd expect from a traditional Left Bank restaurant. Leave room for dessert; the owner once was a top assistant to Gaston Lenôtre. A perfect place for lunch. Michelin has awarded it one star. Closed Saturday lunch, Sundays, and 3 weeks in August. Reservations advised. Major credit cards accepted. 6 Rue de St-Simon, 7e (phone: 45-48-35-74).

Fouquet's Bastille Sister restaurant to the Champs-Elysées institution (see *Cafés*), this post-modern location next to Paris's *Opéra Bastille* offers traditional fare with a modern touch. Closed Sundays. Reservations advised. Major credit cards accepted. 130 Rue de Lyon, 12e (phone: 43-42-18-18).

Gérard Besson Michelin has given this small and formal eatery two stars. The service is impeccable and the classic menu includes specialties such as a savory *poulet de Bresse en cocotte* (casserole-roasted free-range Bresse chicken). Closed Saturdays and Sundays, mid-July to early August, and from December 25 to January 23. Reservations necessary. Major credit cards accepted. 5 Rue Coq-Héron, 1er (phone: 42-33-14-74).

Goumard-Prunier Chef Jean-Claude Goumard relies on a network of Breton and Mediterranean fishermen to provide the finest seafood; his inventive creations have earned him one Michelin star. Closed Sundays and Mondays. Reservations necessary. Major credit cards accepted. 9 Rue Duphot, 1er (phone: 42-60-36-07).

Jacques Cagna This establishment has a quintessential Left Bank look and a mix of nouvelle and classic dishes. The talented eponymous chef always provides an interesting menu at these charming premises on the Left Bank, very near the Seine. *Michelin* has awarded it two stars. Closed most of

August, *Christmas* week, Saturdays (except for dinner twice a month), and Sundays. Reservations necessary. Major credit cards accepted. 14 Rue des Grands-Augustins, 6e (phone: 43-26-49-39).

Ledoyen This grand dowager of Paris dining places has been given a breath of life by a new chef, Ghislaine Arabian, who favors classic cuisine, such as *coquilles St-Jacques* (sea scallops) in cream sauce. There's also an excellent, relatively moderate-priced lunch menu. Michelin has awarded it one star. The view from the upstairs dining room — of the Champs-Elysées but with the trees blocking the traffic — is superb. Closed Sundays. Reservations necessary. Major credit cards accepted. Carré des Champs-Elysées, 8e (phone: 47-42-23-23).

Miravile Gilles Epié's one-Michelin-star cuisine includes such memorable dishes as *lapin aux olives* (rabbit with olives) and other recipes with a Provençal flavor. Closed Saturday lunch and Sundays. Reservations necessary. Major credit cards accepted. 72 Quai de l'Hôtel-de-Ville, 4e (phone: 42-74-72-22).

Morot-Gaudry On the top floor of a 1920s building with a great view of the Eiffel Tower, especially from the flowered terrace. Among the inventive dishes, all very fairly priced, is *pigeon en papillote* (squab steamed in its own juices); many dishes have a Mediterranean accent. One Michelin star. Closed weekends. Reservations necessary. Major credit cards accepted. 8 Rue de la Cavalerie, 15e (phone: 45-67-06-85).

Le Petit Montmorency In his location near the Champs-Elysées, chef Daniel Bouché presents one of the most consistent menus in Paris, offering such specialties as a fresh truffle roasted in pastry (in winter) and a *soufflé aux noisettes* (hazelnut soufflé). Closed weekends and August. Reservations necessary. Major credit cards accepted. 26 Rue Jean Mermoz, 8e (phone: 42-25-11-19).

Le Pharamond This one-Michelin-star restaurant serves only the best Norman food in a beautiful Belle Epoque, timbered townhouse (ca. 1862) that has been declared a historic monument by the French government. Famous for *tripes à la mode de Caen* and *pommes soufflés*. Closed Sundays, Monday lunch, and mid-July to mid-August. Reservations advised. Major credit cards accepted. 24 Rue de la Grande-Truanderie, 1er (phone: 42-33-06-72).

Pile ou Face The name means "heads or tails," but you won't take chances on quality at this one-Michelin-star bistro; super-fresh ingredients come from the owners' own farm. Try the *lapin en marmelade de romarin* (rabbit in a rich rosemary-flavored sauce). Closed weekends, 3 weeks in August, and *Christmas* to January. Reservations advised. Major credit cards accepted. 52 *bis* Rue Notre-Dame-des-Victoires, 2e (phone: 42-33-64-33).

Le Port Alma This elegant establishment, with a view of the Eiffel Tower, offers some of the finest seafood in town, such as baby clams in a thyme-flavored cream sauce. Closed Sundays and August. Reservations necessary. MasterCard and Visa accepted. 10 Av. de New-York, 16e (phone: 47-23-75-11).

Timonerie Be sure to reserve 3 or 4 days in advance in order to dine at this one-Michelin-star restaurant. Specialties include *sandre rôti au chou et pommes de terre* (pickerel with cabbage and potatoes) and a superb chocolate tart. Especially recommended is the very affordable prix fixe lunch. Closed Sundays, Mondays, and 1 week in August and February. MasterCard and Visa accepted. 35 Quai de la Tournelle, 5e (phone: 43-25-44-42).

Le Toit de Passy Not only is the food here good (Michelin has awarded chef Yannick Jacquot one star), but the rooftop view in one of Paris's more exclusive districts is spectacular. Try specialties such as *pigeonneau en croûte de sel* (squab in a salt crust) while dining outdoors. Closed Saturday lunch, Sundays, and *Christmas* week. Reservations necessary. Major credit cards accepted. 94 Av. Paul-Doumer, 16e (phone: 45-24-55-37).

Le Train Bleu Adequate if far from great food and good wine, but with baroque decor so gorgeous that this spot has been made a national monument. And it's in a train station. Open daily for lunch and dinner. Reservations advised. Major credit cards accepted. Gare de Lyon, 20 Bd. Diderot, 12e (phone: 43-43-38-39).

Au Trou Gascon Alain Dutournier created the inspired and unusual cooking that features southwestern French specialties and a vast choice of regional wines and armagnacs. He has moved his bistro to a more elegant neighborhood, but his wife holds down the fort at this one-Michelin-star restaurant; unfortunately, some have found the food uninspired of late. Closed weekends. Reservations advised. Major credit cards accepted. 40 Rue Taine, 12e (phone: 43-44-34-26).

MODERATE

Ambassade d'Auvergne Its young chef creates delicious, unusual, classic Auvergnat dishes with a modern touch (try the lentil salad and the sliced ham), as well as *aligot*, a purée of potatoes and young cantal cheese. Also known for wonderful cakes. Open daily for lunch and dinner. Reservations advised. Major credit cards accepted. 22 Rue du Grenier-St-Lazare, 3e (phone: 42-72-31-22).

Atelier Maître Albert Unlike most other eateries on the Left Bank, this one is pleasantly roomy, with a log fire in winter and a prix fixe menu of classic French cuisine year-round. Notre-Dame looms up in front of you as you walk out the door and onto the quay. Open daily except Sundays for dinner. Reservations advised. Major credit cards accepted. 1 Rue Maître-Albert, 5e (phone: 46-33-13-78).

L'Auberge Nicolas Flanel Believed to be the oldest restaurant in Paris (an inn opened in the half-timbered building in 1407), its menu includes such good, simple fare as grilled tuna, and leg of lamb. Closed Saturday lunch, Sundays, and August. Reservations advised. MasterCard and Visa accepted. 51 Rue de Montmorency, 3e (phone: 42-71-77-78).

L'Avenue This chic brasserie, as fashionable as the district, offers grilled meats, raw oysters, and old-fashioned desserts in a dining room with a view of the Eiffel Tower. Open daily; closed most of August. Reservations advised. MasterCard and Visa accepted. 41 Av. Montaigne, 8e (phone: 40-70-14-91).

Balzar Perhaps because of its location right next to the Sorbonne, this mirrored brasserie has always attracted well-heeled intellectuals. The steaks and *pommes frites* also are worth a visit. Open daily for lunch and dinner; service until midnight. Closed December 25 through January 1, and August. Reservations necessary. Major credit cards accepted. 49 Rue des Ecoles, 5e (phone: 43-54-13-67).

Baracane-Bistrot d'Oulette This reasonably priced bistro has excellent bourgeois cuisine. Try the *pintade* (guinea hen) terrine, or the *daube de boeuf* (beef stew) cooked in red Cahors wine. Closed Saturday lunch, Sundays, and most of August. Reservations necessary. MasterCard and Visa accepted. 38 Rue des Tournelles, 4e (phone: 42-71-43-44).

Bistro de la Grille The decor of this old-fashioned spot in the chic St-Germain-des-Prés district is right out of a Cartier-Bresson photo, and the excellent food, from the *andouillette* (grilled tripe sausage, not for the faint-hearted), to the pot-au-feu, is completely appropriate to the setting. The *première étage* (upstairs) is preferable to the noisy downstairs. Open daily; closed most of August. Reservations advised. MasterCard and Visa accepted. 14 Rue Mabillon, 6e (phone: 43-54-16-87).

Le Bistrot du Sommelier The bourgeois cuisine is excellent and the wine list in this former *Meilleur Sommelier de France*'s bistro is sublime. Closed Saturday evening, Sundays, and August. Reservations advised. Major credit cards accepted. 97 Bd. Haussmann, 8e (phone: 42-65-24-85).

Le Boeuf sur le Toit A haunt of Jean Cocteau and other Paris artists in the 1940s, this eatery off the Champs-Elysées is managed by the Flo group, well known for good value in atmospheric surroundings. Piano bar until 2 AM. Open daily. Reservations advised. Major credit cards accepted. 34 Rue du Colisée, 8e (phone: 43-59-83-80).

Bofinger For magnificent Belle Epoque decor, this is the place; it's one of Paris's oldest brasseries and it is beautiful, even if the food is occasionally dissatisfying. Order onion soup and *choucroute* and you won't be disappointed — and ask to be seated on the ground floor. Open daily. Reservations advised. Major credit cards accepted. 15 Rue de la Bastille, 4e (phone: 42-72-87-82).

Brasserie Lipp This famous café is fashionable for a late supper of *choucroute* and Alsatian beer and for people watching inside and out, although guests not known to the staff sometimes receive less than welcoming treatment. Closed 15 days at *Christmas.* Reservations advised. Major credit cards accepted. 151 Bd. St-Germain, 6e (phone: 45-48-53-91).

Brissemoret Popular with Parisians, this pleasant eatery serves basic quality food at bargain prices: excellent foie gras, raw salmon marinated in fresh herbs, and great sauces (try the breast of duck in wine sauce). Closed Saturdays, Sundays, and most of August. Reservations necessary. Major credit cards accepted. 5 Rue St-Marc, 2e (phone: 42-36-91-72).

La Butte Chaillot Superchef Guy Savoy's bistro in the posh 16th district has starkly modern decor, but features such old-fashioned dishes as roast chicken with mashed potatoes, and an unusual lentil soup with crayfish. Closed August. Reservations advised. Major credit cards accepted. 112 Av. Kléber, 16e (phone: 47-27-88-88).

La Cagouille This Left Bank bistro features fish; try the steamed clams, and the *bar* (sea bass) with vegetables. Open daily. Closed December 25 through January 1. Reservations advised. Major credit cards accepted. 10 Pl. Constantin Brancusi, 14e (phone: 43-22-09-01).

Campagne et Provence The bistro alternative to the fine *Miravile* (see above), this tiny Latin Quarter spot has a lovely *tapenade de lapin* (rabbit with olive purée) and a garlicky mixed green salad. Closed Saturday lunch, Sundays, and most of August. Reservations necessary. MasterCard and Visa accepted. 25 Quai de la Tournelle, 5e (phone: 43-54-05-17).

Canard'avril A friendly place, featuring such French southwestern specialties as roast duck, cassoulet, foie gras, and potatoes sautéed with garlic; there's also a good selection of fish dishes. Closed weekends. MasterCard and Visa accepted. 5 Rue Paul Lelong, 2e (phone: 42-36-26-08).

Le Caroubier A family-run couscous restaurant with some of the best hand-rolled couscous grains in town, accompanied by good vegetables, grilled meat, and a delicious *pastilla,* a flaky pastry with a spicy meat filling. Pour the vegetable broth on the delicate couscous, add a little hot pepper sauce, and you'll feel as if you've been transported to North Africa. Closed Sunday nights, Mondays, and August. Reservations advised. MasterCard and Visa accepted. 122 Av. du Maine, 14e (phone: 43-20-41-49).

Chez André A classic, bustling bistro near the chic shopping of Avenue Montaigne. Although a bit too noisy and crowded, it offers impeccably prepared sole meunière, *blanquette de veau, gigôt d'agneau,* and other traditional dishes. Open daily. Reservations advised. Major credit cards accepted. 12 Rue Marbeuf, 8e (phone: 47-20-59-57).

Chez Marius A real find. The rotund chef really loves his work and the three-dish prix fixe dinner is a great deal. The atmosphere is Old World cozy and the service comes with a smile. Specialties are bouillabaisse and grilled fish. Closed Saturday lunch, Sundays, most of August, and 1 week at *Christmas*. Reservations advised. Major credit cards accepted. 5 Rue Bourgogne, 7e (phone: 47-05-96-19).

Chez René Set in the heart of the Left Bank, this neighborhood bistro offers hearty helpings of regional fare. Charcuterie and an earthy *gratin de blettes* (chard) are among the specialties, and the selection of cheese is not to be missed. There is a room for nonsmokers. Closed Saturdays, Sundays, August, and *Christmas* week. Reservations advised. MasterCard and Visa accepted. 14 Bd. St-Germain, 5e (phone: 43-54-30-23).

Chez Yvette This excellent, small, bourgeois restaurant has good home cooking, lots of choices, and great desserts. Closed weekends and August. Reservations advised. Major credit cards accepted. 1 Rue Alençon, 15e (phone: 42-22-45-54).

La Coupole A big, brassy brasserie, once the haunt of Hemingway, Josephine Baker, and Picasso, it is owned by the Flo group. The atmosphere is still great, the food improving. Open daily until 2 AM. Closed *Christmas Eve,* and August. Reservations advised. Major credit cards accepted. 102 Bd. du Montparnasse, 14e (phone: 43-20-14-20).

Fontaine de Mars A simple, family-style restaurant near the Eiffel Tower with traditional French cooking and specialties such as *quenelles de brochet* (pike dumplings) and chocolate cake. In summer, diners can sup outdoors on the patio. Closed Sundays and August. Reservations advised. Major credit cards accepted. 129 Rue St-Dominique, 7e (phone: 47-05-46-44).

Au Gamin de Paris Combines the coziness of a classic bistro with the chic of a historic Marais building and serves well-prepared, imaginative food. Open daily. No reservations after 8 PM. Major credit cards accepted. 51 Rue Vieille-du-Temple, 4e (phone: 42-78-97-24).

Jo Goldenberg The best-known eating house in the Marais's quaint Jewish quarter, with good, albeit a tad overpriced, chopped liver and cheesecake and a range of Eastern European Jewish specialties. It's also a fine place to sip mint tea at the counter in the middle of a busy day. Open daily. Reservations unnecessary. Major credit cards accepted. 7 Rue des Rosiers, 4e (phone: 48-87-20-16).

La Manufacture The second eatery of two-star chef Jean-Pierre Vigato (of *Apicius*), this starkly modern place in an old cigar factory at the southern edge of Paris offers a reasonable quality/price ratio of traditional fare.

Closed Saturday lunches, Sundays, and 2 weeks in August. Reservations advised. Major credit cards accepted. 30 Rue Ernest-Renan, Issy-les-Moulineaux (phone: 40-93-08-98).

Le Maraîcher This tiny Marais eatery has excellent bourgeois cooking (try the cassoulet) at very reasonable prices. Closed *Christmas* week and August. Major credit cards accepted. 5 Rue Beautrellis, 4e (phone: 42-71-42-49).

La Marée Unobtrusive on the outside, there is great comfort within — also the freshest of fish, the best restaurant wine values in Paris, and fabulous desserts. Michelin has awarded it one star. Closed weekends, holidays, and August. Reservations advised. Major credit cards accepted. 1 Rue Daru, 8e (phone: 43-80-20-00).

Moissonier Little has changed over the past 30 years on the menu of this Lyonnais restaurant across the street from what was once Paris's wine depot — except the prices. The seafood, tripe dishes, and beaujolais, although not innovative, are bourgeois cuisine par excellence. Closed Sunday nights and Mondays. Reservations advised. MasterCard and Visa accepted. 28 Rue Fossés-St-Bernard, 5e (phone: 43-29-87-65).

Le Muniche St-Germain's best brasserie is a bustling place with a rather extensive menu, and it serves until 1:30 AM. Open daily. Reservations advised. Major credit cards accepted. 22 Rue Guillaume-Apollinaire, 6e (phone: 46-33-62-09).

Le Petit Niçois This tiny bistro, serving delicious bouillabaisse, is a favorite of French TV news crews who broadcast from a nearby building. A few good specials vary from night to night. Closed Sundays and Monday lunch. Reservations advised. Major credit cards accepted. 10 Rue Amélie, 7e (phone: 45-51-83-65).

Au Pied de Cochon No more *choucroute* on the menu (sob!). Crowded and colorful 24 hours a day, and its customers enjoy shellfish, pigs' feet, and great crocks of onion soup, all in the old *Les Halles* area. Unfortunately, the food and service aren't what they used to be, and a garish redecoration has mangled most of the old atmosphere. But it still has atmosphere. Open 24 hours a day, daily. Reservations advised. Major credit cards accepted. 6 Rue Coquillière, 1er (phone: 42-36-11-75).

Le Poquelin The excellent bourgeois cooking includes splendid roast duck. Closed Saturdays for lunch, Sundays, and 3 weeks in August. Reservations advised. Major credit cards accepted. 17 Rue Molière, 1er (phone: 42-96-22-19).

Au Quai d'Orsay Fashionable, sophisticated, very French, and very intimate. Traditional bourgeois cooking and good beaujolais. Closed Sundays. Reservations advised. Major credit cards accepted. 49 Quai d'Orsay, 7e (phone: 45-51-58-58).

La Rôtisserie du Beaujolais A de rigueur spot for Paris's "in set" is Claude Terrail's casual canteen on the quay in the shadow of his three-star gastronomic temple, *La Tour d'Argent*. Most of the meat, produce, and cheese served come from Lyons; the Georges Duboeuf beaujolais is superb. Closed Mondays. No reservations. Major credit cards accepted. 19 Quai de la Tournelle, 5e (phone: 43-54-17-47).

Thoumieux A family-run bistro that has been reliable for decades. Come here for tripe, cassoulet, and *boudin aux châtaignes* (blood sausage with chestnuts). Open daily. MasterCard and Visa accepted. 79 Rue St-Dominique, 7e (phone: 47-05-49-75).

La Tour de Monthléry On everyone's favorite Paris bistros list, this establishment in *Les Halles* offers bourgeois cooking. Closed weekends and August. MasterCard and Visa accepted. 5 Rue des Prouvaires, 1er (phone: 42-36-21-82).

Le Valencay A small, popular bistro with classic bourgeois fare and wines by the glass or the bottle. Closed Sundays and August. Major credit cards accepted. 11 Bd. du Palais, 4e (phone: 43-54-64-67).

Yvan Bistro cooking such as *ris de veau aux cèpes* (sweetbreads with boletus mushrooms) and some nouvelle dishes, along with a wonderful cheese selection. Stylish atmosphere and very reasonable prices. Closed Saturday lunch and Sundays. Reservations essential. Major credit cards accepted. 1 Rue Jean-Mermoz, 8e (phone: 43-59-18-40).

Les Zygomates In the out-of-the-way 12th district, this friendly bistro occupies a converted fin de siècle charcuterie with lots of mirrors and marble counters. The menu includes fish, as well as classic bistro meat dishes and gooey chocolate desserts. Closed Saturday lunch, Sundays, most of August, and December 26 to January 4. Reservations necessary. MasterCard and Visa accepted. 7 Rue Capri, 12e (phone: 40-19-93-04).

INEXPENSIVE

L'Ami Jean Good Basque cooking at a good price. Closed Saturday evenings and Sundays. No reservations. No credit cards accepted. 27 Rue Malar, 7e (phone: 47-05-86-89).

Auberge de Jarente This Basque restaurant in the heart of the Marais is the place to sample classic *pipérade* (omelette with ham and tomato), and cassoulet. Closed Sundays, Mondays, and August. Reservations advised. MasterCard and Visa accepted. 7 Rue de Jarente, 4e (phone: 42-77-49-35).

Aux Bigorneaux A souvenir of the old *Les Halles,* this place is frequented by arty types and journalists. Especially recommended are the *foie gras frais maison,* the chicory salad, the steak *au poivre,* the Réserve Maison wine, and the sumptuous desserts. Closed Sundays, Mondays, and for dinner in winter. Reservations advised. Major credit cards accepted. 12 Rue Mondétour, 1er (phone: 40-28-99-11).

Brasserie Fernand A nondescript hole in the wall that produces surprisingly tasty dishes. *Pot-au-feu,* steaks with shallots, and fish pâté all are first-rate, but the real lure is the huge tub of chocolate mousse served for dessert — a chocoholic's fantasy come true. Open evenings only. Reservations advised. MasterCard and Visa accepted. 13 Rue Guisarde, 6e (phone: 43-54-61-47).

La Lozère Some authentic country cooking from the Lozère region in the south of France, which specializes in charcuterie and cassoulet. Closed Sundays, Mondays, and August. Reservations advised. No credit cards accepted. 4 Rue Hautefeuille, 6e (phone: 43-54-26-64).

Polidor Regulars here keep their napkins in numbered pigeonholes, and the place's history includes frequent patronage by such starving artists as Paul Verlaine, James Joyce, Ernest Hemingway, and, more recently, Jean-Paul Belmondo. The *College de Pataphysique,* founded by Raymond Queneau and Ionesco, still meets here regularly for the good family-style food. However, foreigners are often banished to the back room. Closed in August. Reservations unnecessary. No credit cards accepted. 41 Rue Monsieur-le-Prince, 6e (phone: 43-26-95-34).

La Route du Beaujolais It's a barn-like workers' bistro on the Left Bank, serving Lyonnaise specialties and beaujolais wines. Don't miss the charcuterie and the fresh bread here, and try the *tarte tatin* (caramelized apple tart) for dessert. Closed Saturday lunch and Sundays. Reservations unnecessary. MasterCard and Visa accepted. 17 Rue de Lourmel, 15e (phone: 45-79-31-63).

VERY INEXPENSIVE

Bistro de la Gare Michel Oliver offers a choice of three appetizers and three main courses with *pommes frites.* Excellent for a quick lunch. Open daily. No reservations. Major credit cards accepted. Ten locations, including 1 Rue du Four, 6e (phone: 43-25-87-76); 59 Bd. Montparnasse, 6e (phone: 45-48-38-01); and 30 Rue St-Denis, 1er (phone: 40-26-82-80).

Chartier Huge, turn-of-the-century place with lots of down-to-earth food for the money. The famous *pot-au-feu* is still served on Mondays. Open daily. No reservations. No credit cards accepted. 7 Rue du Faubourg-Montmartre, 9e (phone: 47-70-86-29).

Drouot A favorite of locals, the younger member of the Chartier family (see above) proffers simple fare at bargain prices. To avoid a long wait for a table, arrive before 9 PM. Open daily. No reservations. No credit cards accepted. 103 Rue de Richelieu, 2e (phone: 42-96-68-23).

Le Petit Gavroche A hole-in-the-wall bistro-cum-restaurant with a lively clientele and an inexpensive and classic menu. Closed Sundays. Reservations unnecessary. No credit cards accepted. 15 Rue Ste-Croix-de-la-Bretonnerie, 4e (phone: 48-87-74-26).

Le Petit St-Benoît French cooking at its simplest, in a plain little place with tiled floors and curlicued hat stands. Open weekdays. Reservations unnecessary. No credit cards accepted. 4 Rue St-Benoît, 6e (phone: 42-60-27-92).

Au Pied de Fouet This former coach house has had its habitués, including celebrities as diverse as Graham Greene, Le Corbusier, and Georges Pompidou. Service is fast and friendly, and it's a place to order the daily special. Desserts, such as *charlotte au chocolat,* are marvelous. Arrive early; it closes at 9 PM. Closed Saturday evenings, Sundays, 2 weeks at *Christmas* and *Easter,* and August. No reservations. No credit cards accepted. 45 Rue de Babylone, 7e (phone: 47-05-12-27).

> ## EXTRA SPECIAL
>
> Although we've noted the existence of *Fauchon* as a shopping destination in *Quintessential Paris* (see DIVERSIONS), we would be remiss in omitting it from the restaurant listings. On the first floor of the 30 Place de la Madeleine location is *Le 30,* a charming garden-style restaurant that serves first-rate seafood and veal dishes, along with some spectacular desserts. And for nonpareil pastries, coffee, and a wide variety of light lunches or snacks, folks in the know head for the basement. Mornings begin at 8 AM here with an American- or French-style breakfast (offering over 40 different types of coffee); lunchtime (in the same space) features reasonably priced daily specials (to attract shoppers from nearby department stores). In the afternoons (until about 5 PM), the setting serves as a tearoom, offering the house's celebrated pastries. Chocolate *opéra* cakes and macaroons in many hues, as well as *millefeuilles* and other custardy concoctions, are sold by the slice and can be sampled here, Paris's "in" place for standup snacking; there also are casual communal tables.

CAFÉS

Paris without cafés would be like Rome without the Colosseum, Dublin without pubs, or New York without Broadway. The corner café is the glue that holds the French neighborhood together; it's a place for coffee and gossip, or just a spot to sit and watch the world go by. And, possibly best of all, it's a place that's also easy on the wallet — no matter the francs conversion rate.

There are over 5,000 cafés in Paris (approximately 1 for every 400 residents and their dogs), but we have a few favorites.

PARIS'S BEST CAFÉS

Café Costes A post-modernist design (inspired by Fritz Lang's *Metropolis*) located in the Beaubourg district near the *Centre Georges-Pompidou,* this café was the trendiest of trendsetters for *branché* (with-it) Parisians; now its fame is such that it rated a mention in *Time* magazine. Open daily. Major credit cards accepted. 4 Rue Berger, 1er (phone: 45-08-54-38 or 45-08-54-39).

Café de la Paix Designed by architect Charles Garnier to complement his baroque *Opéra,* this grande dame is best for afternoon tea; keep your eye out for the elusive pastry cart and sometimes elusive service. Open daily. Major credit cards accepted. 12 Bd. des Capucines and 2 Rue Scribe (2 entrances), 9e (phone: 40-07-32-32).

Fouquet's Arguably, Paris's best-located café — it's a part of the eponymous regal restaurant (now declared an official historic monument) — this institution on the Champs-Elysées is far from perfect. (The drinks are too expensive; the sidewalk is often too crowded; the bar carries a sign offensive to women; and the downstairs dining is forgettable one night and simply mediocre the next.) But if there is still magic in the world, it comes from sitting here at dusk and watching the lights come up on the Arc de Triomphe. Open daily 9 PM to midnight. Major credit cards accepted. 99 Av. des Champs-Elysées, 8e (phone: 47-23-70-60).

Ma Bourgogne Set beneath the vaulted arcades of the Place des Vosges, this is a great spot for an afternoon stop, not for food, but for the view of Paris's most beautiful square. Closed Mondays. MasterCard and Visa accepted. 19 Pl. des Vosges, 4e (phone: 42-78-44-64).

Le Piano Zinc Tiny and authentic, this 1900s-era hole-in-the-wall (with a zinc-top, horseshoe-shape bar) has a regular — though eclectic — clientele of artists and workers. Central to Marais shopping, museums, designer boutiques, and the Hôtel de Ville, it's well worth the detour. Closed August. No credit cards accepted. 49 Rue des Blancs-Manteaux, 3e (phone: 42-74-32-42).

Le Select Opened in 1925 during the height of Paris's Jazz Age, this was the first Montparnasse café to stay open all night. Edna St. Vincent Millay adored it. So did Erik Satie and Leonard Foujita, and in 1927 Isadora Duncan got into a fistfight here with an American newspaperman (history records the dancer won by a decision). The café hasn't changed much since, and has one of the liveliest early-morning-coffee and midnight scenes imaginable. Open daily until 2 AM year-round. MasterCard and Visa accepted. 99 Bd. du Montparnasse, 6e (phone: 42-22-65-27).

Le Voltaire Opposite the *Louvre* and close to the *Musée d'Orsay,* this tiny café along the Seine is an often-overlooked gem. It has a very rich literary history as the place where Baudelaire wrote *Les Fleurs du Mal* (he lived at No. 29), Wagner wrote *Die Meistersinger* (his home was at No. 22), and Willa Cather wrote her Pulitzer Prize–winning novel, *One of Ours* (she resided at No. 19). Closed Sundays, Mondays, and the month of August. No credit cards accepted. 27 Quai Voltaire, 7e (phone: 42-61-17-49).

WINE BARS

Choosing a place to drink is not a pressing problem in Paris. Following is a selection of watering holes to suit a variety of tastes and thirsts. Prices tend to be higher than in the United States, with a *café crème* or a glass of red wine costing $3 or more in the more expensive establishments. The moderate ones charge $2 to $3 for the same, and you pay less than $2 in the inexpensive spots.

EXPENSIVE

Au Chai de l'Abbaye At this wine bar in the heart of the St-Germain-des-Prés you can opt for a fine Meursault at around $12 per glass, or settle for an excellent Côtes de Brouilly for $5; the food includes a variety of salads, omelettes, and charcuterie. Open daily. Closed most of August. No reservations. MasterCard and Visa accepted. 26 Rue de Buci, 6e (phone: 43-26-68-26).

Harry's New York Bar The son of the original Harry, who opened this celebrated establishment in 1911, is still at the helm here. And the memories of past patrons like Ernest Hemingway, Gertrude Stein, and George Gershwin are almost as tangible as the university flags and banners that hang from the paneled walls. Open 10:30 AM to 4 AM every day but *Christmas*. Reservations unnecessary. Major credit cards accepted. 5 Rue Daunou, 2e (phone: 42-61-71-14).

Willi's An enterprising Englishman set up this smart little wine bar, a pleasant walk through the Palais Royal gardens and only minutes from the *Louvre*. The wine selection — a list of 150 — is one of the best in Paris, with an emphasis on Côtes du Rhône. The chef creates some appetizing salads as well as a *plat du jour*. Closed Sundays. Reservations unnecessary. Major credit cards accepted. 13 Rue des Petits-Champs, 1er (phone: 42-61-05-09).

MODERATE

L'Ecluse This unassuming wine bar looking onto the Seine has fathered several others, more sophisticated, in the Rue François-Ier, at the Madeleine, at the *Opéra* (both the *Garnier* and the *Bastille*), in *Le Forum des Halles,* and in Neuilly. Its red velvet benches and wooden tables — not to mention its bordeaux and its fresh, homemade foie gras and spectacular chocolate cake — remain unchanged. Open daily. No reservations. Major credit cards accepted. 15 Quai des Grands-Augustins, 6e (phone: 46-33-58-74), and several other locations in Paris.

Au Franc Pinot A restaurant has operated on this spot for 350 years, making this Paris's oldest "wine bar." In a lovely setting on the Ile St-Louis, the bar offers regional wines, many from the Loire, and delicious snacks. Closed Sundays, Mondays, August, and daily from 2 to 7 PM. No reservations. Major credit cards accepted. 1 Quai Bourbon, 4e (phone: 43-29-46-98).

Le Pain et Le Vin An imaginative wine bar with 40 wines by the glass, and daily hot luncheon specials. It's operated by four top Parisian chefs, including Alain Dutournier of *Le Carré des Feuilliants* and *Le Trou Gascon*. Closed Sundays and August. Reservations unnecessary. Major credit cards accepted. 1 Rue d'Armaille, 17e (phone: 47-63-88-29).

Le Repaire de Bacchus A tiny wine bar specializing in unusual regional wines, displayed in crowded rows. You can buy wine by the bottle to take home or on a picnic, or sample them at the counter with cheese and charcuterie. Closed Sundays and Mondays. Reservations unnecessary. Major credit cards accepted. 13 Rue du Cherche-Midi, 6e (phone: 45-44-01-07).

Zimmer Centrally located, this is the place to stop off for a drink before or after a show at one of the nearby theaters. Open daily. Reservations unnecessary. Major credit cards accepted. 1 Pl. du Châtelet, 4e (phone: 42-36-74-04).

INEXPENSIVE

Bistrot des Augustins Just across the street from the booksellers on the Quais, this old-fashioned café with an excellent *plat du jour* at lunch has fine beaujolais and other wines by the glass. Open daily; closed August. No reservations. No credit cards. 39 Quai des Grands-Augustins, 6e (phone: 43-54-41-65).

Le Bouchon du Marais One of the capital's newer wine bars, it specializes in wine from the Loire valley (the owner has a vineyard in Chinon) and simple light snacks. Closed Sundays, August, and daily from 3 to 6 PM. No reservations. No credit cards accepted. 15 Rue François-Miron, 4e (phone: 48-87-44-13).

Caves Saint Gilles A Spanish wine bar, near the *Picasso Museum,* serving generous *tapas* (try the *piperade,* a Basque omelette), rioja and sangria by the glass, and an ample *plat du jour*. Open daily. Closed August. Reservations accepted for a full meal at lunch only. No credit cards accepted. 4 Rue St-Gilles, 3e (phone: 48-87-22-62).

La Cloche des Halles The dim lighting and dark wood paneling at this cozy establishment only add to the pleasure of sampling the wine here. Those with a hunger pang can sample the generous cheese platter or try a plate of charcuterie. Closed Saturday evenings, Sundays, and August. 28 Rue Coquillière, 1er (phone: 42-36-93-89).

L'Enoteca An Italian wine bar in the Marais, with Italian fare at lunch, and a vast assortment of Italian wines by the glass or bottle. Open daily. Closed part of August. No reservations. 25 Rue Charles-V, 4e (phone: 42-78-91-44).

Espace Hérault Attached to the Hérault *département*'s tourist office, it features wines from France's Languedoc region, accompanied by simple dishes from the same area. Closed Sundays and August. Reservations unnecessary. MasterCard and Visa accepted. 8 Rue de La Harpe, 5e (phone: 43-54-11-40).

Jacques Melac An old-fashioned wine bar run by a young, extravagantly mustachioed man from the Auvergne, who bottles and sells his own rustic wines and even stages a harvest celebration in honor of the restaurant's vineyard. Note the sign above the bar that asserts that water only should be used for cooking potatoes. Closed Monday evenings, weekends, and August. No reservations. No credit cards accepted. 42 Rue Léon-Frot, 11e (phone: 43-70-59-27).

Juveniles This friendly spot has excellent wine and top-quality snacks, as well as several fine sherries. The British owners have a loyal Anglo-American following. Closed Sundays. MasterCard and Visa accepted. 47 Rue de Richelieu, 1er (phone: 47-97-46-49).

La Palette A Left Bank hangout on a tiny square, with outdoor tables during the summer, it stays lively with a young crowd until 2 AM. Closed Sundays, holidays, and August. Reservations unnecessary. No credit cards accepted. 43 Rue de Seine, 6e (phone: 43-26-68-15).

Le Passage The wine bar with everything: excellent wine (try the chinon), jazz, a varied menu, and friendly service. Closed Saturday lunch, Sundays, and most of August. No reservations. MasterCard and Visa accepted. 18 Passage de la Bonne-Graine, 11e (phone: 47-00-73-30).

Relais Chablisien As the name implies, this wine bar, with its wood-beamed ceilings and warm atmosphere, specializes in chablis. Sandwiches and snacks also are available. Closed weekends and 2 weeks in August. Reservations advised for meals. Major credit cards accepted. 4 Rue Bertin-Poirée, 1er (phone: 45-08-53-73).

Le Rouge-Gorge Near the antiques shops of the St-Paul *quartier*, this place has innovative, changing "thematic" menus that feature the wines and foods of a particular region for a 2-week period. Closed Sundays and August. No reservations. No credit cards accepted. 8 Rue St-Paul, 4e (phone: 48-04-75-89).

Le Rubis A tiny corner bar with an old-fashioned atmosphere and a selection of about 30 wines. With your glass of wine try the pork *rillettes,* a savory meat pie made on the premises. Closed Saturdays after 4 PM, Sundays, and 2 weeks in August. No reservations. No credit cards accepted. 10 Rue du Marché-St-Honoré, 1er (phone: 42-61-03-34).

Le Sancerre An hospitable spot featuring sancerre and nothing but sancerre. Simple lunches of omelettes, charcuterie, apple tarts, and *petits goutés* (snacks) such as goat cheese marinated in olive oil, are the perfect accompaniment for bottles of excellent red, white, and rosé. Closed Saturday evenings, Sundays, and August. No reservations. Major credit cards accepted. 22 Av. Rapp, 7e (phone: 45-51-75-91).

Au Sauvignon The no-nonsense couple who run this tiny corner bar seem to be in perpetual motion, pouring the sauvignon (or the white quincy and beaujolais nouveau in November and January) and carving up chunky sandwiches with bread from the famous *Poilâne* bakery not far away. Closed Sundays, 2 weeks in January, *Easter,* and August. No reservations. No credit cards accepted. 80 Rue des Sts-Pères, 7e (phone: 45-48-49-02).

La Tartine One of the old, authentic bistros, where Trotsky was once known to sip a glass or two of wine. There's a colorful local clientele and a good selection of wine by the glass. Closed Tuesdays, Wednesday mornings, and most of August. Reservations unnecessary. No credit cards accepted. 24 Rue de Rivoli, 4e (phone: 42-72-76-85).

Taverne Henri IV A selection of nearly 20 wines are offered by the glass, along with generous servings of simple food such as open sandwiches of ham, cheese, sausage, or a terrine of wild boar. Closed Saturday evenings, Sundays, and August. Reservations unnecessary. No credit cards accepted. 13 Pl. du Pont-Neuf, 1er (phone: 43-54-27-90).

TEAROOMS

Yes, you have crossed the Channel, but even in Paris, taking tea is a revitalizing mid-afternoon break from frantic sightseeing and window shopping. The *salon de thé* originally was the refuge of patrician Parisian ladies, who lingered over ambrosial pastries and fragrant, steaming cups of *cerise* (cherry) tea between social calls. Today, tearooms still lure many a Parisian and visitor alike to partake of their caloric delights. Here is a sampling of some of the best in town: *L'Arbre à Canelle* (57 Passage des Panoramas, 2e; phone: 45-08-55-87) offers a scrumptious chocolate-pear and apple tart in a stylish setting. Those with discriminating tea tastes frequent *A La Cour de Rohan* (59-61 St-André-des-Arts, 6e; phone: 43-25-79-67), which offers over 20 varieties — described in almost religious detail. You'll find a *plus raffiné* Belle Epoque atmosphere at *Ladurée* (16 Rue Royale, 8e; phone: 42-60-21-79); it would be a shame to ignore the masterfully decorated petits fours, marrons glacés, and macaroons. Nowhere in Paris is tea taken more seriously than at *Mariage Frères* (30-32 Rue du Bourg-Tibourg, 4e; phone: 42-72-28-11; and 13 Rue des Grands-Augustins, 6e; phone: 40-51-82-50); with a supply of 450 different kinds of tea, it's perhaps wisest to close your eyes and choose a blend at whim. Neoclassical art, tranquil ambience, and classical music all contribute to the success of *A Priori Thé* (35-37 *Galerie Vivienne,* 2e; phone: 42-97-48-75), conveniently located across the street from the Bibliothèque Nationale in the *Galerie Vivienne.* The *Tea Caddy,* one of the oldest tea shops in Paris, is very British — from its name to its fine teas and scones (14 Rue Julien-le-

Pauvre, 5e; phone: 43-54-15-56). *Tea and Tattered Pages,* a combination tearoom and used-English-books store, is a great place to pick up some reading for a rainy day (24 Rue Mayet, 6e; phone: 40-65-94-35). And the *Hôtel Crillon* is one of the city's most elegant spots in which to take very expensive afternoon tea (around $25) complete with an assortment of sublime pastries.

AND FOR CHOCOHOLICS The best hot chocolate in Paris, if not the universe, is served at *Angelina* (226 Rue de Rivoli, 1er; phone: 42-60-82-00, and 10 Pl. de Mexico, 16e; phone: 47-04-89-42). Make sure to ask for *chocolat l'Africain,* a dessert made with delicious dark chocolate.

Diversions

Exceptional
Experiences for the
Mind and Body

Quintessential Paris

We hear a lot of complaints about Paris these days. Traffic. Pollution. The once harmonious, elegant sweep of Haussmann's boulevards are, say critics, increasingly disregarded, marred by such modern intrusions as La Défense, the futuristic-looking business center that obstructs the skyline to the west, or the Big Mac invasion that is threatening the sanctity of the corner café.

A century ago, the Eiffel Tower had its critics, too, and while it may be necessary to look a little harder these days to find the Paris of Proust and Hemingway, happily it still exists. We still encounter with reassuring regularity the Frenchman and his dog on a morning stroll to the *pâtisserie*. An organ grinder still plays for Sunday crowds in the Place des Vosges. Piaf sing-alongs occur nightly in Montmartre bistros. And just when we begin to despair that this century has erased the best of the old, and wonder what the next will possibly retain, we happen upon the nonpareil Paris bistro, a perfect little red-awninged gem, hidden away on a tiny, sun-dappled square.

Paris is, after all, still Paris, the quintessential City of Light, and life. Yes, it is more crowded than when Gershwin immortalized it in music. Yes, it becomes more expensive with each passing season. But when the lights rise along the Seine or the Bois de Boulogne is filled with the fresh, crisp scent of chestnuts, you really wouldn't want to be anywhere else.

ILE ST-LOUIS Joined by a footbridge to the Ile de la Cité, the place where Paris began, this island floats like a medieval oasis between the Left and Right banks in the middle of the Seine. Once home to the likes of Voltaire, Rousseau, and Baudelaire, the narrow cobblestone lanes that radiate from the island's single lengthwise street (Rue St-Louis-en-l'Ile) are among the most coveted and expensive of Paris real estate. The center street, a narrow one-way lane, is lined with shops and charming restaurants, some with stone walls and vaulted ceilings, as well as a *fromagerie* (cheese shop) or two. Try the *Montecristo*, a superb, yet inexpensive, Italian trattoria, the *Franc Pinot* wine bar, or the outrageous (and loud) *Brasserie de l'Ile St-Louis* for the best views of Notre-Dame across the Pont St-Louis footbridge. No trip here would be complete without generous samplings of the island's own Berthillon ice cream. Served in two company-owned parlors on the island and several other local *glaciers,* Berthillon has become a legend in its own time — handmade, rich mixtures with inspired combinations of ingredients (try the crunchy chocolate nougat — you'll swoon with happiness!). So confident are they of their reputation that Berthillon not only steadfastly refuses to expand off the island, they insist on closing altogether during the prime ice cream–consuming month of August.

LUXEMBOURG GARDENS Every day is Sunday in Hemingway's favorite park, where Parisians stroll with babies in prams, children "race" miniature sailboats in the fountains, and young lovers sit on benches beneath the trees. George Moore may have captured the mood best when he wrote in his *Memories of My Dead Life,* "I loitered in the Luxembourg Gardens to watch the birds and the sunlight . . . and began to wonder if there was anything better in the world worth doing than to sit in an alley of clipped limes smoking, thinking of Paris and myself." Enchanting as is the idea of doing absolutely nothing here, there is in fact plenty to do in this 46-acre garden. Requisitioned in 1615 by Marie de Médici and designed, in part, by Salomon de Brosse, today it's a popular jogging spot; there are six tennis courts (available on a first-come, first-served basis); and for children, there's a puppet theater near the orchards, pony rides, a small carousel, a playground, and toy sailboats for cruising around the Médicis fountain. Honey is still produced by the garden's hives, where a beekeeping course is taught in summer by a priest. Enjoy the serenity. The 20th century hasn't made its mark here — yet.

CAFÉ SOCIETY If you've ever read a novel, or ever thought of writing one, you shouldn't leave Paris without visiting one of its thousands of cafés. Those along the Boulevard St-Germain are as well-known for the inspiration and comfort they have afforded generations of novelists and intellectuals as for the thick *serré* coffees they serve.

Among the city's most celebrated hangouts are the *Café Les Deux Magots,* reputed by some to have the world's best hot chocolate (we give the nod to *Angelina's,* on the Rue de Rivoli, opposite the Tuileries, and at its other location in the Palais de Congrès, near the Porte Maillot métro), and the place where Sartre drank whiskey while de Beauvoir nursed a Coke. Down the street is the revived *Café Le Flore,* an exceptional breakfast stop for brioche and *oeufs brouillés* (scrambled eggs) before wandering through the bookstores and chic clothing boutiques that line the boulevard. Across the street, the old *Brasserie Lipp* has been a popular *choucroute*-and-conversation spot for actors and politicians for over a century. And the neighborhood continues to attract a lively arts and tourist crowd. Be warned, though: The price of "membership" in café society is high (as we went to press, the price of a cup of coffee in some of the best-known cafés was $4), and service can be excruciatingly slow and indifferent. But then, you never know — the same muse who inspired Sartre may be seated at the table next to yours.

FAUCHON AND PLACE DE LA MADELEINE *Fauchon* is one of the good things about Paris that only keeps getting better. Born in 1886 as a simple pushcart, *Fauchon* grew over the years to be so much a bastion of the privileged that one of its stores was bombed by radicals back in 1978. With a complex of shops and eating establishments extending from Nos. 26 to 30 on the Place de la Madeleine (central phone: 47-42-60-11), the legendary food purveyor stocks some 20,000 items, from Cambodian peppers and African mangoes to New England clam chowder. Here, food is art, and the window displays are the stuff of which dreams (and picnics) are made. (At *Christmas,* the glittering still-life tableau slows traffic to a crawl on this corner, drawing nearly as many gawkers as New York City's *Lord & Taylor* department store's holiday windows.) One *Fauchon* shop—No. 26—specializes in the most beautiful fruits and vegetables available anywhere, plus pâtés, terrines, and as many other incomparable culinary items as even the most jaded gourmet's palate could conceive. The sculptured pâtés are so finely detailed that it's almost a shame to eat them; even grapes are displayed as if they were the crown jewels. There also is a trattoria on the first floor (remember that we'd call this the second floor) that offers a variety of pasta dishes, salads, and other light luncheon food that can be eaten at tables or on stools at chic counters.

Another member of the *Fauchon* food trilogy—No. 28—carries breads, pastries, and candies. The third incarnation, the grocery (No. 30), is where all of Paris congregates for a variety of delicious reasons. The main floor is stocked with house brand vinegars, olive oils, teas, and coffees, while the rest of the building is given over to an excellent restaurant and a deliciously decadent stand-up snack and dessert spot (see *Eating Out* in THE CITIES for details on both).

Although discerning shoppers will find several other smaller places in the neighborhood with better prices and more patient service, *Fauchon* is still a good place to get a delicious souvenir of your visit to enjoy back home: a pound of house blend coffee, a tin of aged sardines from Brittany, or a decanter of peaches soaked in armagnac. We particularly admire Fauchon vinegar (try the tarragon) and *tchando* (lotus) tea. *Fauchon* also ships anywhere. All branches are closed Sundays.

In Paris, the tradition of window shopping is called *léche-vitrine,* literally, "window licking." You'll understand why after a walk around the shops fringing the Madeleine. Across from *Fauchon,* you'll find the *épicerie Hédiard,* specialist in exotic fruits; *Maison de la Truffe,* the world's largest truffle retailer; and *Caviar Kaspia,* a retail caviar vendor with a small restaurant upstairs. And Alain Senderens's *Lucas-Carton,* one of Paris's Michelin three-star restaurants, is just a few steps away across from the Madeleine.

PLACE DES VOSGES In the heart of the Marais, Paris's most beautiful and oldest (1605–1612) square remains a most privileged and prestigious address. Among the 39 houses that grace the red-brick quadrangle are the *Maison de Victor-Hugo* (No. 6) and *L'Ambroisie* (No. 9), one of Paris's three-star restaurants. With its vaulted arches and arcades, Place des Vosges was also the model for the Places Dauphine, Vendôme, and later, de la Concorde. This location was the site of *l'Hôtel des Tournelles,* where Henri II was killed in a jousting tournament. In 1612, it became known as Place Royale; in 1800 the square was baptized Vosges in honor of the first French *département* to pay all its taxes to the new French Republic.

Today, the square is a garden spot for area residents and tourists alike. The Marais (the name means "marsh," which it was when the city was founded) is to Paris what Greenwich Village is to New York City, with its sense of history, its jumble of interesting shops, restaurants, and museums, and its historical architecture. Directly behind the Place des Vosges are synagogues designed by Alexandre-Gustave Eiffel and Art Nouveau architect Hector Guimard. The Marais bristles with art galleries and museums: *Musée Carnavalet* (devoted entirely to the history of the city of Paris, the largest municipal museum in the world), *Musée Picasso,* and *Musée de la Chasse et de la Nature.* The area is also home to Paris's largest Jewish population; the colorful Rue des Rosiers is chockablock with restaurants and shops that remind one of a street in central or Eastern Europe.

RUE DE SEINE/RUE DE BUCI MARKET Paris's markets provide some of its great sensory pleasures, and the lively little sixth-*arrondissement* morning market that begins at the eastern end of Rue de Buci and winds around the corner onto Rue de Seine is a typically tantalizing example. From early morning, the scents of freshly baked bread and creamy camembert waft above neatly arranged spears of white asparagus, seas of super-slim green beans, carts filled with nothing but wild mushrooms, and an array of fruits worthy of a still-life by Gauguin. A fishmonger shouts out prices of the day's catch, glistening and fresh *comme l'oeil.* At 81 Rue de Seine is an old-fashioned *charcuterie,* pleasingly cluttered with hams hanging from ceiling beams, prepared dishes, and pâtés — the makings of divine picnics. Next door (also No. 81) is an excellent cheese shop; try their *fromage frais* and goat cheeses. Around the corner on Rue de Buci (No. 8), foie gras terrines of all sizes glitter like jewels in the windows of *J. Papin,* a sleek, modern *traiteur* (caterer). For cakes, homemade candies, and *fruits glacé* (glazed fruit), try *La Vieille France* (No. 14), one of Paris's oldest *pâtisseries* (pastry shops), founded in 1834. Have a light lunch and glass of wine at *Au Chai de l'Abbaye* (No. 26), or gather up an armful of market goodies and head south to the Luxembourg Gardens for a *déjeuner sur l'herbe* — but sit on a bench; the grass is off limits!

BOULEVARD ST-MICHEL In the glitter of streetlamps, and the evening glow from floodlit Notre-Dame, there is a simmering mix of arguing students, drumming youths, and strumming guitars, roasting chestnuts, and sizzling street-corner crêpes along the Boul' Mich (as Parisians call it) — a feast that hasn't moved since Hemingway's day. Latin no longer is the lingua franca of this quarter, but you'll hear plenty of Greek, Arabic, Farsi, and Wolof, and sharing billboard space in front of the multilingual movie theaters are posters for the latest films from India — or from the *Cannes Film Festival.* The bookstalls along the Seine hold anything from a first edition of Proust to a paperback mystery from 1962 — or a single, illuminated page from a medieval manuscript.

RUE DU FAUBOURG-ST-HONORÉ AND RUE ST-HONORÉ Like the *Grand Bazaar* of Istanbul, the souk of Marrakesh, and the agora of ancient Athens, the mile-long stretch of designer sidewalks between the president's palace and the Palais-Royal is one of the world's great shopping experiences. It has the finest names in everything, and an unsurpassed array of specialized retailers of chocolate, leather, and lingerie. Try *Au Nain Bleu* for a miniature tea set in Limoges porcelain, *Hermès* for an equestrian-print umbrella, or *Raymond* for gold-plated faucets. Nearby, on Place de la Madeleine, visit *Fauchon* for plum mustard or a salmon mousse sprinkled with caviar, and if you can't live without something nobody else could have, tour the galleries and antiques dealers, and stop in at that ultimate purveyor of the unique — *Le Louvre des Antiquaires* on the Place du Palais-Royal.

Romantic Hostelries an Hour or Less from Paris

Who doesn't fantasize about a welcoming country inn or a fairy-tale château with a swan-filled moat and acres of gardens and woodlands? These hostelries just outside of Paris exist in a certain harmony with their settings; they seem to be a part of local life rather than something aside from it. They also have a special warmth. And the staff has an ability to make you feel that you count and that they care. Excellent cuisine often is a feature, though not always.

BAS-BRÉAU, Barbizon Fashionable, well-heeled Parisians have been coming to this mid-19th-century inn since shortly after Robert Louis Stevenson lived and wrote here. Located in the village that gave its name to a school of 19th-century painters including Théodore Rousseau, Corot, and Millet, this is a perfect place to idle away a fall weekend, or at least a Sunday afternoon. A member of the prestigious Relais & Châteaux group, it boasts 12 rooms, 8 suites, and a separate villa, all decorated *à l'ancienne* with modern bathrooms. And the dining room, warmed by a flickering fire during fall and winter, serves first-rate food — worth the half-hour drive from Paris even if you don't plan to spend the night. Try the *langouste rôtie* *au sel de Guérande* (rock lobster roasted in salt) or, in the fall, game dishes such as *noisettes de chevreuil* (medallions of venison) or *pâté chaud de grouse* (warm pâté of grouse). Closed 3 weeks in January. Information: *Hôtellerie du Bas-Bréau*, 22 Rue Grande, Barbizon 77630 (phone: 60-66-40-05; fax: 60-69-22-89).

L'ESCLIMONT, St-Symphorien-le Château Set on 150 acres of private woodlands and landscaped French gardens near Chartres, this 16th-century fairy-tale castle has 48 rooms, including 6 romantic circular suites in the turrets. There are tennis courts and a pool; though the restaurant is a bit pricey, the food is good, if not always memorable — but the gardens are worth the visit (Parisians arrive here by helicopter for Sunday lunch, touching down neatly on the expansive lawn). Forty-five minutes from Orly airport. Information: *L'Esclimont*, St-Symphorien-le Château, Auneau 28700 (phone: 37-31-15-15; fax: 37-31-57-91).

FORESTIÈRE/CAZAUDEHORE, St-Germain-en-Laye A superb garden setting just 20 minutes from Paris, it's one of the Ile-de-France's best-kept secrets — an agreeable inn with 6 apartments and 24 rooms, and a refined restaurant featuring classic and Basque cuisine. Restaurant closed Mondays. Information: *Forestière/Cazaudehore*, 1 Av. du Président-Kennedy, St-Germain-en-Laye 78100 (phone: 39-73-36-60 for hotel; 34-51-93-80 for restaurant; fax: 39-73-73-88).

TRIANON PALACE, Versailles Attached by private gardens to Versailles, this renovated palace is one of France's most historic hotels. Its vaulted-ceilinged marble dining room, resembling a great mirrored ballroom, has played host to the likes of Woodrow Wilson, Proust, Colette, and Marlene Dietrich. Romantic legends abound here. Sarah Bernhardt used to arrive in a horse-drawn carriage, wrapped from head to wooden leg in tulle and feathers. And when King Edward VIII abdicated the throne of England for the woman he loved, he and the former Wallis Simpson honeymooned here. Chef Gérard Vié (formerly of *Les Trois Marches*) presides over the kitchens; the beauty salon and spa (described as "a beauty kingdom") are an exclusive Givenchy operation stocked with his signature cosmetics and perfumes; and a hotel conference center, shops, a tennis park, and underground parking are among the amenities. Restaurant closed Sundays, Mondays, and August. Information: *Trianon Palace*, 1 Bd. de la Reine, Versailles 78000 (phone: 30-84-38-00 for hotel; 39-50-13-21 for restaurant; fax: 39-51-66-55).

Shopping Spree

For centuries, France has been producing some of the world's most fashionable clothing, its most delicious food and wine, and its most bewitching perfumes. And all of these items benefit from that same soupçon of Gallic flair and good taste that characterize just about everything else to which the French put their hearts and hands. So it's no wonder that shopping in this country — and especially in its capital — is such a delight.

Below is a list of those special things any shopper worth his or her salt would be hard-pressed to pass up. For information on specific shops, see *Shopping* in THE CITY.

ART GALLERIES Concentrated in St-Germain-des-Près.

CLOTHING The haute couture designers who put Paris on the map as the center of the fashion world still are flourishing in the French capital, and still welcoming those able to afford their distinctive and luxurious made-to-order clothing. However, they often sell much less expensive clothing of very high quality in couturier boutiques, usually at the same address. Haute couture can be found in the streets around the Champs-Elysées: Avenue George-V, Avenue Montaigne, Rue François-Ier, and Rue du Faubourg-St-Honoré.

Boutiques abound here; the attractive and innovative clothing that the French so nicely call *votre bonheur,* "your happiness," is stocked at thousands of small boutiques throughout the city.

Boutiques are especially numerous on Avenue Victor-Hugo, Rue de Passy, Boulevard des Capucines, in the St-Germain-des-Près area, in the neighborhood of the *Opéra,* in the *Forum des Halles* shopping center, around the Place des Victoires, and on or near the Rue des Rosiers in the Marais district. The Rue d'Alésia has several blocks devoted solely to discount fashion shops.

And for those in search of high-fashion bargains, the concept of selling at a discount is gradually catching on in France, and new designs from the top couturiers are available a season (sometimes only a few months) later at many outlets.

It's true that many Americans living in France buy their own lingerie in the US, swearing that American products are not only better made and better fitting but even less expensive and prettier than their French counterparts. But the lacy, frilly, silk undergarments sold in France, often covered with polka dots or dripping with ribbons, are the stuff of which fantasies are made, and lingerie makes a delightful souvenir.

Department stores carry a wide selection of brands, styles, and sizes and display their wares clearly, making choices simpler than in small shops, where much of the stock may be tucked in boxes behind the counter.

Though men's clothing is not generally considered to be a good buy, and many a male has gone into shock after looking at a price tag, for some, the blend of classic styling and French flair is irresistible. And for babies and older children, gorgeous hand-smocked and hand-decorated clothing can still be found in Paris, but at prices that are painfully high. For all but the most indulgent grandparents, the best idea is to head for department stores, which generally display a wide and top selection of charming togs for tots and teens, often decorated with motifs that make them look very French.

CRYSTAL AND CHINA Paris has crystal and china to make the humblest table gleam like a royal banquet hall, and one of the best ways to get an overview of the nation's best is to take a stroll along the length of the Rue de Paradis. The entire street is lined with stores specializing in objects related to what merchants here call "the arts of the table." Near the Gare de l'Est and the Gare du Nord, this area is less than chic. Nevertheless, it yields some sparkling treasures.

FOOD AND WINE At any given point in Paris, it's possible to put together a sumptuous picnic by making exactly four stops: the closest *charcuterie,* or butcher shop, often much like a deli; the *fromagerie,* or cheese store; the *marchand de vin,* or wine merchant; and the *boulangerie,* or bakery. Usually, these shops will be within a block or two of one another, sometimes right next door.

JEWELRY Most of the world's greatest jewelers have outlets in Paris and several are clustered around the elegant Place Vendôme, which is a dazzling place to window shop, if not to pick up an heirloom or two.

KITCHENWARE In a country that reveres cooking among the highest of the arts, it is not surprising to find an abundance of kitchen items at nearly every turn. Pots and pans that are almost sculptural in their classic beauty are everywhere, as are odd-looking gadgets that perform tasks that most cooks never even imagined. Department stores provide an overview of both the most traditional and the latest utensils in the world of French cookery.

LEATHER GOODS It is a pleasure to shop for leather goods in Paris, especially in the best establishments, where every piece of merchandise from key cases to steamer trunks is impeccably designed and perfectly crafted. Bear in mind, however, that lower-quality leather goods are probably more expensive and not as well made as comparable items in the US.

Americans should be aware that some exotic skins that are sold legally in France — including certain species of alligator, crocodile, ostrich, and lizard — could be seized on arrival back home, since these animals are on the endangered-species list in the United States. The best Parisian stores will steer American shoppers to merchandise that meets US import laws, but it's still wise to check the latest regulations with the US Fish and Wildlife Service before leaving home.

PERFUME For centuries, the French have been making enticing scents that are synonymous with luxury and romance, and around the world, in all languages, the adjective that springs most quickly to mind to modify the word "perfume" is "French." Consequently, it's not surprising that perfume heads the shopping lists of visitors to Paris more than any other item.

But today, with virtually all names and sizes of French perfume available in US stores, is there any reason beyond this mystique to buy French perfume in France?

The answer is yes. By shopping in the right places and following the rules for getting tax refunds as described below, it's possible to save significant money — and to pay as much as 40% less than the price of some of France's most expensive and sought-after perfumes. Even without the additional reduction afforded by the tax refund, in fact, the cost of French perfume in a department store is roughly 90% of what you would pay stateside.

Do not be taken in by the flashy Tax Free signs sported by perfume stores all over the country. Most shops, the major department stores included, sell basically the same brands and sizes at rates set by the manufacturers. Regardless of where you shop, the perfume becomes tax-free only after you have purchased enough of it at a single store to qualify for the tax refund set up by the government. The exception is airport duty-free shops, which sell without tax even on small bottles of inexpensive perfumes; the selection is more limited than in Paris stores, however.

SHOES France is a country for shoe fiends, and it is full of places to buy footwear that is not only stylish but also — probably because the French walk a good deal themselves and refuse to clump around in ugly shoes — comfortable.

HOW TO GET A TAX REFUND

The values available to visitors in Paris on certain merchandise become even more compelling when the refund offered by the French government of its special value added tax (VAT) — 18% and up for some "luxury" goods — is added to existing bargains.

To qualify, visitors must be at least 15 years of age, must reside outside the European Community, and must have visited in the country for less than 6 months. No refunds are offered for purchases of food, wine, or tobacco.

To receive a refund, a visitor must spend at least 2,000F (currently about $370) in a single shop, and must show a passport to prove eligibility. The clerk will then give the buyer an export sales document in triplicate, which must be signed and saved, and an envelope addressed to the store. When leaving France, both the forms and the purchased goods must be taken to the French Customs *détaxe* (tax refund) booth. Note that tax formalities must be taken care of *before* checking baggage and *before* going through passport control at an airport or *before* boarding a train at a station.

The same person who signed the refund forms in the store must present the envelope and the three sheets to the customs officials (who will return one, countersigned, to the buyer in case of later difficulties). The traveler will receive a check for the tax refund mailed from the store. Sometimes, if the buyer pays by credit card, the store makes out a credit slip for the amount of the tax and processes the credit after receiving the validated refund forms from French customs.

It is now possible to receive an immediate refund (in local currency) at Charles de Gaulle and Orly airports if you bring the appropriate paperwork with you. And large department stores such as *Galeries Lafayette, La Samaritaine, Bon Marché,* and *Au Printemps* have an arrangement so that visitors can receive a refund from a designated VAT desk right in the store.

MARKETS AND MOVEABLE FEASTS

Going to market is so much a part of Parisian life and culture that it should probably be on every tourist's itinerary. Aside from the rich feast for the eyes — perfectly piled pyramids of oranges, sunbursts of yellow-white endive, and stands of steaming-hot *choucroute* — Paris markets offer enlightening glimpses of the Gallic manner and mentality. Note the brassy produce vendor crooning, "Deal of the century — four avocados for 10 francs," or the rosy-cheeked cheese man serving up a wink with the camembert. There'll be a buxom matron, basket in hand and dog in tow, huffing indignantly at a skinny chicken. Paris's markets are not only the most brilliantly stocked and colorful in the world, they are ubiquitous. No matter where in the city you are, you're only a short stroll from one of them.

Paris's first market appeared during the 5th century on the Ile de la Cité; it was followed by small markets at the old gates of the city, many specializing in a single food item. Today, there are 70 open-air and covered food markets in Paris, plus about 10 market streets, and the central wholesale market — *Les Halles de Rungis,* 13e, successor to *Les Halles,* and now the world's largest wholesale market. Most numerous are the open-air roving markets that set up early in the morning 2 or 3 days a week on sidewalks or islands of major boulevards, only to tear down again at 1:30 PM, when they close for the day.

A few tips to the novice: Take along a string bag or basket, since most merchants don't provide bags. Go in the morning, when the produce is freshest and the scene is the liveliest. The general rule is don't touch the merchandise. Vendors take pride in doing the choosing for you. Most markets and market streets are closed Mondays. Below is a small sampling of markets worth visiting.

MARCHÉ BATIGNOLLES An open-air market existed here, in the 17th *arrondissement* near Place Clichy, for decades before the area was annexed by the city of Paris in 1860. The old covered market built in 1867 came down 9 years ago to make way for the current modern structure. *Batignolles* is noteworthy for its reasonable prices — due, no doubt, to its somewhat out-of-the-way location (a bit west of the Montmartre Cemetery) — and for having more stands (68 in all) than any other covered market. There's a fine selection, including a cluttered stand with Italian specialties, one featuring exotic fruit (*Godreau*), an Alsatian selling *choucroute* and sausages, and a small stand with prepared Oriental items. More food shops line the streets surrounding the market. There's a good charcuterie, *Le Cheneau* (44 Rue des Moines), and *Le Terroir,* an inviting wine shop, a few shops away. From here, follow Rue Lemercier to Rue Brochant, turn left at the bakery (which makes a wonderful rye bread *ficelle*), and walk to the Square des Batignolles, one of the 20 small garden parks built by a protégé of Haussmann named Alphand; a perfect picnic site, it comes complete with duck pond, tiny waterfall and bridge, and stone sculptures.

RUE MONTORGUEIL This busy, cobblestone market street not far west of the *Centre Georges-Pompidou* is all that remains of "the belly of Paris," the old *Les Halles* wholesale food market, which was relocated south of the city to Rungis more than 20 years ago. Some of Paris's chefs still do their marketing here. And even if *Montorgueil* lacks some of the character and intrigue of the erstwhile *Les Halles,* there's still a lot of value to be found here. Most worth a visit is the spruced-up *Pâtisserie Stohrer* (No. 51), allegedly Paris's oldest pastry shop, founded in 1730. The decor is magnificent, particularly the ethereal murals painted on glass in 1865 by Paul Baudry, an artist responsible for decorating parts of the Paris *Opéra.* The pastries and prepared foods — including pâtés and individual quiches — of present owner François Duthu are admirable. There are plenty of fruit and vegetable sellers nearby, and farther on is *Ballotin,* a tiny, pristine chocolate shop. Near the start of the street (toward *Le Forum des Halles*) there's an Oriental fruit stand where litchi, cherimoya, and other exotics can be found. You can picnic at the park at the end of the street, where a maze of green trellises and stone animals occupy ground on which the old wholesale market once stood. If the landscape is not to your liking, the surrounding view should be: With the magnificent 16th-century Eglise St-Eustache on one side and the futuristic shapes and mirrored surfaces of *Le Forum des Halles* on the other, this is one of the most arresting views of old and new Paris.

RUE MOUFFETARD Most popular of all Paris market streets, *Mouffetard* is criticized by locals for its high prices, dubious quality, and circus atmosphere. But this steep, winding street — about halfway between the Jardin du Luxembourg and the Jardin des Plantes, and invaded in recent decades by ethnic restaurants and tacky clothing shops — retains an old-time flavor and appeal, as well as some very good purveyors. Best known here is *Fachetti* (No. 134), the Italian charcuterie at the bottom of the street, with its appetizing array of hams, pasta, and prepared foods. Farther up the hill, on a small side street, is the African market where fascinating exotic fruits and vegetables, dried fish, and other curiosities can be found. Off another side street are two shops specializing in hams and sausages of the Auvergne region. There's also a fancy food shop, *l'Epicerie* (46 Rue Daubenton), selling a good foie gras for considerably less than you'll pay in the shops at La Madeleine. Back on Rue Mouffetard, there's a small *charcuterie* worth a visit (No. 120), and there's no lack of good bread and cheese along the street. A cheese shop at the top of the street, *l'Assiette aux Fromages* (No. 27), has a small garden café in the back where cheese and other items are served. From Place de la Contrescarpe at the top of Rue Mouffetard, follow Rue Lacépède east to the Jardin des Plantes (see *Walk 1: Gardens, Bridges, and Islands*, DIRECTIONS).

GRENELLE From the merchant's point of view, this open-air roving market is the best in Paris, due in part to its affluent clientele and its sheltered location under the elevated métro in the center of Boulevard de Grenelle. Before strolling through this market, stop in the *Poilâne* bakery (at the corner of Grenelle and Rue Clodion) to sample this bread maker's famous sourdough loaf. Once in the market, you'll find 141 generously stocked stands, among them a stall with huge rustic baskets of loose farm eggs, and one with tables filled with nothing but mushrooms, wild and cultivated. Another offers eight varieties of oysters. Plenty of fresh fruit and cheese is sold here; there also are a handful of stalls with pâtés and other prepared picnic-worthy fare. The market extends to La Motte–Picquet métro stop, only a 3-block walk from the Champ-de-Mars park in the shadow of the Tour Eiffel. If your menu lacks a sweet or pastry (items frequently not found at the roving markets), stop at *La Petite Marquise* (50 Av. de La Motte–Picquet) for one of its butter-rich cakes. They're expensive, but worth it.

The best and most enjoyable market here is probably the one set up on Wednesday and Saturday mornings on the Avenue du Président-Wilson between Place d'Iéna and Place de l'Alma, both of which have métro stops. Butchers, bakers, and cheese and flower sellers abound here, along with all types of fresh fish, lettuce and herbs just pulled from the ground and trucked in from farms outside the city, and wonderful fruits and other vegetables. Other good roving markets appear in the Place Monge on Wednesdays, Fridays, and Sundays; on the Boulevard Raspail on Tuesdays and Fridays; and on the Boulevard Edgar-Quinet on Wednesdays and Saturdays. Every neighborhood has one, and everyone has his or her favorite.

An Odyssey of the Old: Antiques Hunting in Paris

The history of France may best be seen in fortresses and châteaux and the Bastille, but it is best felt by holding a fragment of a sculptured choir stall or an Art Deco soup ladle, by touching the satiny surface of a marquetry wedding chest or by slipping on the signet ring that once belonged to a scheming marquise. Such morsels of the nation's past can be savored at some 100-plus Parisian antiques shops and auction houses or at fairs and markets held throughout the city.

SOURCES FOR ANTIQUES IN PARIS

SHOPS In every neighborhood of Paris you'll stumble across small, often slightly dusty shops where the best of the old is the offering. Some are true *antiquaires,* antiques dealers who handle pieces of established value and pedigrees. Others are *brocanteurs,* secondhand dealers, whose stock may run the gamut from Second Empire snuffboxes to broken 78-rpm Edith Piaf records. Many dealers belong to either the *Syndicat National des Antiquaires* (National Antiques Dealers' Association) or the *Syndicat National du Commerce de l'Antiquité* (National Association of Antiques Businesses), two highly reputable guilds whose members have pledged to tell the truth about all items they are selling.

For an important purchase, the wise buyer will request a certificate of authenticity. With furniture, in particular, the dealer should be precise about just which parts have been restored and how; a number of "antiques" are really superbly carpentered composites of partly salvaged pieces, and there is a thriving industry in the recycling of genuinely ancient wood into pieces of "antique" furniture that were actually born yesterday.

A trend of the past decade has been the clustering of individual shops into *villages d'antiquaires,* which are something like shopping centers for antiques, with dozens of dealers housed under a single roof. The prototype is the giant *Louvre des Antiquaires* (2 Pl. du Palais-Royal, 1er; phone: 42-97-27-00; open daily except Mondays, and Sundays in the summer), whose 250 different shops are in an old Paris department store. Others in Paris include *La Cour aux Antiquaires* (54 Rue du Faubourg-St-Honoré, 8e; phone: 42-66-38-60; open daily except Sundays and Monday mornings), *Village Suisse* (78 Av. Suffren, 15e; phone: 43-06-69-90; open Thursdays through Mondays), *Village St-Honoré* (91 Rue St-Honoré, 1er), and *Village St-Paul* (entrance on Rue St-Paul just off the Quai des Célestins, 4e; phone: 48-87-91-02). *Le Carré Rive Gauche,* an association of more than 100 antiques shops, is located in the square of streets formed by Quai Voltaire, Rue de l'Université, Rue des Sts-Pères, and Rue du Bac, 7e.

Other good hunting grounds include Boulevard St-Germain, Rue Bonaparte, and Rue Jacob on the Left Bank; and Rue du Faubourg-St-Antoine, Rue St-Honoré, Rue du Faubourg-St-Honoré, Avenue Victor-Hugo, Rue La Boëtie, and Rue de Miromesnil on the Right Bank.

The richness and tradition of the French antiques trade have spawned a high degree of specialization, both by genre and by period. Some shops deal exclusively in dolls, maritime instruments, chimneys and mantel-pieces, locks and keys, or postcards. Several antiquarians in Paris stock only items from the 1950s. Passionate collectors with a one-track mind should consult the *Guide Emer* (50 Rue/Quai de l'Hôtel-de-Ville, Paris 75004; phone: 42-77-83-44) for information about where in the whole of France to indulge their most exotic whims.

EXPOSITIONS, FAIRS, AND SALONS Paris's most prestigious antiques salon, the *Biennale International des Antiquaires,* is held astride September and early October in even-numbered years in the *Grand Palais.* With its stock of the finest pieces available in Europe and a range of exhibitors that includes all the top dealers from France and abroad, the *Biennale* may set the tone of the market for the following 2 years.

The *Foire Nationale à la Brocante et aux Jambons* is a curious event that takes place in March and September every year and mixes antiques, handi-crafts, and regional foods from all over France; fairgoers do lots of wine tasting, cheese nibbling, and bric-a-brac browsing. This party is held at Ile-de-Chateau, and is organized by *SNCAO,* 18 Rue de Provence, Paris 75009 (phone: 47-70-88-78).

In Ivry-sur-Seine, the *Foire Internationale Brocante Antiquitè* (*FIBA*) attracts over 1,000 exhibitors every March, June, and September. Orga-nized by *SODAF,* 2 Placette Fauconnières, Ivry-sur-Seine 94200 (phone: 46-71-66-14).

Less impressive, but nonetheless worth a visit if you happen to be here in late November or early December, is the *Salon des Antiquaires,* held in various locations annually (phone: 45-85-01-85).

FLEA MARKETS Paris's best-known and largest of its *marchés aux puces* — liter-ally, "markets with fleas" — is the *Marché aux Puces de St-Ouen* (better known as *Puces de Clignancourt*), located at the Porte de Clignancourt, 18e. This incredible collection of some 3,000 stalls is actually a maze of different submarkets, including *Biron, Paul Bert, Vernaison,* and *Serpette,* all sprawled over a vast area and encompassing everything from rather elegant little shops to ramshackle lean-tos and rickety tables or blankets spread on the curbstone. It's easy to get lost here, so stay close to your companions or give each other a precise time and place at which to rendezvous. There are several cafés and even a little restaurant (*Chez Louisette,* in *Marché Vernaison*) where a Piaf sing-alike croons on Sunday afternoons. The Paris tourist office sells an official guide to this market (*Guide Officiel & Practique des Puces*) for 50 francs, and a map is sold at the market. The market is open Saturdays, Sundays, and Mondays from 9 or 10 AM (some stands open as early as 8 AM) to around sundown (in summer, this can be as late as 8 PM).

Lesser known and lower brow are *Les Puces de Montreuil* (literally "the fleas of Montreuil"), held on Saturdays, Sundays, and Mondays at the Porte de Montreuil, 11e; and *Les Puces de Vanves,* held on Saturdays and

Sundays at the Porte de Vanves, 14e. Both run from early morning to sunset, or later. Both also consist mostly of *brocanteurs,* people dealing in secondhand items. *Vanves* sprawls along the sidewalk and around a corner for several blocks; you have to venture well along the street before you begin to see items that are more than other people's old junk. Some of the items offered here turn up later in the *Puces de St-Ouen* with higher price tags attached. But there are some treasures to be found here, including a lot of Art Deco items and old French linen. The *Montreuil* is even more lowbrow than *Vanves,* crowded with peddlers selling everything from an old espresso machine and African beads (in the same stall) to spare automobile parts. Though there are not many great antiques to be found here, the occasional bargain does turn up, especially in used clothing and furniture. Those in the market for a 19th-century armoire will find a good selection here, and many pieces can be dismantled for shipment.

AUCTIONS Once something of a professional club for dealers only, auctions — known in French as *ventes aux enchères* — have become the favorite indoor sport of the *haute bourgeoisie* in the last few years, and in the *salles des ventes* (salerooms) of France, there are fewer bargains around than there used to be. However, those who know their market may still save as much as a third of the retail price; and even for those who don't, auctions are hard to beat for pure theater.

But the auction situation in France is a bit different than those in the US, Great Britain, and Ireland, for all sales take place under the aegis of a government-authorized auctioneer known as the *commissaire-priseur.* And Paris's venerable auction house, *Hôtel Drouot,* is basically a cooperative managed by a guild of *commissaires-priseurs,* and it is they who are known for their probity and expertise, rather than salerooms or specific companies. By law, French auctioneers are responsible for the authenticity of any item they sell for 30 years after the sale.

The *Hôtel des Ventes Drouot-Richelieu,* on the Right Bank not far from Boulevard Montmartre, is the center of the auction world in Paris. Some 600,000 lots go through its 16 salerooms every year, and the activity is frantic. If you find yourself in a room full of plumbers' fittings or vintage cognacs when what you really wanted was antiques, just go up to the next floor. Information: *Hôtel des Ventes Drouot-Richelieu,* 9 Rue Drouot, Paris 75009 (phone: 48-00-20-20; fax: 48-00-20-33). Sales also are held at the *Drouot-Montaigne,* 15 Av. Montaigne, Paris 75008 (phone: 48-00-20-80 or 48-00-20-20).

The weekly *Gazette de l'Hôtel Drouot* (on sale on newsstands everywhere) prints a calendar of auction sales all over France, as well as a running tally of the results (10 Rue du Faubourg-Montmartre, Paris 75009; phone: 47-70-93-00).

A recent bidding-free variation on the auction theme is the *dépot-vente,* a saleroom where private sellers leave lots on consignment with a dealer who sets the price and takes a 15% commission. These generally are well patronized by bargain-hunting professionals. The largest is the immense *Dépôt-Vente de Paris,* 81 Rue de Lagny, Paris, 20e (phone: 43-72-13-91).

Casinos Royale

Forbidden by Napoleonic decree within 100 kilometers (about 60 miles) of Paris, there are only two "legitimate" gaming houses within easy reach of the city. These establishments draw a crowd that is a heady mixture of Parisian chic and Arab sheik. The scenario is pure Hollywood. In fact, behind all the glitter is a system of tight surveillance by the Brigade des Jeux, France's special branch of gaming police, and a gambling code that regulates everything from the odds on the slot machines to the dinner jacket on the croupier — which has (by law) no pockets. The result is an almost totally aboveboard industry, though internecine squabbles among operators have occasionally evoked memories of Chicago in the 1920s. Players are nonetheless fairly certain to lose their money according to the inexorable laws of mathematics.

Passports are required for admission, which is limited to those 18 and older. Though marathon games of chemin de fer are allowed to continue until the players drop, most French casinos open in mid-afternoon and close at 3 or 4 AM, day in and day out. Dress has become far more casual in recent years, but there still are many casinos where jacket and tie are de rigueur for gentlemen; in any case, it's always better to err on the side of decorum. A number of the larger casinos have glamorous, first-rate restaurants right on the gaming room floor; their waiters discreetly reheat the food of those kept away from their meal by a winning streak.

The staples of the French casino diet are roulette, baccarat, and *boule;* craps and blackjack increasingly are in evidence, the result of creeping Americanization. If you're not familiar with the rules or the vocabulary, many casinos will provide an explanatory booklet. And still others have roving *chefs de partie* (game chiefs), who will be more than happy to help a player who doesn't mind looking like a greenhorn in the midst of all that savoir faire.

ENGHIEN-LES-BAINS Though inside Napoleon's 100-km zone, this lakeside establishment — part of Lucien Barrière's glittering gaming empire — does have roulette as well as all the other requisites of a world class casino. A recent face-lift has restored its Art Deco elegance. Gaming begins daily at 3 PM and continues well into the night. A rather steep entry fee and hefty minimum betting requirements discourage dilettantes; the gambling here is serious and the crowd is relatively chic. The small café in the gaming room offers light meals and afternoon tea. Arrive from Paris by taxi (a 20-minute to 1-hour ride north, depending on traffic) and the management will exchange your cab receipt for its equivalent in chips. (The casino also is easily reached from the Gare du Nord.) If you hit it big, invite the house to sup with you at the neighboring *Duc d'Enghien,* one of the best restaurants in the area surrounding Paris. There are three meeting and conference rooms (for 35 to 600 guests) and a theater seating 700. A chip's throw away is the *Grand* hotel and the Thermal Bath, somewhat dated monuments to the turn-of-the-century elegance of this resort. Information: *Casino d'Enghien,* 3 Av. de Ceinture, Enghien-les-Bains 95880 (phone: 34-12-90-00; fax: 34-12-41-70).

FORGES-LES-EAUX, Seine-Maritime Just outside Napoleon's roulette-free zone, Forges attracts all the capital's players who don't want to risk the wheels at the city's various *clandés,* as its clandestine gaming dives are called. Those who can't face the predawn drive back to Paris can stay at the *Continental* hotel, right in the casino complex — and those who lose enough in the course of the evening are guests of the management. Information: *Casino de Forges,* Av. des Sources, Forges-les-Eaux 76440 (phone: 35-09-80-12).

Learning the Culinary Arts: Cooking Schools

In Paris, visitors can study cooking with famous chefs such as Gaston Lenôtre. They can gain hands-on experience at the most classic of all cooking schools — Paris's Le Cordon Bleu. Travelers who want to look behind the scenes at restaurant kitchens or to visit the wholesale markets where the chefs themselves shop can go on tour with Robert Noah (see below). Some schools — such as Paris's ritziest offering — L'Ecole de Gastronomie Française Ritz-Escoffier — will tailor special courses for groups. And for those who have only an afternoon or two to devote to the pursuit of better cooking skills, afternoon demonstrations are offered by some schools, particularly the Ritz and Cordon Bleu. The course is limited only by one's vision and by one's command of French, a knowledge of which goes a long way toward making the experience meaningful, even though translators are usually available. Programs tend to be casual and are geared to novices and experts alike. The point is to go with an open mind and a willing spirit, ready to acquire a few additional culinary skills and authentic French experiences — and have a good time besides.

CFT FERRANDI The only Paris cooking school (Centre de Formation Technique or CFT) to offer professionally motivated foreigners preparatory courses for a CAP, the French government's culinary certification. Though its basic course runs for 9 months (5 days a week) and is recommended only for the most serious students, shorter programs also are offered. They include twice-annual week-long pastry and cuisine courses. Though it is a private school (owned by the Paris Chamber of Commerce), *Ferrandi* courses have been endorsed by such famous French chefs as Joël Robuchon and Pierre Troisgros. Information: *CFT Ferrandi,* 11 Rue Jean Ferrandi, Paris 75006 (phone: 49-54-29-03).

LE CORDON BLEU This famous school has been instructing an international group of students in French cooking and pastry making since 1895. During the summer, special 5-week courses are offered in cooking and pastry, while 11-week sessions that give credits toward certificates and diplomas are available during the year. Visitors may reserve a few days ahead for single afternoon demonstrations, with menus available about 30 days in advance for each month's program. There also are intensive 4- or 5-day sessions during holiday periods — *Christmas, Easter,* and throughout the summer. Both the demonstration and intensive courses often are translated into English; there are even classes for children 10 years and older. Students are responsible for their own lodging. Information: *Le Cordon Bleu,* 8 *bis* Rue Léon-Delhomme, Paris 75015 (phone: 48-56-06-06; in the US, 800-457-2433 or 212-308-4067; fax: 48-56-03-96).

ECOLE DE GASTRONOMIE FRANÇAISE RITZ-ESCOFFIER Escoffier was to food what Daimler was to automobiles. Today, the *Ritz* hotel, where the legendary chef Escoffier made his debut in the last century, houses the ultimate cooking school. Courses last 1 to 6 weeks and involve 25 hours of instruction weekly. There also is a course in *pâtisserie* — the art of cake, ice cream, chocolate, and candy making — and a 12-week program for professionals. Instruction is in French and English. Information: *Ecole de Gastronomie Française Ritz-Escoffier,* 38 Rue Cambon, Paris 75001 (phone: 42-60-38-30; fax: 40-15-07-65).

ECOLE LENÔTRE Working in groups of up to a dozen under France's best-known and most respected pastry chef, Gaston Lenôtre, professionals and serious amateurs study French pastry, chocolate, bread, ice cream, *charcuterie,* and catering in the huge, modern, spotless Lenôtre laboratory in the suburb of Plaisir, about 17 miles (28 km) outside Paris. Courses, which are conducted in French, generally last 5 days and include breakfast and lunch (though students are responsible for their own lodging and transportation). Reserve at least 6 weeks in advance. Information: *Ecole Lenôtre,* 40 Rue Pierre-Curie, Plaisir 78370 (phone: 30-81-46-46; fax: 30-54-73-70).

PARIS EN CUISINE Travelers who want to visit the wholesale market in the outskirts at Rungis, tour the kitchens of such well-known Paris restaurants as *Taillevent* or *Chiberta,* attend cooking classes with top chefs like Michel and Pierre Troisgros or Michel Guérard, or get an inside view of a chocolate shop, a *charcuterie,* a *boulangerie,* or a *pâtisserie* can arrange individual or group visits led by Robert Noah, an American based in Paris with distinguished contacts in the French food world. The tours are excellent for those who do not speak French, for Noah is a careful translator and groups are small (usually about ten students, depending on the program). Reserve several months in advance. Students are responsible for their own lodging. Information: *Paris en Cuisine,* 49 Rue de Richelieu, Paris 75001 (phone: 42-61-35-23; fax: 42-60-39-96). Noah also publishes a lively, informative newsletter about food and wine in France. Information: *Paris en Cuisine,* PO Box 50099, St. Louis, MO 63105.

PRINCESS ERE 2001 A well-appointed apartment in Paris and a château in Normandy are the sites for 1- to 6-week classes for groups of six students offered by the outgoing, enthusiastic Princess Marie-Blanche de Broglie. In the capital, these include demonstration courses that deal with cooking professionally, the harmony of wines and foods, pastry, the art of entertaining, and French regional cooking. Courses may be arranged in English, French, and Spanish, with translations supplied as necessary. Paris programs run year-round, except August; students are responsible for their own lodging. Reserve at least 1 month in advance. Information: *Marie-Blanche de Broglie, Princess Ere 2001,* 18 Av. de La Motte-Picquet, Paris 75007 (phone: 45-51-36-34; fax: 43-47-38-68).

Celebrated Cathedrals and Châteaux Within an Hour of Paris

For half a millennium, the Gothic cathedral and the Renaissance château reigned as the most sublime reflections of the French spirit. As their massive stone shadows colored the lives of entire towns and surrounding countrysides, these structures were the peaceful statements of the power, both religious and secular, that was France.

The Gothic mode took shape during the middle of the 12th century and then spread throughout Western Europe. With its vaults and spires straining heavenward and its pointed arch, which the sculptor Rodin called "a pair of hands in prayer," the cathedral was a celebration of both God and engineering. Searching for ever greater elevation and ever more light, its architects replaced the massive walls of earlier styles with airy windows and raised the vaulting higher and higher like stakes in some Olympian poker game. The result was a whole new system of stress and support, characterized most obviously by the famous *arc boutant,* flying buttress.

The onset of the Hundred Years War in 1337 put an end to the golden age of Gothic cathedral building. But the end of the conflict in the middle of the 15th century marked the beginning of the château building years, when new generations of royalty subjected Paris and its surrounding countryside to an orgy of regal real estate development. And as decoration replaced defense as a prime architectural motivation, the once stolid and brooding medieval fortress gave way to the fanciful wonder that became the Renaissance château.

The Cathédrale de Notre-Dame, Sacré-Coeur, and the Conciergerie are described in detail in *Special Places* in THE CITY. Here are some of our favorites within a short drive of Paris.

BASILIQUE DE ST-DENIS Located north of Paris (off the A1 highway, less than 2 miles/3 km north of Porte de la Chapelle), this is one of the great, albeit one of the least visited, of the city's ecclesiastical monuments.

Considered the cradle of French Gothic style, the basilica is noteworthy not only as an architectural milestone, but also for its magnificent tombs. Among those who were buried here are Clovis, the first King of the Franks; Dagobert; Charles Martell; and Pepin the Short. Elaborate Renaissance structures, many of them created by the sculptor Germain Pilon, represent Catherine de Médici and Henri II, Louis XII and Anne de Bretagne, and most moving of all, Louis XVI and Marie-Antoinette. Most of the tombs now are empty — the royal remains were exhumed during the Revolution and heaped into a nearby communal grave. Regular guided tours of the transept are available (there is a charge). Visitors may also rent headphones with commentary in one of several languages. Information: *St-Denis Tourist Office,* 2 Rue de Strasbourg, Paris 93200 (phone: 48-09-83-54).

CHÂTEAU DE FONTAINEBLEAU, Fontainebleau, Seine-et-Marne Set in the midst of a verdant forest 39 miles (63 km) south of Paris, Fontainebleau was built, expanded, redecorated, or otherwise touched by all the greats of French royalty. François I transformed it from a hunting lodge to a palace, Henri IV created its lakes and carp-filled pond, Louis XIII was born here, Louis XV was married here. And Napoleon turned Louis XIV's bedroom into his own throne room, signed his abdication here, and bade farewell to his Old Guard from the great Horseshoe Staircase. The most beautiful sections of the interior are the Gallery of François I and the Ballroom — but Josephine's bedroom and Marie-Antoinette's boudoir are worth a look as well. Open daily except Tuesdays from 9:30 AM to 12:30 PM and from 2 to 5 PM. Information: *Syndicat d'Initiative,* 31 Pl. Napoléon-Bonaparte, Fontainebleau 77300 (phone: 64-22-25-68), or the *Château* (phone: 64-22-27-40).

DOMAINE DE VAUX-LE-VICOMTE, Melun, Seine-et-Marne On the evening of August 17, 1661, Louis XIV's superintendent of finance, Nicolas Fouquet, proudly welcomed his 23-year-old king to see the new castle on whose construction he had just spent his entire personal fortune. Serenades especially composed by the renowned Lully, a new stage production by Molière, a fabulous five-course banquet, and a fireworks display all heralded the occasion. Three weeks later, the jealous and fearful Louis XIV had Fouquet clapped into jail for life on trumped-up charges and hired his former superintendent's architect, painter, and landscaper to whip him up a pied-à-terre called Versailles. Vaux-le-Vicomte, Fouquet's castle, is today the largest private property in France; its magical, stylized gardens alone cover more than 125 acres. And it is full of lovely fountains, placid pools, sculptured lawns, and fields of flowers that look like giant illuminated medieval manuscripts. The Vaux-aux-Chandelles (Vaux-by-Candlelight) tours show off all of the château's splendors at their most dramatic. The tours take place on Saturdays at 9:30 PM from June through September. Information: *Service Touristique,* Domaine de Vaux-le-Vicomte, Maincy 77950 (phone: 60-66-97-09).

CHÂTEAU DE VERSAILLES, Versailles, Yvelines Many consider Versailles the most magnificent of all the French châteaux, and it's just 13 miles (21 km) southwest of Paris. In 1682 Louis XIV, called the Sun King because of the splendor of his court, took a small château used by Louis III, enlarged it, and really outdid himself. The vast, intricate, formal gardens, designed by the great Lenôtre, cover 250 acres and include 600 fountains, for which a river had to be diverted. Besides a nucleus of a thousand nobles, Louis XIV's retinue consisted of some 9,000 men-at-arms and an equal number of servants; at any given moment, between 5,000 and 6,000 people were living here, which only begins to suggest the scale of this royal commune. Seeing it all in one visit is about as relaxing as running the *Boston Marathon*, but, before you drop, be sure to squeeze in the cream-and-gold Chapel where the kings said mass, the State Apartments, the fabled Hall of Mirrors, and the Royal Suites. On the grand green grounds is the Grand Trianon, a smaller palace often visited by Louis XIV, and the Petit Trianon, a favorite of Marie-Antoinette, who also liked Le Hameau (the hamlet), a model farm where she and her companions played at being peasants. More than 20 additional rooms — the apartments of the dauphin and the dauphine — are open to visitors Thursdays through Saturdays. Between May and September, on specified afternoons, the 600 jets of water in the 50-odd fountains and pools in the park outside the palace are all turned on; it's a spectacular sight. Versailles is accessible by public transportation from downtown Paris. Open daily except Mondays from 9 AM to 5 PM; guided tours in English are available from 10 AM to 3:30 PM. Admission charge. Information: *Office du Tourisme,* 7 Rue des Réservoirs, Versailles 78000 (phone: 30-84-74-00).

Euro Disneyland:
An American in Paris

Just 20 miles (32 km) east of Paris (35 minutes from Paris by train; an hour by car) — yet light years away from some of the magnificent châteaux described above—this French version of the altogether all-American attraction is worth a detour for some. (Mickey and friends have thoughtfully provided several first-rate hotels for those who can't tear themselves away from the Magic Kingdom.) To aficionados of the Disney properties in the US — *Walt Disney World* and *Disneyland* — this is a place to touch base with all of your favorite characters, — and perhaps to wish upon an *étoile* before returning to Paris.

In spite of considerable controversy, more than 10 million visitors passed through the $4.5 billion European home-away-from-home of Mickey, Minnie, Donald, et al., in its first year alone. Familiar Disney attractions include Main Street USA, Frontierland, Adventureland, Fantasyland, and Discoveryland (known as Tomorrowland in the US parks), although there are some French additions, such as a fire-breathing dragon at Sleeping Beauty's castle and a theater that features both videos and live entertainment (it turns into a disco at night). Disney-philes can enjoy such facilities as six theme hotels, plus a campground, restaurants, shops, an 18-hole golf course, and *Festival Disney*, an entertainment center and the site of the terrific *Buffalo Bill Wild West Show*. The site can be reached by a 35-minute *RER* (regional express train) ride from Paris — passengers disembark at *Euro Disneyland*'s entrance. There also is a shuttle service from Charles de Gaulle and Orly airports (the park site is in between the two) to carry visitors to the park's hotels, and the *TGV* (*train à grande vitesse*) is expected to serve the park from Paris next year.

Note: This *Disney* park and its hotels are much pricier than their US counterparts. It's open year-round. For hotel reservations information (in English), call 49-41-49-10 or send a fax to 49-30-71-00. You can make reservations in the US by calling 407-354-1846. All hotels have specially adapted rooms for the handicapped, as well as rooms for nonsmokers. All rooms accommodate up to four people, and the log cabins at Camp Davy Crockett can bed down six. At *Euro Disneyland*, expect to pay from $150 to as much as $350 per night for a double room.

Great Golf Nearby

Food, wine, castles, and cathedrals are what first come to mind when thinking about France — not golf. But golf has been a tradition in Gaul since 1856, when the first course was laid out in Pau (in the Pyrénées). Since that time, the game has grown enormously in popularity. At the end of last year, there were 470 courses around the country. In fact, except for England and Scotland, France has more courses than any other country in Europe (and by next year, there will be *more* here than in Scotland!).

Not only is the countryside around Paris enticing for an afternoon excursion, but also for a round of golf. The four courses listed below are open to visitors.

EURO DISNEYLAND This 18-hole competition-level course in Marne-la-Vallée, just 20 miles (32 km) east of Paris, is part of its "megaresort" project (which, when complete, will be nearly one-fifth the size of Paris). The Ron Fream design is laid out around a lush landscape including manmade lakes with stepped tees and characteristic mouse-ear–shape sand bunkers. Greens fees are $40. Information: *Euro Disneyland,* Marne-la-Vallée 77777 (phone: 44-57-04-43).

GOLF CLUB DE CHANTILLY Known for food and lace, Chantilly is also famous for the Château de Chantilly, the home of French kings, and this elegant club, only 5 minutes from the historic castle. With its Old World charm and aristocratic ambience, its two British-designed, 18-hole courses (both 6,820 yards) wind through an impressive forest just 25 miles (40 km) north of Paris. Non-members may play for a fee on Mondays, Tuesdays, and Wednesdays. Closed Thursdays. Greens fees are $70. Information: *Golf Club de Chantilly,* Vineuil–St-Firmin, Chantilly 60500 (phone: 44-57-04-43).

GOLF NATIONAL Owned and operated by the *Fédération Française de Golf,* this huge public golf complex is in St-Quentin-en-Yvelines, southwest of Paris. The first of its three courses, the 18-hole, 7,400-yard *Albatros* (designed by Hubert Chesneau and Bob Von Hagge), opened in 1990. This stadium course is host to the *French Open.* Water hazards abound. Greens fees range from $35 to $55. Information: *Golf National,* 2 Av. du Golf, Guyancourt 78280 (phone: 30-43-36-00).

GOLF DES YVELINES Set in a protected park, this 18-holer is a par-72 forest course, 28 miles (45 km) southwest of Paris. Its clubhouse is in a château. Greens fees are $35 during the week, $50 on weekends. Information: *Golf des Yvelines,* La Queue-en-Yvelines 78940 (phone: 34-86-48-89).

Game, Set, and Match:
Tennis Around Paris

Like the United States, France has seen an enormous increase in the interest in tennis over the past 20 years — as a sport for spectators and participants alike. The prime surface of choice is red clay, although there are a fair number of all-weather and hard courts in the countryside around Paris. Though it can be hard to get court time in the city itself, conditions are far less crowded outside the capital. For more information on tennis courts in Paris, see *Tennis* in THE CITY.

The many tennis clubs in France — of which the most famous by far is Paris's *Racing Club,* unquestionably one of the greats among the world's athletic clubs — are organized by *département* or league. Most require annual membership, and virtually all are closed to outsiders who aren't personally acquainted with a member. However, some are less exclusive than others, and occasionally it's possible for business associates to provide an entrée. The clubs listed below are located close to the capital.

AUBERVILLIERS, Seine-St-Denis Open year-round (except August), the *Tennis Forest Hill* offers lessons for an hour and a half each day in blocks of 4 days on 18 indoor courts. Information: *Tennis Forest Hill,* 111 Av. Victor-Hugo, Aubervilliers 93300 (phone: 48-34-75-10).

BOIS-LE-ROI, Seine-et-Marne With 9 hard courts outdoors and 2 indoors, the *UCPA* offers a 7-hour weekend instruction program year-round. Information: *UCPA,* Rue de Tournezy, Bois-le-Roi 77590 (phone: 64-87-83-00; to reserve a court, 64-87-83-07).

BOULOGNE, Hauts-de-Seine At the *Tennis Club de Longchamp,* down the road from *Roland Garros Stadium,* in the Bois de Boulogne on the outskirts of Paris, it is possible to enroll for weekly instruction sessions on the 3 hard courts. There is a golf course nearby. Information: *Tennis Club de Longchamp,* 19 Bd. Anatole-France, Boulogne 92100 (phone: 46-03-84-49).

NANTERRE, Hauts-de-Seine Weekend lessons are possible here year-round at the *Tennis Club Forest Hill La Défense.* Various periods of instruction and weekend lessons are available on the 10 hard courts. Information: *Tennis Club Forest Hill La Défense,* 9 Av. Liberté, Nanterre 92000 (phone: 47-24-67-67).

VILLEPINTE, Seine-St-Denis The *Villepinte Tennis Club* has 7 clay and 6 hard courts, with possibilities for indoor and outdoor play year-round. Weekend and extended courses are offered. Information: *Tennis de Villepinte,* Rue du Manège, Villepinte 93420 (phone: 43-83-23-31).

TOURNAMENT TENNIS The "French Open" or *Championnats Internationaux de France,* locally known as the *"Roland Garros"* after its home stadium, takes place during the last week of May and the first week in June in Paris. It is the world's premier red-clay-court tournament and one of the four *Grand Slam* events (the other three being *Wimbledon,* the *US Open,* and the *Australian Open*), attracting most of the top international men and women players. Tickets for the early matches generally are easy to obtain at the box office or by mail through the *Fédération Française de Tennis Billetterie* (Service Reservation, BP 33316, Paris 75767; phone: 47-43-48-00); tickets for the finals are reserved a year ahead.

River Cruising: Sailing Up the Seine

The Seine cuts through the heart of the French capital, dividing the right and left banks and harboring the two islands where the city began. Among our favorite ways to pass a soft summer afternoon or evening is cruising on one of its many glass-domed tourist boats or canal cruisers.

Everyone knows about the *bateaux-mouches* that parade from morning to evening along the Seine between the Pont de l'Alma and the Pont de Sully at the eastern end of Ile St-Louis; they look horribly touristy from afar, but once you're on board you'll gain an entirely new perspective of Paris. Less well known, but perhaps even more charming, are the morning and afternoon cruises along the Canal St-Martin, between the métro stops at Jean-Jaurès and Bastille, and the full-day excursions on the Canal de l'Ourcq, which take in some lovely green areas starting at the Paris-Bassin de la Villette near the métro stop at Jean-Jaurès. Information: *Office du Tourisme*, 127 Champs-Elysées, Paris 75008 (phone: 47-23-61-72).

From April to September the *Batobus* — a small cruise barge, more like a miniature *bateau-mouche* — travels up and down the Seine from near the Eiffel Tower to the Hôtel de Ville, making several stops which are marked by signs on the *quais*. Information: *Batobus* (phone: 47-23-61-72).

There are also two companies offering longer cruises starting on the Seine, traveling to and through Paris's old canal networks, routes by which basic provisions were once delivered to the capital from the provinces. Starting mornings at the quay near the *Musée d'Orsay,* the 3-hour trips pass from the Seine to the Bastille and navigate an underground tunnel below the Place Bastille, resurfacing on the Canal St-Martin and finally docking at La Villette, the sciences and industries complex. In the afternoons, the route is reversed. Information: *Paris Canal* (phone: 42-40-96-97) or *Canauxrama* (phone: 46-07-13-13).

A Shutterbug's Paris

The historic corners and places of Paris, its gardens and regal buildings, the serene Seine — all afford shutterbugs myriad photo opportunities throughout the city. Even a beginner can achieve remarkable results with a surprisingly basic set of lenses and filters. Equipment is, in fact, only as valuable as the imagination that puts it into use.

LANDSCAPES The Paris architecture is so varied and picturesque that it is often the photographer's primary focus. Be sure to frame your subject appropriately, however.

Although a standard 50mm to 55mm lens may work well in some landscape situations, most will benefit from a 20mm to 28mm wide-angle. Sacré-Coeur and the Place de la Concorde are just two of the panoramas that fit beautifully into a wide-angle format, allowing not only the overview, but the opportunity to include people or other points of interest in the foreground.

PEOPLE As with taking pictures of people anywhere, there are going to be times in Paris when a camera is an intrusion. People are often sensitive to having a camera suddenly pointed at them, and a polite request, while getting you a share of refusals, will also provide a chance to shoot some wonderful portraits that capture the spirit of the city as surely as the scenery does. For candid shots, an excellent lens is a zoom telephoto in the 70mm to 210mm range; it allows you to remain unobtrusive while the telephoto lens draws the subject closer. And for portraits, a telephoto can be used effectively as close as 2 or 3 feet.

For authenticity and variety, select a place likely to produce interesting subjects. The courtyard of the *Louvre* and its glass pyramids is an obvious spot for visitors, but if it's local color you're after, visit the Marais, Montmartre, or the Ile St-Louis. Or capture a picture of chic and outrageously clad commuters hopping the métro at rush hour or rushing home with a baguette or a bunch of flowers. Aim for shots that tell what's different about Paris. In portraiture, there are several factors to keep in mind. Morning or afternoon light will add richness to skin tones. To avoid the harsh facial shadows cast by direct sunlight, shoot in the shade or in an area where the light is diffused.

NIGHT If you think that picture possibilities end at sunset, you're presuming that night photography is the exclusive domain of the professional. If you've got a tripod, all you'll need is a cable release to attach to your camera to assure a steady exposure (which is often timed in minutes rather than fractions of a second).

For situations such as evening strolls along the Seine or a moonlight ride on a *bateau-mouche,* a flash usually does the trick, but beware: Flash units are often used improperly. You can't take a picture of Notre-Dame from the Ile St-Louis with a flash. It may reach out as far as 30 feet, but that's it. On the other hand, a flash used too close to your subject may result in overexposure, resulting in a "blown out" effect. With most cameras, strobes will work with a maximum shutter speed of 1/125 or 1/250 of a second. If you set the exposure properly and shoot within range, you should come up with pretty sharp results.

CLOSE-UPS Whether of people or of objects, close-ups can add another dimension to your photography. There are a number of shooting options, one of which is to use a 70mm or a 210mm lens at its closest focusable distance. Unless you're working in bright sunlight, a tripod will be worthwhile. If you are very near your subject and there is a good deal of reflective light, it may pay to underexpose a bit in relation to the meter reading.

If you do not have a telephoto lens, you can still shoot close-ups using a set of magnification filters. Filter packs of one-, two-, and three-time magnification are available, converting your lens into a close-up lens. Even better is a special macro lens designed for close-up photography.

A SHORT PHOTOGRAPHIC TOUR

Here are some of Paris's picture-perfect places.

ARC DE TRIOMPHE A daytime shot of this massive structure at the head of the Champs-Elysées at the Place de l'Etoile can be appealing, but a more memorable picture can be taken at dusk. If you stand on the Champs-Elysées, you can get a side-angle shot of the arch as it glitters against the deepening colors of the sky.

CENTRE GEORGES-POMPIDOU From the brightly colored blue and yellow tubes that wrap around it to the amusing papier-mâché sculptures in the interior garden (we especially like the pair of Parisian-red lips that spout water), every photo taken here is a keeper. In the summertime, you can snap a shot of street entertainers who perform such feats as juggling and fire-eating.

EIFFEL TOWER Some may feel that this well-known symbol of France has been photographed ad nauseam, and perhaps so. The challenge for the innovative shutterbug is to try looking at the same old thing from a different angle. If you walk down the steps of the Palais de Chaillot and frame your picture horizontally, you'll capture the lean, minimalist curves in an almost dizzying perspective. And if your plans call for a climb up the tower (and they should), stop at the second level and have someone take a corny but how-can-you-leave-Paris-without-it picture of you with a section of the black steel erector-set structure and all of Paris in the background.

FAUCHON Mouth-watering displays of meat, poultry, baked goods, spices, and exotic produce from every corner of the world tempt the eye as well as the palate. Everything is artistically arranged to dazzle — and it does. Be sure to use a flash when shooting indoors, and try including customers as well as store staff in your photo — shots of shoppers selecting mustards and attendants cutting choice wheels of cheese for Sunday brunch exemplify Paris every bit as much as its splendid monuments.

LUXEMBOURG GARDENS This is the perfect place to get a shot of children frolicking in the grass, office workers basking in the noonday sun, and couples, blissfully oblivious to the rest of the world, embracing. And nowhere else in the city will you find as many species of animals to photograph — cats, dogs, and birds alike seem to enjoy a daily outing almost as much as their owners.

NOTRE-DAME CATHEDRAL The spectacular cathedral where Napoleon and Henri IV were crowned is among the most popular photo spots for tourists and French alike. Here's a place to try out a wide-angle lens to get the expanse of the grand entrance flanked by flying buttresses. Other interesting pictures can be taken of the ornately carved front doors or from a side street looking up at the soaring arches or at the grotesque gargoyles. The stained glass windows are especially beautiful when photographed at sunset, with the last rays casting shadows across the nave of the church. Interior shots generally require a flash, unless the camera's shutter speed is very slow and the lens is open wide.

PÈRE-LACHAISE A jaunt to a cemetery just to capture a few headstones and mausoleums on film may sound a trifle morbid, but one visit to this unique site will change your mind. Cobblestone paths, flowering trees, a weeping willow or two, plus cavalries of cats form the backdrop for the thousands of gravesites in this, the final resting place of such luminaries as Chopin, Oscar Wilde, and Sarah Bernhardt, among other famous and infamous bodies.

PLACE DE LA CONCORDE This extraordinary square, bordered by eight impressive statues that represent the regions of France, is crowned by its magnum opus, the Obelisk of Luxor. Use a wide-angle lens to best capture the square's formidable grandeur. The corner where Avenue Gabriel meets the Rue de Rivoli affords an incomparable vista. Try to ignore the hundreds of cars whizzing by—or better yet, come back at dusk, when the street-lamps begin to glow and the City of Light puts on its best face.

PLACE DES VOSGES If there were a competition for Most Beautiful Square in the World, Place des Vosges could vie for the title. Delightfully serene, this enclosed area of picturesque homes (including Victor Hugo's) is an oasis of beauty (albeit in a not-so-shabby neighborhood) in the French capital. Once the royal palace of Henri IV, the courtyard now houses many upscale shops. If you enter the Place from the Hôtel Sully, you will be able to get a good shot of a section of the square. Then point your camera upward and zoom in on the lovely architecture: red-brick façades, gables, and windows, some of them stained glass.

SEINE Almost any shot of the Seine makes a lovely photo and, with pictures of the *bâteaux-mouches* chugging along, you can't go wrong. Snap from almost any bridge, anchoring the shot with the slender trees and distinctive buildings that line the river. An especially fine view is from the Ile St-Louis — aim your camera toward Notre-Dame and shoot.

Directions

Introduction

Paris is a city for walkers. With 20 distinct *quartiers* and *arrondissements,* each revealing a different aspect of Parisian life, the most often described city on earth still manages to defy the clichés it has engendered. Even for those who think they have seen it all, there will always be an unexpected discovery, whether it is one of the less celebrated of the nearly 150 museums that grace the city, a surprising side street off a major thoroughfare, or perhaps one of the hundreds of unassuming — but wonderful — neighborhood cafés.

The mood of the city changes with the seasons. Paris under the slate gray skies of winter, with bare chestnut trees gracing an elegant boulevard is quite different from Paris in the full bloom of spring, when its numerous parks and well-tended gardens burst into glorious color. (Be aware, however, that this riot of blossoms normally comes far later in the season than the creator of "April in Paris" would have you believe.)

From the circuit of famous monuments that loom like stage sets, the grace notes of France's aristocratic past, to the continual joie de vivre of its fluid street life, to the quiet enclaves of an unassuming little café on the Left Bank, one is constantly reminded that beauty is treasured here. Paris is the spectacle of l'Etoile, with its 12 lanes of traffic defying each other in a daily test of wits and will. It is children sailing their miniature boats in the Luxembourg Gardens. On a busy afternoon in the Tuileries, if you squint your eyes, it appears more like an Impressionist painting by Renoir. Paris also is the silent eloquence of its cemeteries, where homage is regularly paid to painters, poets, musicians (including American rock stars), and philosophers.

To explore this grande dame of European capitals, here are seven walks that encompass some of the most interesting and accessible *arrondissements,* each offering a different perspective on the city.

Paris is arranged in a kind of spiral, which was part of Baron Haussmann's brilliant master plan. The visionary architect/city planner was appointed in 1853 by Napoleon III to transform the layout of the city. The result, a uniform classical elegance surrounded by graceful parks and promenades, has gained it the almost uncontested title as the most beautiful city in the world.

These walks visit the 1st *arrondissement,* with the *Louvre* and the Tuileries providing a contrast to the former market district of *Les Halles;* and the gentrified Marais district (the Jewish quarter of the city), the elegant Place des Vosges, *Le Centre Georges-Pompidou,* and the historic Hôtel de Ville in the 4th *arrondissement.* In addition, they meander through the student center, the botanical gardens, and the 6th *arrondissement* on the Left Bank, as well as Notre-Dame and the city islands, Ile de la Cité and

Ile St-Louis. Visit the historic square at St-Germain-des-Prés, once the domain of the existentialists, and the beautiful Luxembourg Gardens. Also on the Left Bank, tour the Eiffel Tower area and, adjacent, Les Invalides, where Napoleon is buried; and nearby on the Right Bank, wander through the elegant 8th *quartier* with its gastronomic palaces like *Maxim's* and well-known monuments such as the Arc de Triomphe and the majestic Place de la Concorde. We also go to Place Pigalle, long reputed to be Paris's "sin street," and the nearby 18th *arrondissement* in the north, to stand above the city at Sacré-Coeur, in the heart of Montmartre.

Though some of the terrain will no doubt be familiar to repeat visitors, the point of these walks is to wander and discover detours off the beaten track. The joy and challenge is to use these suggestions as a guide, and to make them a variation on your own theme. Just think of yourself as a painter, with Paris as your palette of inspiration. And enjoy.

Walk 1: Gardens, Bridges, and Islands

At the turn of the century, the most pleasant way to arrive at the Jardin des Plantes (Botanical Gardens) was by steamboat, gliding up the Seine past the *Louvre* and Notre-Dame; these days one must settle for a local bus or the métro to the Gare d'Austerlitz (station). The magnificent 46-acre gardens are in the 5th *arrondissement* on Paris's Left Bank, and they border the Latin Quarter and the Seine. Originally founded by Louis XIII in 1626 as a Royal Garden of Medicinal Herbs, they met with such hostility from the medical community that for years the land lay fallow. Later, the gardens were revived and enlarged to include — in addition to medicinal herbs — live animals, minerals, research laboratories, and a library. During the 19th century, the complex grew to include a museum of natural history; today, the vast range of facilities here enjoys a worldwide reputation for teaching and research.

The gardens boast a varied collection of plants and trees from all over the world. There is an alpine garden, an ecological park, and a tropical plant complex, as well as examples of French and English garden landscape design. Some of the oldest trees in Paris can be found here, including a 200-year-old American sequoia, a ginkgo from China, an iron tree from Persia, and a cedar of Lebanon, 40 feet in circumference, that was supposedly brought from Syria as a seedling in 1735. After wandering up the main promenade and the winding paths, cross over to the Quai St-Bernard. Along the river are the Tino Rossi Gardens, with an open-air sculpture museum boasting several impressive works, including Zadkine's *Development of Form*. Parisians come here to stroll and to walk their dogs; students from the university (across the boulevard) come to relax between lectures. From here one can also enjoy a spectacular view of the Ile St-Louis, one of two important islands in the middle of Paris (see below). For now, just take a seat on one of the benches and watch the barges floating by and the light shifting over the bridges.

Continue along the path bordering the quay and walk toward Notre-Dame. The tall, modern glass-and-aluminum building on the left is the *Institut du Monde Arabe* (Institute of the Arab World), which houses a museum, a library, a cultural center, and a rooftop café (offering excellent cappuccino) — and splendid city views. The institute was created by France and 20 Arab countries as a cultural exchange, and a means of providing more cooperation with and a better understanding of Arab culture. The building itself is a good example of Paris's modern architecture. Designed by architect Jean Nouvel, it has a spectacular façade of 240

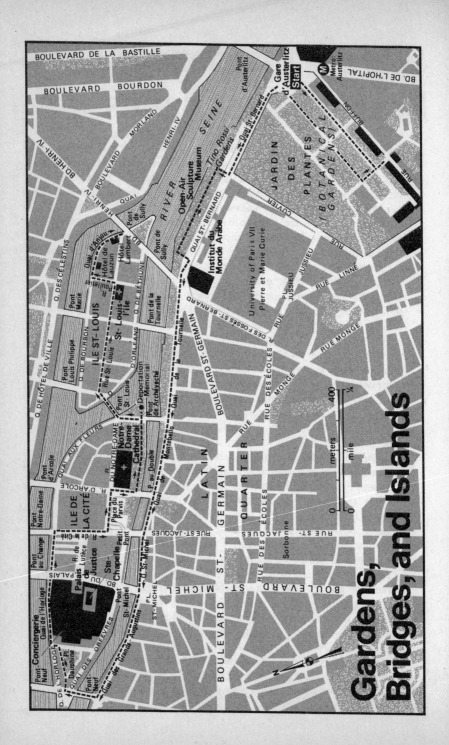

Gardens,
Bridges, and Islands

light-sensitive geometric panels that automatically filter the sunlight. Across the street along Quai de la Tournelle, at No. 15, is *La Tour d'Argent* (see *Eating Out,* THE CITY,) definitely Paris's second-best-known restaurant (after *Maxim's*).

Continue along the riverside quays, whose names change at practically every intersection (for example, Quai de Montebello becomes Quai St-Michel, and so on). In all, there are more than 40 quays that run for several miles alongside the Seine. Many date from the Middle Ages, when boats were the quickest, safest, and most efficient way to bring goods into the city. The quays were divided into separate docking areas for wine, coal, grain, and other items. Nowadays, some 30 bridges cross the Seine, while numerous métro tunnels go under the river.

While walking along the Seine, with Notre-Dame on the right, browse among some of the green, boxlike bookstalls that line both sides of the river. These *bouquinistes* (booksellers) are a Paris institution, but while there were probably some real bargains here a few decades ago, these days be happy to find new postcards that sell for only 1 franc each, or some vintage versions in pastel tints for a bit more. The books are rather pricey, but this is still an interesting stop. The stalls have no fixed hours, so you may find shops that seem closed or look deserted; probably the owner has just walked next door to have a coffee with a colleague.

Walk farther along the Left Bank to the hubbub of the Place St-Michel intersection, with its raucous mix of milling students from the nearby Sorbonne, bustling bookstores, sidewalk cafés, and Middle Eastern snack bars that constitute Paris's Latin Quarter. A stop into 5 Place St-Michel, a branch of a *Gibert Jeune* bookshop, may yield, among other things, some interesting cookbooks. Continuing along the Seine on the Quai des Grands-Augustins, turn right at the next bridge, the Pont-Neuf, said to be the oldest span in Paris. Dating from 1578, its construction began during the reign of Henri III and was completed by Henri IV. Before the Revolution, the Pont-Neuf was the greatest thoroughfare in Paris, attracting beggars, vaudeville acts, medicine shows, and other assorted entertainments. Here it was possible to do almost anything — from having a tooth extracted to getting a poodle trimmed. It was almost certain that if you were looking for somebody, native or foreign, you would surely run across him or her here.

The Pont-Neuf intersects the Ile de la Cité on the right. This island in the middle of Paris is a major historic site, with the Palais de Justice (law courts), Sainte-Chapelle, the Conciergerie (the former prison, today the police headquarters), and the magnificent Notre-Dame cathedral located here. Stroll through the Place Dauphine, just ahead as you turn right off Pont-Neuf. Dating from 1607, this charming square was named after Louis XIII when he was the dauphin. It was one of Henri IV's three urbanization projects; there is a splendid statue of the very popular king on the Pont-Neuf, overlooking the Seine. The original statue was erected by his widow, Marie de Médici, but was melted down during the Revolution and converted into cannon. By way of retaliation, Louis XVIII ordered a statue of Napoleon and one of General Desaix to be melted down in order to provide material for the new statue of the king. But the sculptor commissioned by Louis XVIII, an ardent follower of Bonaparte, had the last laugh: He stashed a small statuette of Napoleon and various written articles favoring the emperor inside his finished sculpture.

Make a note to have a meal at *Paul* (15 Pl. Dauphine; phone: 43-54-21-48), an unassuming restaurant with family-style seating and friendly service. Try the roast duck with cherries and roasted apples. Closed Mondays; reservations advised. Just across the way is *Fanny Tea* (20 Pl. Dauphine; phone: 43-25-83-67), as intimate and cozy as your grandmother's parlor, but with definite Gallic touches. It is the perfect place to have a pot of tea and one (or several) of their warm apple tarts. An ideal escape on a rainy day or a spot to recharge one's batteries.

Henri IV (25 Pl. Dauphine; phone: 43-54-44-53) is still one of Paris's most popular inexpensive and no-frills hotels, more for the student or the eternal bohemian. To give you some idea of how many students and/or eternal bohemians there are in the world today, it is necessary to book a room here at least 3 months in advance!

Head east from the Place Dauphine along Quai de l'Horlage and walk around the Conciergerie, the former prison (now police headquarters) that housed Marie-Antoinette and many others before they were taken to the guillotine.

The entrance to the Palais de Justice is around the corner, on the Boulevard du Palais. Now the law courts, it was the first seat of the Roman military government, then the headquarters of the early French kings. Inside one of its courtyards, to the left after entering, is one of the jewels of Paris, the 13th-century Sainte-Chapelle of King Louis IX (St-Louis). The chapel, built to house the Sacred Crown of Thorns and other holy relics (many of which now are in Notre-Dame), has 15 splendid stained glass windows — with practically no walls in between — and a rose window, all under a 247-foot spire. Sainte-Chapelle is especially impressive in sunny weather.

Walk east along Rue de Lutèce; a pleasant pedestrian mall, its benches afford a welcome respite for foot-sore explorers. Farther east on the island, cross the Rue de la Cité to reach Notre-Dame, the magnificent cathedral (begun in 1163) that has become (to the world's imagination), the quintessence of Gothic architecture. Its steeple rises 285 feet above the ground, and the entire structure is supported by a series of flying buttresses that were, at the time of their construction, considered an architectural marvel. Note the exquisite stained glass windows, the 37 chapels, the archaeological crypt, and the organ, which dates from 1730. It was here that Napoleon was crowned, and where Victor Hugo's famous hunchback lived.

The views from the church's tower, reached by climbing 397 steps, are still the finest in the city; a popular tourist spot, they rarely offer any solitude. Its great bell, the 16-ton Bourdon of Notre-Dame, is one of the largest in existence — though not quite as large as the one at Sacré-Coeur. After viewing the church, walk through the park on the riverfront to the easternmost tip of the island. Cross the street to the Square de l'Ile de France to the Mémorial de la Déportation. The entrance to this unusual installation is below street level and is easy to miss because of the dozens of Notre-Dame tour buses parked outside. Worth seeking out, the memorial is a moving tribute to the 200,000 French citizens who were exterminated in concentration camps during World War II. Sometimes there is a survivor of one of the camps who unofficially acts as a volunteer guide, giving a short tour in several languages. Though he does not demand a fee, it is customary to give him a few francs.

Retrace your steps toward Notre-Dame and cross Pont St-Louis to the neighboring Ile St-Louis. Until the beginning of Louis XIII's reign, this island was still uninhabited pastureland and was composed of two islets: a small one called Ile aux Vaches (Isle of Cows) and a larger one, known as Ile de Notre-Dame. In an ambitious engineering project — begun in 1614 and completed in 1664 — the isles were joined, equipped with streets, and surrounded with stone quays. Described by Anatole France almost a century ago as "a pleasantly quiet and elegant backwater of Paris life," these days it is considered a desirable (albeit exclusive) place to dwell, accessible to the heart of the city, yet apart from it. Still quaint and serene, it is a fine place to ramble. In addition to its classic 17th-century architecture, it offers several refreshing views of Paris. A special bonus is to indulge in an ice cream at *Berthillon* (31 Rue St-Louis-en-l'Ile), pricey but worthy of its reputation as the best in the city, if not the world. Flavors change with the season, but the plum armagnac and espresso, chocolate and orange, and cassis sorbet are highly recommended. During the summer, there always is a line stretching around the corner. Since it is closed during August, as well as on Mondays, Tuesdays, and school holidays, a more dependable place to get your Berthillon fix might be *Le Flore en l'Ile,* a tea house/café at the foot of the Pont St-Louis (42 Quai d'Orléans). Enjoy the cozy ambience inside, or buy a cone from the outdoor vendor and enjoy it while taking a leisurely stroll around the island.

The island is small enough to walk in its entirety from quay to quay, and offers a relaxing place to sit by the riverside, write a postcard alongside a fisherman hauling in his catch, or sip a coffee with businesspeople reading *Le Figaro* during their lunch hour. Rue St-Louis-en-l'Ile is the main street, which runs down the middle of the island and is the site of several small hotels, restaurants, and quaint shops. Seasoned travelers will enjoy the *Ulysse* bookstore (No. 26), which specializes in travel books, with an extensive inventory of both new and used books. Owner Catherine Domain speaks English and is very helpful in providing information. At No. 21 is the Eglise St-Louis-en-l'Ile, built between 1664 and 1726, and distinguished by its unusual iron clock. The ornate interior is in the 17th-century Grand Siècle style, adorned with wood, gilt, and marble (closed Sunday afternoons and Mondays). The great political caricaturist Honoré Daumier lived at No. 9 for a time. Turn left along Rue Poulletier. Along the Quai d'Anjou on the north side of the island are several old mansions of note: No. 17, for example, is home to the Hôtel de Lauzun, built in 1657. Its typical, austere 17th-century façade belies the excessiveness of its interior, with its cut-velvet walls, golden nymphs, and elaborate ceilings. Its original owner was an army caterer, but during the 1800s, many poets and writers lived here, among them Baudelaire, Rilke, and Théophile Gautier. Today, it is used by the city of Paris for official receptions. No. 7 is still the site of the Pastry and Bakery Syndicate, founded in 1801.

The walk concludes outside the Hôtel Lambert (2 Rue St-Louis-en-l'Ile) at the corner, near the Pont de Sully. It was built in 1640 by Le Vau, principal architect to Louis XIV, who also did the early work on the Eglise St-Louis and many of the other buildings on the island. No expense was spared in creating this magnificent home for Nicholas Lambert de Thorigny, who was known as Lambert the Rich. In 1742, Voltaire completed his *Henriade* while visiting here; during the next couple of centuries it became a girls' school, and later a depot for military stores, before returning again to private ownership.

Walk 2: Montmartre

Until it officially became part of the city of Paris at the turn of the century, Montmartre, in the 18th *arrondissement,* was a secluded, picturesque village, with no more than 1,000 inhabitants living on the tree-lined Butte, amidst a charming landscape of windmills, vineyards, and pleasant country houses. Construction of the Basilique du Sacré-Coeur — which began in 1875 — heralded a brighter future after the devastating defeat in the Franco-Prussian War of 1870–71, and gave the remote village new prominence. Ironically, the church wasn't completed until 1910 and wasn't consecrated until 1919, following World War I.

Located on the site of the ancient abbey of Montmartre, the enormous, grandiose structure is visible for many miles around Paris. While some marvel at its beauty, there are many who think its Roman-Byzantine–influenced design is definitely mediocre from an architectural point of view; some critics have gone so far as to describe it as a giant salt or pepper shaker.

It was built at a cost of about 36 million francs (not at the value of today's franc!), pretty expensive considering the relatively lower 6-million-franc price tag for the Eiffel Tower; monies were raised mostly by subscriptions and government subsidy. The foundations for Sacré-Coeur alone cost 3½ million francs, since the 83 masonry columns that support the structure had to be sunk over 100 feet into the soft soil of the Butte to bear their weight. The foundations are so strong that it has been said that even if the hill were taken away, the church would remain intact. The 19-ton Sacré-Coeur bells, purported to be the heaviest in the world, can be heard at least 20 miles away.

During the 19th century, Parisians came to Montmartre to wander at leisure through the steep footpaths along the Butte. These days, crowds of tourists from all over the world make that same trek, trying to recapture a glimpse of "Gay Paree." For those who can't manage the climb, there is a funicular railway at the bottom of the hill. Or take the "tourist train" that weaves up through the surrounding streets, passing other points of interest as well.

Supposition has it that the name Montmartre is derived from "Mon Mars," the name of the temple dedicated to the god of war. Other historians argue that it was named for another temple dedicated to Mercury. Just as battles rage over Montmartre's history, it seems fitting that this naturally fortified area has been a refuge for armies battling Paris's attackers over the centuries.

During the mid-1800s, Montmartre was home to many aspiring artists; they chose the area partly because of its good light and, more importantly, its inexpensive lodgings. Braque, van Gogh, Renoir, Toulouse-Lautrec,

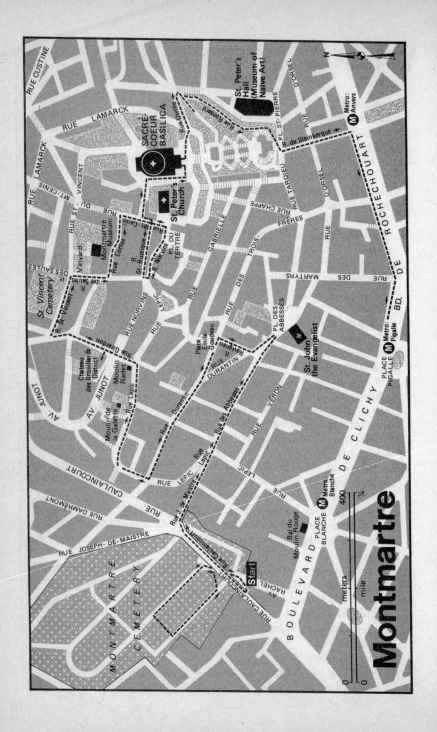

Montmartre

RUE CUSTINE

RUE LAMARCK

RUE LAMARCK

RUE LAMARCK

SACRÉ-COEUR BASILICA

Rue Utrillo

Rue Paul

St. Peter's Hall (Museum of Naive Art)

PL. ST-PIERRE

R. de Steinkerque

Metro: Anvers

RUE ST-VINCENT

RUE DU MT-CENIS

St. Peter's Church

RUE TARDIEU

RUE D'ORSEL

RUE D'ORSEL

RUE DE ROCHECHOUART

Montmartre Museum

Vinyard

R. Cortot

R. St-Rustique

R. Norvins

PL. DU TERTRE

RUE GABRIELLE

RUE CHAPPE

FRÈRES

RUE DES SAULES

St. Vincent Cemetery

R. des Saules

R. St-Vincent

RUE NORVINS

RUE LEPIC

RUE DES TROIS.

RUE DES

MARTYRS

RUE DES MARTYRS

BD. DE

AV. JUNOT

Château des Brouillards District

Moulin Radet

Rue Girardon

Place Émile-Goudeau

Rue Ravignan

RUE

PL. DES ABBESSES

St. John the Evangelist

PLACE PIGALLE

Metro: Pigalle

AV. JUNOT

Moulin de la Galette

Rue Lepic

Rue Durantin

RUE DURANTIN

RUE VÉRON

RUE CAULAINCOURT

Rue Durantin

Rue Lepic

Rue des Abbesses

RUE LEPIC

RUE

DE CLICHY

RUE LEPIC

RUE DAMRÉMONT

RUE

Rue J. de Maistre

Rue Tholozé

Metro: Blanche

RUE JOSEPH-DE-MAISTRE

Bal du Moulin Rouge

PLACE BLANCHE

MONTMARTRE CEMETERY

RUE CAULAINCOURT

Rue Rachel

Start

RUE RACHEL

meters   400

mile   ¼

0

0

BOULEVARD

N

and Utrillo all made their homes here at one time; in fact, many of their paintings of street scenes were inspired by this neighborhood. Following World War II, the erection of many taller, modern buildings caused Montmartre to lose its sleepy village quality. Once known for its charming windmills, sadly, only two or three of the original ones remain. And although the area's famous nightclub, *Le Moulin Rouge* (immortalized in many a canvas by Lautrec), is designed as a windmill, it never actually was one.

The "real" surviving windmills have their own unique historical anecdotes. In 1833, the Moulin de la Galette was the place villagers came to get fresh cow's milk and tasty rolls. Père Debray, the proprietor, was also fond of dancing and began selling dance lessons to his customers in addition to bread and milk. Supposedly, this is how the dance hall of the Moulin de la Galette came into being. Over the next 20 years it became quite the nightspot, doubling in size; and since its popularity inspired the opening of other dance halls and clubs, many agree that the toe-tapping M. Galette should be credited with making Montmartre the center of nightlife in Paris.

This walk begins in the southwest corner of the *arrondissement* at the Cimetière Montmartre (Montmartre Cemetery), which dates from the 17th century, when it served as the parish cemetery. Although smaller than the Père Lachaise and Montparnasse cemeteries, it is the final resting place for many illustrious people, and is equally rich in monuments and statuary. Among those who were buried here are Emile Zola (whose remains were later transferred to the Panthéon in 1908), Edgar Degas, Vaslav Nijinsky, François Truffaut, Heinrich Heine, and Hector Berlioz. (The composer has the distinct advantage of being buried between his first and second wives. He arranged this by having one wife exhumed from a prior burial place and taken to Montmartre to wait for him.)

The grounds are entered by descending the steps leading down from Rue Caulaincourt and passing under a busy, low-hanging overpass. Until 1888, the cemetery blocked direct access into Paris, necessitating the construction of a bridge that would link the Boulevard de Clichy with Rue Caulaincourt. Unfortunately, the span was built directly over some of the older monuments, barely grazing their tops.

Up a few steps at the Carrefour du Croix, a tall column marks the burial spot of the victims of the coup d'état of 1851. There are several tombs of interest: The red granite tomb of Zola has a bust by Solari; nearby, the tomb of Castagnary features a fine bust by Rodin. Turn around and walk under the bridge and up the stairs; turn left to find the grave of Dalida, the popular French singer of the 1960s, who shocked her fans by taking poison. Fresh bouquets are still left here year-round, and on the right, just before reaching her grave, there is an unusual statue. The property of Dr. Guy Pitchal, Dalida's psychiatrist, it is a headless bust holding a pipe, with a lifelike death mask behind it that appears to follow you as you pass it.

Walk out the main entrance again, up the steps to the right and cross the bridge. Look for the *Terrasse* hotel and turn right on Rue Joseph-de-Maistre. Walk down this street toward the busy Rue Lepic, a good venue for observing typical Parisian lifestyle. Continue along Rue Joseph-de-Maistre to Rue des Abbesses and the Place des Abbesses. On the right is St. John the Evangelist, a distinctive brick church built in 1904. It is the first church in Paris to be built with reinforced concrete, a forerunner of the modern style of architecture now represented in many of the city's newer buildings. En route, take a break at one of the *pâtisserie*/tearooms, or buy a slice of quiche to eat along the way. From the Place des Abbesses, walk up the steep Rue Ravignan, an ancient street that was once part of the only road that led from Paris to the abbey above. A few steps from here is the Place Emile-Goudeau, site of the Bateau-Lavoir, the famous artists colony where Picasso, Braque, and other "modern" artists painted in adjoining studios. These simple, wooden dwellings later earned the moniker "Villa Médici of Modern Art." After Picasso and his group moved on, the equally impressive "Ruche" (beehive) took root, with such fledgling artists as Léger, Modigliani, and Soutine seeking inexpensive studios in which to live and work. Unfortunately, these famous shanties burned down in 1970, but many were rebuilt (at No. 13) as artists' studios and apartments. Even for those not artistically inclined, this is a good place to pause and watch the Parisian street scene. The *Tim* hotel (on the square at 11 Rue Ravignan; phone: 42-55-74-79) is a good local base to stay in Montmartre. When leaving the square, turn right at Rue Garreau (which becomes Rue Durantin); turn right again into the upper end of Rue Lepic. At the top of a small incline is a view of one of the area's surviving windmills, the Moulin de la Galette, which has topped the Butte for more than 6 centuries (it is no longer accessible to the public). Walk to the corner of Rue Girardon to the *Moulin Radet,* another survivor, now an Italian restaurant. Turn left, following Rue Girardon to a descending stairway; at the bottom of the steps, turn right on Rue St-Vincent, where, enclosed by high walls, is the cemetery of the same name. At the crossing of Rue des Saules and Rue St-Vincent is *Au Lapin Agile* (phone: 46-06-85-87; closed Mondays). Formerly an inn where crowds assembled at the turn of the century to hear local poets read their own works, and later frequented by Picasso and other painters of the time, it remains a popular cabaret attracting an international crowd who love a good French sing-along. Originally called the *Cabaret des Assassins,* it takes its present name from the artist A. Gill, who painted a rabbit on a signboard advertising *"poèmes et chansons."* The name stuck.

Across the street is a modest vineyard, owned by the community and still in use today. It is here that a festive grape harvest takes place on the first Saturday in October. About 500 bottles of a red wine (Clos Montmartre) that makes no pretense of being exceptional are produced here. During the festival, the wine is sold at a special fund-raising auction at the Town Hall (1 Pl. Jules-Joffrin) for about 150 francs per bottle.

Turn south on Rue des Saules to Rue Cortot and turn left to find the *Musée Montmartre* (12 Rue Cortot; phone: 46-06-61-11). This simple, rustic-looking building, dating from the 17th century, houses a rich collection of paintings, drawings, and documents, depicting life in the quarter (open daily, except Mondays, 2 to 6 PM). At No. 6 is the house where the composer Erik Satie lived. An enjoyable detour with some interesting examples of architecture is the Château des Brouillards neighborhood around to the left off Rue Girardon, home to many French celebrities. At the end of Rue Cortot, look to the left down the descending walkway for a magnificent view of the northern suburbs of Paris. Turn right at the steps and go to Place du Tertre, which unfortunately has become a tourist trap; crowded with souvenir market stalls, it is all but impossible to really appreciate the charming 18th-century houses surrounding the square. While art is a tradition in this area, the plethora of portrait artists who hawk their wares here have become a matter of controversy, as the government is now deciding whether to regulate the number of licenses issued.

And speaking of tourist traps, be sure to check the prices at the local cafés carefully; many of them take advantage of visitors. From the Place du Tertre, wander past the shops along Rue Norvins; turn right at Rue Lepic and immediately right again onto the narrow and often deserted Rue St-Rustique, a good place for a leisurely stroll before encountering the crowds at Sacré-Coeur.

Back at the Place du Tertre, note l'Eglise St-Pierre (St. Peter's Church) on the left. One of the oldest churches in Paris, it was founded by Louis VI in 1134, and completed during that century. It has been added to, rebuilt, and revived so many times since then that there is a real contrast in architectural styles — though a few sections of its original Gothic roots remain. It is interesting to note the sharp contrast of this simple church with the massive scale of Sacré-Coeur. Just to the back of St-Pierre, on the site of the ancient cemetery, is the Jardin du Calvaire (Calvary Garden), which is no longer open to the public. For a magnificent view of the city (especially on a clear day), bear left and walk a short distance toward the Sacré-Coeur terrace. Unfortunately, the vendors who clog the steps of Sacré-Coeur often obstruct the view of Paris.

At Sacré-Coeur, it is still possible to make the very steep ascent into the dome for a view that is about equal to that from the top level of the Eiffel Tower. A stroll through the vast interior of this famous church, with its capacity of 8,000, is a must experience.

When leaving Sacré-Coeur's grounds, avoid the busy stairs directly in front and descend instead via the scenic steps called "Rue" Maurice-Utrillo at the east of the Sacré-Coeur terrace. (If a break from the crowds is in order at this point of the tour, turn right for a stroll through the church's terraced gardens.) At the bottom of the steps, turn right and head down another set of steps called "Rue" Paul Albert and follow Rue Ronsard south, noting on the right St-Pierre Halle (St. Peter's Hall), a fine 19th-century iron structure that houses a children's museum (*Musée en*

Herbe) on the ground floor and the *Museum of Naive Art* on the first floor. At Place St-Pierre, turn right to the Montmartre carousel; turn left and head down Rue de Steinkerque, the heart of Paris's fabric district, recognizable by the abundance of yard goods and trimming supply stores, and the crowds of needle-and-thread aficionados. Farther down Rue de Steinkerque is Boulevard de Rochechouart, a wide shopping street with a large métro station to the left, where it seems all of the immigrant population of Paris comes to buy clothes at bargain prices, mostly at the stretch of *Tati* shops (a chain of clothing boutiques).

It is important to realize that there is an upper Montmartre and a lower Montmartre, and nothing depicts lower Montmartre better than Place Pigalle, with its dubious strip of entertainment spots lining the edge of Boulevard de Clichy, the western continuation of Boulevard de Rochechouart. If planning a visit here, remember that Place Pigalle comes to life only at night. The American author Henry Miller immortalized it in several of his books during the late 1930s and early 1940s. But it earned its original image as "sin street" with the first burlesque cabaret, *Chat Noir,* founded in 1884. These days, Boulevard de Clichy and its tacky neon surroundings have become more of a cliché.

Walk 3: The Grandeur of Paris

This walk begins just off the Champs-Elysées, on Avenue Winston-Churchill, site of the *Petit Palais* and the *Grand Palais*. The *Grand Palais,* a magnificent building with an Ionic colonnade, mosaic frieze, and three porches conceived and built from the designs of three different architects, has long been used for a variety of annual industrial exhibitions and shows, and is now a cultural center where such temporary exhibitions as the *Paris Book Fair* are held. The back of the *Grand Palais* is the science museum and planetarium, called the *Palais de la Découverte* (on Av. Franklin-D.-Roosevelt).

The *Musée du Petit Palais,* now a museum of fine arts, is architecturally distinguished by an ornamental flat glass dome. The Grand and Petit palaces were built for the *1900 Paris International Exposition,* replacing the former Palais de l'Industrie.

Walk to the Seine and across the Pont Alexandre-III, which was built at the same time as the palaces. This single-span bridge, with its numerous gilded statues, is a fine example of popular 19th-century steel architecture and ornate style. Walk down the busy Avenue du Maréchal-Galliéni along the vast tree-lined Esplanade toward the Hôtel des Invalides. Les Invalides was founded by Louis XIV in the 1670s as an asylum for wounded and aged soldiers; initially intended to house 4,000, it more often was a refuge for twice that number. The classically balanced buildings were designed by Libéral Bruant. The royal church (Eglise du Dôme), constructed from 1675 to 1706, is topped by an elaborate golden dome designed by Mansart and built between 1843 and 1861. This houses the tomb of Emperor Napoleon I. The monument is surrounded by 12 huge white marble statues, interspersed with 54 flags, each symbolizing another of Napoleon's victories. The church has an impressive courtyard, and frescoes that are worthy of note. If time allows, visit the *Musée Rodin* (see *Special Places* in THE CITY).

Back at Les Invalides, walk north toward the Seine along the pleasant Rue Fabert. Turn left at Rue St-Dominique, with its lineup of cafés, greengrocers, wine shops, *pâtisseries, boucheries,* and *boulangeries.* Neighborhood folk casually go about their business, more often than not ignoring the fact that the magnificent Eiffel Tower is right in their own backyard. If you're ready to rest and sample some Parisian sweets, stop at *La Cour du Sable* (111 Rue St-Dominique). It is an exceptional *pâtisserie,* where walkers should indulge in a tart of fresh orange slices (*tarte à la orange*) or the simple cheese tart (*tarte du fromage*). There is a choice of

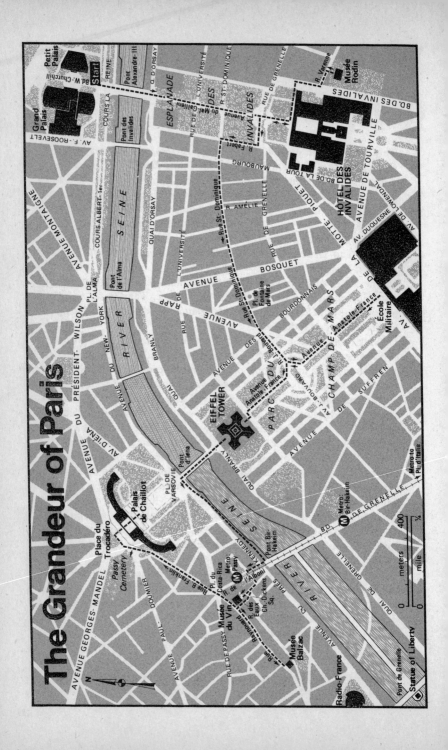

two restaurants at which to lunch, depending on your mood — and the availability of a table. The small (only four tables) *L'Auverge Normande* (No. 127) specializes in *produits du terroir,* or rural cuisine. Next door, *La Fontaine de Mars* (No. 129) is a family bistro that serves Provençal cooking in a friendly atmosphere. The simple and tasty dishes include grilled sardines, fresh foie gras, a changing plat du jour, and a delicious ice cream dessert with chocolate sauce and meringue. Continue on Rue St-Dominique — the neighborhood shifts from a French ambience to an Italian one, as you pass the heavy-arched Place des Fontaine de Mars with its adjacent fountain.

Cross the busy intersection of Avenue de la Bourdonnais and Place du Général-Gouraud and walk ahead to Avenue Joseph-Bouvard, which leads directly to the extensive grounds of the Champ-de-Mars. In 1793 a guillotine was erected at its northeast corner. A good way to soak up some of the history of this area is to visit l'Ecole Militaire (the French Military Academy), the impressive complex to the left. Originally built to accommodate 500 soldiers-to-be, it has been through many transitions over the centuries — alternatively used as a barracks, then headquarters of the Imperial Guard, and back to a training school once again. It is one of the best examples of 18th-century French architecture, with its distinct 2-story Corinthian columns and handsome gilded dome. Not long after it opened in 1752, Napoleon I was among its many students.

The Champ-de-Mars was the scene of a battle in 888 between the Parisians and the Normans, who were ultimately defeated. From 1770 to 1900, the area was the place for both military reviews and the great *Paris International Expositions* of 1867, 1878, 1889, and 1900. In 1908, it was transformed into a park in order to be more in keeping with the high class residences that were built in the surrounding neighborhood.

Although all of those international exhibitions were significant, it was perhaps the 1889 exhibition that was most memorable, as it commemorated the centenary of the 1789 French Revolution. The newly erected Eiffel Tower was unveiled as a monument to that event. During the exhibition period, more than 25 million people visited the unusual tower, which at 984 feet was (until the construction of the 1,284-foot-high Empire State Building in New York City in 1930) the tallest structure in the world. Controversial and despised by many, it was nearly torn down in 1909 when its first 20-year lease expired, only to be saved when the invention of the wireless gave it a new lease on life — as a radio transmitter. Beneath the tower's north pillar is a statue by Antoine Bourdelle of Alexandre-Gustave Eiffel, its architect and engineer.

Having ceremoniously celebrated its 100th anniversary in 1989, the Eiffel Tower continues to make its glorious presence known at the northwestern end of the Champ-de-Mars, facing the Palais de Chaillot on the opposite bank of the Seine. Be sure to view the tower from as many perspectives as possible. Walk down the middle of the Champ-de-Mars, with its tree-lined paths and children's park; from there note the graceful lines and impressive craftsmanship of Eiffel's work, even more fascinating as one climbs the stairs to the second level to take an elevator to the top. On an exceptionally clear day, it is possible to see for about 50 miles. There are three restaurants within the tower, but the *Jules Verne* (open daily for lunch and dinner; phone: 45-55-61-44) is the one that we recommend, though it is pricey and requires reservations a month or two in advance.

After leaving the tower, walk across the Pont d'Iéna facing it, which leads to the Place du Trocadéro and the Palais de Chaillot (both of which can be visited at the end of this walk). After crossing the bridge, don't take the easy route straight ahead, but turn left and walk along the footpath bordering the Seine, avoiding the noise and traffic of the upper level of the Avenue du Président-Kennedy. This route offers yet another view of the Eiffel Tower, as well as a skyline of the high-rise buildings to the west in a tableau that looks something like Paris confronting Manhattan.

The walk along the river ends at Pont de Bir-Hakeim. Follow the steps up to the right, where there is a pedestrian tunnel and another bridge across noisy Avenue du Président-Kennedy leading to Rue de l'Alboni.

Walk up Rue de l'Alboni; before the steps to the Passy métro stop, turn left at Place Alboni and right on Rue des Eaux. At the end of the street at Rue des Eaux at Place Charles-Dickens is the *Musée Du Vin* (Wine Museum; 5-7 Pl. Charles-Dickens; phone: 45-25-63-26). Located in the cellar of the former Abbey of Passy, which was built during the second half of the 14th century by St. Francis of Paule, the museum couldn't be better situated. During that time, many of the hills around Paris were found to be covered with vineyards and several, operated by local monks, produced some very good wine. Between 1650 and 1720, mineral water sources were discovered here, which explains the name Rue des Eaux (Street of Waters). Passy became a very famous thermal site and was visited by such luminaries as Benjamin Franklin and Jean-Jacques Rousseau. The abbey was destroyed after the Revolution, but during the 1960s the foundations were rediscovered by a Parisian restaurateur, who transformed the space into wine cellars in order to supply the restaurants of the Eiffel Tower. The museum, which opened in 1981, now hosts the wine brotherhood (Conseil des Echansons de France), an order dedicated to the promotion of high-quality French wines.

Within its cave-like environment, the museum displays interesting scenes depicting the history of wine — from harvesting to bottling — as well as examples of vintage pressing equipment, casks, corkscrews, and labels, that give the visitor a good overview of oenology. One can also buy wines, champagnes, and spirits at prices lower than those at many of the wine shops, or visit the tasting room to enjoy a simple lunch served with a selection of wines by the glass or bottle. (A free glass of wine is included in the admission price.) Private parties, complete with traditional wine tasting ceremonies, can also be arranged. Even for those familiar with

Paris, a visit to this museum is a unique experience. Open daily from noon to 6 PM.

For an interesting detour, take a round trip from the Passy métro stop to the Pasteur métro stop (toward Nation). This is one of the city's most scenic rides, beginning in "Le Seizième" (the 16th *arrondissement*), one of Paris's richest, most elegant neighborhoods. The main part of the ride goes aboveground for several stops, crossing over the Seine and affording a great view of the Eiffel Tower. The ride along the Boulevards de Grenelle and Garibaldi at second-story level provides a refreshing perspective of Parisian life. To get to the Passy métro after leaving the *Wine Museum*, go back down Rue de l'Alboni to the first corner and turn left.

Those who decide against the métro excursion should walk up the steps through the narrow passageway (on the right side of the square as you leave the museum) and make a left onto Rue Raynouard to the *Maison de Balzac* (No. 47). The plain exterior of his house belies the flamboyant excesses of its renowned inhabitant; the treasures in art and antiques he once accumulated are no longer to be found, as they were sacrificed to creditors during his colorful life. However, this unassuming house is a testament to his hard work, evidenced by the manuscripts and memorabilia on display in the museum-library (closed Mondays and holidays).

As you ramble around this well-tended neighborhood, complete with discreet doormen and private roads, remember that the Passy quarter is the city home to Paris's wealthy class. For a change of scene, walk back past the Place du Costa-Rica and up Rue Benjamin Franklin (he was the US Ambassador to France from 1776 to 1785); note the *Café Franklin* on the corner. On the left above Place du Trocadéro is the terraced Cimetière de Passy, enclosed by high walls. Among the prominent people buried here are artists Edouard Manet and Berthe Morisot, composers Debussy and Fauré, and the actor Fernandel. Proceed to the large open space of Trocadéro to fully appreciate still another view of the Eiffel Tower and the Left Bank, as well as the elegance of the stunning, white-stone Palais de Chaillot. Its dazzling twin pavilions and sweeping horizontal lines contrast nicely with the verticality of the Eiffel Tower. Housed in the palace complex are the national theater, the *Cinémathèque,* and several museums: the *Museum of French Monuments,* the *Museum of Man,* the *Maritime Museum,* and the *Cinema Museum.* The gardens are a nice place around which to stroll and unwind, and at night, the verdant area takes on a whole new look when its powerful fountains are illuminated.

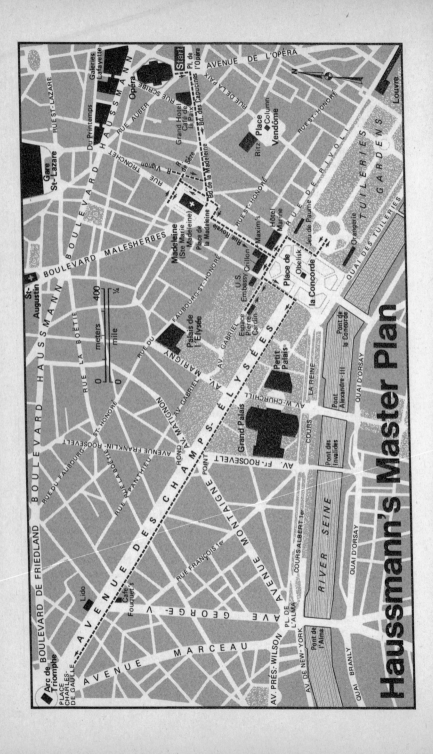

Haussmann's Master Plan

Walk 4: Haussmann's Master Plan

In the middle of the 19th century, Napoleon III gave his urban planner, Baron Georges-Eugène Haussmann, an order: Clean up Paris. The emperor wanted to eliminate the city's warren of narrow streets, which had become the scenes of riots by rambunctious crowds. Haussmann proceeded to tear down much of the capital to make way for broad, tree-lined boulevards, and rather than destroying the city, he created a unique urban unity. His best work was on the Right Bank, where the avenues spread out from the rococo *Opéra.*

This walk begins at the *Opéra,* which, when it was completed in 1875, was touted as the largest theater in the world (though with a capacity of only 2,156, it holds fewer people than the *Vienna Opera House* or *La Scala* in Milan). Designed by Charles Garnier, it covers nearly 3 acres and took 13 years to complete. At one time visitors could enter only if attending a performance; but today its magnificent interior and special exhibitions are open to the public (call first to find out days and hours; phone: 47-42-57-50, ext. 3514). The Place de l'Opéra is intersected by the Boulevard des Capucines and five other main avenues that lead to many of the city's — and the world's — most elegant shops. Just behind the *Opéra,* on Boulevard Haussmann, are Paris's two major department stores, or *grands magasins: Printemps* (No. 64) and *Galeries Lafayette* (No. 40). Shoppers can spend hours wandering from one cosmetic counter to another on the main floor before entering any one of a number of elegant galleries carrying high-fashion designs — at prices to match. Both stores are open Mondays through Saturdays from 9:30 AM to 6:30 PM.

Just outside these department stores are rows of sidewalk displays with clothing and various products for sale. Be sure and shop carefully, as these are operated by private vendors who are not affiliated with the stores.

From the Place de l'Opéra, walk southwest along the Boulevard des Capucines toward La Madeleine. At the corner of Rue Scribe is the monumental 19th-century *Grand* hotel (2 Rue Scribe), which houses the famous *Café de la Paix* (you can also enter at 12 Bd. des Capucines), where generations have come to watch the diverse parade of passersby. Just next door was the equally popular (but no longer standing) *Grand Café.* It was here, on December 28, 1895, that the first public showing of a motion picture was held. In 1990s parlance, it was a bomb; only 33 people (the house held 100), paying 1 franc each, attended the program of 10 short films.

Past the Rue Scribe on the right, where the grand boulevards come to an end, is the Church of St. Mary Magdalene, or La Madeleine. This late Roman adaptation of a Greek temple, constructed between 1764 and 1842, is surrounded by an imposing group of massive Corinthian columns. In 1806, Napoleon Bonaparte had it consecrated as a "Temple of Glory." The bronze doors are adorned with illustrations of the Ten Commandments, and inside there are many distinctive murals and sculptures. It is currently undergoing renovation, but unlike the ugly metal and wood paneling that covers the *Louvre* and Luxembourg Palace reconstructions, the renovation of the Madeleine, scheduled for completion as we went to press, was carried out behind an amusing life-size Impressionist painting of the actual church front. It catches the eye of the *flâneur* (stroller) from as far as the Place de la Concorde. Some will probably even miss it when it is gone.

While other neighborhoods pay homage to haute couture, the Madeleine quarter pays homage to *haute gastronomie*. Near this temple of worship are several culinary "temples" that cater to their own following of gourmands. Just opposite the small flower market next to the Madeleine métro station—and also across the street—is *Fauchon* (26 to 30 Pl. de la Madeleine; phone: 47-42-60-11), with its distinctive chocolate brown logo emblazoned on the walls and canopies of its complex of shops. Whether you choose just to look or to partake, this is the ultimate movable feast. For a detailed description of this gastronomic landmark, see *Quintessential Paris* in DIVERSIONS and *Eating Out* in THE CITY.

Also on Place de la Madeleine (across Rue Tronchet) is *Hédiard* (21 Pl. de la Madeleine; phone: 42-66-44-36), another gastronomic emporium on a smaller scale, with exotic spices, flavored vinegars and oils, and at least 30 varieties of tea. The wine cellar offers an extensive selection (sorry, no bargains). Closed Sundays.

Still in an eating mode, *Maison de la Truffe* (19 Pl. de la Madeleine; phone: 42-65-53-22) is the place to come from November to March for the best fresh truffles. Otherwise, there are preserved truffles from which to choose, and rich foie gras, exotic fruit, and a variety of charcuterie (closed Sundays). *Creplet-Brussol* (17 Pl. de la Madeleine; phone: 42-65-34-32) is regarded as one of the city's best cheese shops. Although the windows are filled with a lot of fancy packaged cheeses, the classic collection of aged brie and fine raw milk camembert, among others, is inside (closed Sundays and Mondays).

In the same building is *Caviar Kaspia* (phone: 42-65-33-52), a simple, straightforward store that specializes in (what else?) caviar. Choose from a selection of well-priced pressed caviar, excellent smoked salmon, and tasty fresh blinis. If you like, go upstairs to their elegant, informal restaurant and sample a few dishes along with a frosty glass of vodka (open from 9 AM to midnight daily except Sundays).

Cross back to *Fauchon* at the corner of Rue de Sèze. Enter Rue de Sèze and turn left on Rue Vignon. Not far from the corner is *La Maison du Miel*

(The House of Honey; 24 Rue Vignon, off La Madeleine; phone: 47-42-26-70), which has been operated by the Galland family at this location since 1908. Devoted totally to honey and honey products, it produces about one-fourth of the 53 tons of honey sold here each year. There are many varieties from which to choose and sample tastings are available (closed Sundays). Just across the street is *La Ferme Saint-Hubert* (No. 21; phone: 47-42-79-20), a compact little shop that has extraordinary varieties of cheese and a friendly staff to advise you. They have one of the best selections of roquefort, dozens of goat cheeses (*chèvres*) from which to choose, and a fine assortment of reasonably priced house wines, as well as bread from the famous *Poilâne* bakery. For a unique experience, visit their adjoining lunchroom/restaurant, which offers special *dégustation* (sampler) plates of cheese and raclette (a melted cheese dish from Switzerland served with boiled potatoes, pickled onions, and *cornichons*) in the evening. Closed Sundays and Mondays.

Return to Rue de Sèze; continue along Rue Vignon and turn right on Boulevard de la Madeleine and then left on Rue Royale. Walk down Rue Royale, past the chic shopping street of Rue du Faubourg-St-Honoré (see *Quintessential Paris,* DIVERSIONS). Directly ahead is *Maxim's* (at No. 3); long a legend for its Belle Epoque decor and atmosphere, it remains a formal and exclusive bastion of fine dining (see *Eating Out,* THE CITY).

At the corner of Rue Royale and Place de la Concorde are two stately mansions designed by Gabriel, with colonnades similar to those at the *Louvre.* The pavilion across the street on the left is the Hôtel de la Marine, now headquarters of the French navy. The pavilion at the right is shared by the French Automobile Club and the *Crillon* hotel, with its discreet sign and elegant gold C's on the door (see *Checking In,* THE CITY). Directly in front is Place de la Concorde, dominated by its famous obelisk. Considered to be one of the finest public squares in the world, with its eight massive statues designed by Gabriel, representing provincial capitals in France, and its two bronze fountains, Place de la Concorde is bounded on the left by the Tuileries Gardens, nearby the Seine and the Concorde Bridge, and on the right by the Avenue des Champs-Elysées. Looking in any direction at this point will bring you face to face with one of the major monuments of Paris.

The central monument of the square is the Obelisk of Luxor. At 75 feet high and weighing more than 220 tons, it is quite similar to its London counterpart, Cleopatra's Needle. The obelisk was presented by the government of Egypt to the government of Louis-Philippe and was erected on its present site between 1834 and 1836. It had quite an ambitious journey: It was removed from the Temple of Luxor and brought to the Nile; it was then shipped 600 miles to Alexandria, where it crossed the Mediterranean and traveled up the Atlantic to Cherbourg, and was finally transported by road through Normandy to Paris. In this same square in 1793 stood a guillotine that took the lives of some 3,000 victims of the Reign of Terror, including King Louis XVI, his queen, Marie-Antoinette, and other members of the royal family. The site was originally called Place Louis-XV, and, afterward, the Place de la Révolution. It was then renamed Place de la Concorde, but altered once again to Place Louis-XVI until 1830, when its present name was restored. The name "Concorde" was given to erase the memory of the deeds performed here.

Cross the street to the Tuileries, a lovely park framed at its western end by two small museums, the *Jeu de Paume* and the *Orangerie,* flanking a large pond that's usually surrounded by children and young couples; at the eastern end of the Tuileries is the *Louvre,* one of the world's greatest museums (see *Special Places* in THE CITY). Cross the Place de la Concorde — carefully, and preferably not directly across the heavily trafficked square — to the park-like, tree-lined street, which is the eastern end of the Champs-Elysées, the most famous thoroughfare in Paris. It was first called the Grand Allée du Roule and, afterward, the Avenue des Tuileries. The American Embassy is on the right at 2 Avenue Gabriel. At No. 1 is *L'Espace Cardin* (phone: 42-66-11-70), a theater complex and restaurant owned by fashion designer Pierre Cardin, who is also the owner of *Maxim's.* You might want to return and see a theatrical or musical performance, or else sample the buffet at the restaurant, with its amusingly funky decor (open daily).

As you continue down the Champs-Elysées, set in a large garden off to the right is the Palais de l'Elysée. A magnificent structure that dates from 1718, it has been the residence of the French president since 1873.

Just ahead is the Rond-Point des Champs-Elysées, a large, circular, flower-filled place at the intersection of Avenues Matignon, Franklin-D.-Roosevelt, and Montaigne. The city of Paris once actually ended at this point; beyond the Arc de Triomphe, there was nothing but suburbs.

It was only after the construction of the *Grand Palais* and *Petit Palais* (they are just to the left) for the *1900 Paris International Exposition* that the Champs-Elysées became the scene of numerous street festivals. Though now considered one of the great promenades of the world, before 1830 it was unsafe to walk here after dark. The only lights were from a few gas lamps, candles shining from small retail shops, and the red lanterns of the orange vendors' stands. These days, many of the bright lights belong to fast-food franchises, which intrude on the ambience of this high-rent neighborhood.

Once lined only by private hotels and mansions, the area grew to include banks, corporate headquarters, luxury shops, and a number of automobile dealers; during the last few decades, many large cinemas with attached shopping complexes were built on both sides of the broad street, as well as more restaurants and cafés to accommodate the growing number of visitors. *Café Fouquet's* (pronounced Foo-*kett*) is on the left (99 Champs-Elysées, at the corner of Av. George-V; phone: 47-23-70-60). It is definitely the most famous of the cafés along the route, for decades the place for *tout* Paris to see and be seen (open daily).

Directly ahead is the Arc de Triomphe, and Place Charles-de-Gaulle (l'Etoile). The large, circular traffic hub from which 12 avenues radiate into various parts of the city is the centerpiece of Baron Haussmann's inspired master plan. The famous arch — as synonymous with Paris as the Eiffel Tower — crowns the long vista of the Champs-Elysées. Conceived by Napoleon I to commemorate his victories of 1805–6 and later in memory of the Unknown Soldier, it was at the time the largest monument of its kind in the world. In front of the arch are four amazing groups of statuary symbolizing triumph, peace, resistance, and departure. A 260-step climb up to the platform at the top is rewarded by a magnificent view of the city, including the Champs-Elysées and the Bois de Boulogne. (The platform can also be reached by elevator.) A small museum under the platform contains souvenirs relating to Napoleon I, the Arc de Triomphe, and both world wars.

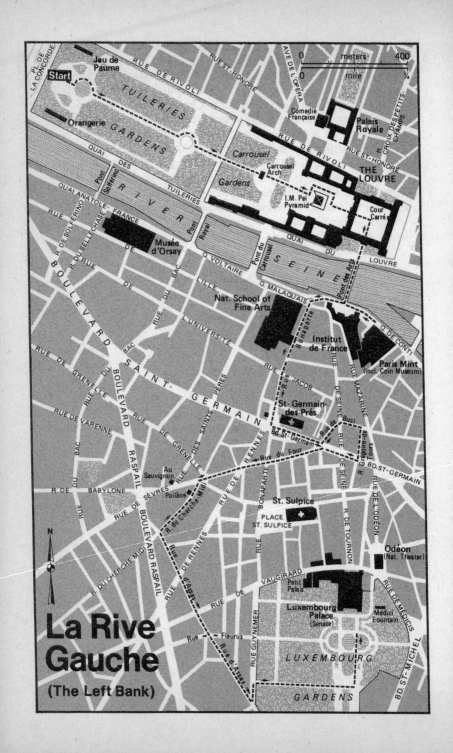

La Rive Gauche

(The Left Bank)

Walk 5: La Rive Gauche (The Left Bank): From the Louvre to the Latin Quarter

Begin this walk on the Right Bank, at the main entrance to the Tuileries Gardens, at the east side of the Place de la Concorde. Designed by Lenôtre, the celebrated landscape gardener of Louis XIV, the main path of the gardens crosses through the center and leads straight to the *Louvre*. The Tuileries were originally commissioned in 1563 by Catherine de Médici, the queen mother, who wanted an Italianate park next to the palace (now the *Louvre*) that she shared with King Henri II. These were to be no ordinary gardens; they would include fountains, a maze, a grotto, and a menagerie. It is said that the Tuileries epitomize formal French design. Years later, sensual sculptures by Maillol were placed on the lawns, as were busts of prominent figures, like Lenôtre, and mythical figures, like Mercury, the messenger of the gods, who sits here atop his winged horse.

The Tuileries were enlarged in 1889 with more garden space created on the site of the former Tuileries palace, which was destroyed by the Communards during the Revolution. It remains the most popular promenade in Paris, most likely because of its central location. Nannies stroll with baby carriages; lovers embrace on benches; mimes entertain among groves of trees; lines of schoolchildren wait for ice cream cones at a kiosk; and in a nearby pond, charming miniature sailboats complete this idyllic Parisian parkscape.

As you enter, on the immediate left is the *Jeu de Paume,* and on the right, the *Orangerie.* Each of these elegant pavilions was built during the Second Empire and has served as an art gallery since the turn of the 20th century. Before the main works of the collection were moved to the *Musée d'Orsay,* the *Jeu de Paume* was known for its Impressionist exhibitions. The *Orangerie* holds temporary exhibitions, in addition to housing the prestigious Walter-Guillaume collection, which includes works by Picasso, Matisse, Cézanne, Modigliani, Renoir, Monet, and others. For more information see *Special Places* in THE CITY. The museums in the Tuileries are closed on Tuesdays.

To the left outside the Tuileries is Rue de Rivoli, with its uniformly designed 19th-century arcades of bookstores, cafés, hotels, and boutiques.

To the far right are the quays bordering the Seine. Walk a while, look back, and enjoy the panoramic view, impressive despite the renovations currently taking place around the *Louvre* complex (which should be complete by 1996). The *Louvre* enjoys the distinction of being the largest museum in the world, and when the renovation is completed — including an ambitious plan for a new bridge and pedestrian pathway linking the *Musée d'Orsay* and the Palais Royale — that distinction will surely be unrivaled (also see *Special Places* in THE CITY).

Stroll around the glass pyramid, designed by I. M. Pei, for an entirely updated perspective of the former fortress/palace. Some (like us) believe that the Egyptian-inspired design is out of place here. Continue straight ahead to the last building, the Cour Carrée (Square Court), considered to be the most impressive of the old *Louvre* buildings. Walk through the elegant courtyard and out the door to the right toward the Seine. Enjoy the impressive view across the Pont des Arts (Bridge of Arts), taking in the domed complex of the Institute of France across the river, on the Left Bank. Cross the Pont des Arts to the institute, which encompasses several prestigious academies. Designed by Levau and opened in 1688, it was a poor contrast to his more illustrious monument across the Seine (the *Louvre*). Even though the buildings were meant to complement one another, the institute was actually considered one of the prominent architect's failures.

The institute has had an interesting history as a college for scholars, and is notorious for its former exclusion of women and for the notable male candidates it has refused. Among the rejects were Descartes, Pascal, Molière, Proust, Balzac, and Zola. Today, it accepts women members; author Marguerite Yourcenar was the first to be admitted (in 1980). The institute incorporates the French Academy and the schools of Fine Arts, Literature, Science, and Political Science.

To the left of this rarefied intellectual complex is the Hôtel des Monnaies (Paris Mint), a fine, unpretentious building by Antoine, who lived here until his death in 1801. The *Musée de la Monnaie,* with its wonderful collection of coins and exhibitions on the art of engraving, is on the premises (closed Mondays and holidays; phone: 40-46-55-33). Walk west along the Quai de Conti and then the Quai Malaquais to the National School of Fine Arts at the corner of Rue Bonaparte. This former monastery was founded in 1608 and closed down in 1791. It later became the *Museum of French Monuments,* displaying busts and statues from other monuments that had been destroyed. The school was created at the time of the Revolution by the union of the Painting and Sculpture Academy and the Architecture School. Although the museum was closed in 1816, it is still possible to tour the courtyard today to see some of the monuments (entrance is at 14 Rue Bonaparte).

Turn up Rue Bonaparte to see rows of exclusive and pricey antiques shops and art galleries. This narrow street dates to 1250, and today it can barely accommodate the steady flow of city traffic crossing from the Left to the Right Bank. Walk a bit farther to the Boulevard St-Germain. On the left is the Eglise St-Germain-des-Prés; to the right is the *Café Les Deux Magots* (No. 170), said to be the birthplace of Surrealism. Just next door is *Café de Flore* (No. 172), long the existentialist hangout where Jean-Paul Sartre and Simone de Beauvoir held court over *café espresso*. Each is worth a visit, depending on where your nostalgic loyalties lie, and if you don't mind paying inflated prices to soak in the ambience of people watching people, which is basically what happens here. On weekend nights, this stretch of boulevard is the place to get a front-row seat to watch the lively stream of street entertainers — from mimes to fire eaters to acrobats. *Café de Flore* is closed in July; *Café Les Deux Magots* is closed in August.

Across the street at *Brasserie Lipp* (No. 151; phone: 45-48-53-91), politicians rub well-tailored elbows with the fashion and publishing crowds who work in the surrounding quarter. It is so crowded that one's only chance to sample the house specialty of *choucroute* is in the Siberia section in the upper dining room. This Alsatian combination plate of sausages, smoked meat, and sauerkraut found its way into the French capital during the middle of the 19th century, when there was a large immigration of people from the Alsace region into Paris. Many of them opened brasseries (which are beer halls distinguished by their brass dispensers). There are reports these days that even some *Lipp* regulars are saying the food here has lost much of its charm, so why not just settle for a glass of Alsatian beer and take in the atmosphere. Closed Mondays and in July.

Cross the street once again and visit the unassuming St-Germain-des-Prés, the oldest church in Paris. Originally founded about 543 by Childebert I, it belonged to the powerful Benedictine Monastery of St. Germain. It was built on the advice of St. Germain, the Bishop of Paris, who is buried here.

After leaving the church, turn left down Boulevard St-Germain, taking a left at Rue de Buci. This is where Paris's most expensive, and usually jam-packed, market street begins. Here (each morning until noon) are a jumble of fruit, vegetable, and *fromage* vendors alongside fish dealers, bread sellers, and meat merchants. If you don't want to grab a bite here — or would like to sit down — why not go to where many of the market vendors themselves go: *Orestia's* Greek taverna (4 Rue Grégoire-de-Tours; phone: 43-54-62-01), around the corner. Here you will squeeze into rickety chairs and sit at a long table with tourists and locals from all walks of life. Founded in 1929, this place is as busy and noisy as it is welcoming and friendly. Try the mixed appetizer plate, and if you want to please the waiter, order retsina, the unique resin-flavored wine called the "Blood of the Gods."

Walk south on Rue Grégoire-de-Tours and turn right at Boulevard St-Germain onto Rue du Four, which leads to a busy crossroads. For a delightful shoppers' detour, continue into Rue de Sèvres, or turn left to Rue de Rennes; either way, this area has shop after shop of fashionable clothing by such famous designers as *Issey Miyake* (201 Bd. St-Germain), *Dorothée Bis* (33 Rue de Sèvres), and *Sonia Rykiel* (6 Rue de Grenelle). Or stop for a bite at *Au Sauvignon* (80 Rue des Sts-Pères, at the corner of Rue de Sèvres; phone: 45-48-49-02). Try their special sandwiches, with either the thin-sliced *jambon* (ham), a light pâté, or a mellow *chèvre* (goat cheese), served on bite-size pieces of delicious bread from *Poilâne*. Try a glass of either red or white sauvignon, bottled especially for the café. Closed Sundays, 2 weeks in January, *Easter,* and the month of August.

Those who enjoyed the bread should visit the *Poilâne* bakery shop, around the corner from the café, at 8 Rue du Cherche-Midi. There will probably be lines of customers waiting to buy the trademark flour-dusted sourdough loaves. Available also by the slice, it is sold by the ounce. Their apple tarts are also worth tasting. If the place is not too hectic, visit the basement and watch the bread being mixed, kneaded, and baked in ancient wood-burning ovens. Open from 7 AM to 8 PM daily, except Sundays.

Walk past *Poilâne* and turn left at the upcoming street, Rue d'Assas, which will lead to a side entrance of the Luxembourg Gardens and the adjacent palace. Along the way, there are interesting shops, galleries, and old bookstores through which to browse. *J-C & C* (16 Rue d'Assas) is an aromatic tea shop with a good selection of tea and coffee, as well as an unusual selection of tea-flavored honey and jam.

Continuing down Rue d'Assas, briefly turn left onto Rue Fleurus, where Gertrude Stein once resided with Alice B. Toklas at No. 27. There were many spirited salons held here, with the likes of Picasso and Hemingway sparring for attention.

Continue down Rue d'Assas and enter through the gate of the Luxembourg Gardens on Rue Guynemer. These surrounding streets were originally part of the garden complex, developed after 1870. The Jardins du Luxembourg were built in 1613 on the site of an ancient Roman encampment, and a 13th-century convent of Chartreux. When the monastery was demolished in 1790, the surrounding gardens were enlarged and remodeled. There are several entrances to this park: Boulevard St-Michel, Rue de Vaugirard near the historic *Odéon* theater, Rue Guynemer, and the Avenue de l'Observatoire.

The impressive Palais du Luxembourg at Rue de Vaugirard was originally built between 1615 and 1620 for Marie de Médici, mother of Louis XIII. It was inhabited by successive generations of the royal family until the time of Louis XVI. During the dark days of World War II, it served as German Air Force headquarters. It now houses the French Senate. Guided tours of the palace are conducted on the first Sunday of the month; for information, contact the Caisse Nationale des Monuments Historiques (admission charge; phone: 44-61-21-70).

The Petit Palais next door is now the home of the President of the

Senate, and it includes the original Hôtel de Luxembourg that Marie de Médici presented to Cardinal Richelieu as a residence.

These gardens are, after the Tuileries, one of the more favored of the Parisian promenades, particularly during the summer when many outdoor concerts are held here. Each section of the park is different, with tennis courts, pony rides, a large fountain with toy sailboats gliding by. A relief of Leda and the Swan is one of the more original examples of the statuary; located near the Médicis fountain, it is worth seeing. In addition to the ubiquitous park benches, there are hundreds of chairs that people can freely move to a spot of their choice. This is indeed a tranquil setting in which to conclude this tour of the Left Bank.

For those who aren't tired, cross the Boulevard St-Michel and walk toward the Seine (about a block). Here is the center of Parisian student life, the Latin Quarter — so named because classes used to be conducted in Latin — an area rife with cafés that welcome scholars (very few of whom speak Latin these days) and visitors alike. The boulevard opens up onto a square, dominated by the Eglise de là Sorbonne, with university buildings surrounding it. Founded in 1256, the Sorbonne is the oldest university in Paris; although it still has a certain cachet, it has fallen far behind the Grandes Ecoles in prestige. Many of the most famous institutions of French intellectual life, including the Collège de France, Ecole Polytechnique and Lycée Louis le Grand, where Molière, Voltaire, and Robespierre studied, also have their headquarters in this neighborhood.

Behind the Sorbonne, the Rue St-Jacques leads to Rue Soufflot, named in honor of Germain Soufflot, the original architect of the vast, domed Panthéon. Commissioned by Louis XV in 1744 and finished only in 1789 the church is of interest mainly because it houses the remains of Voltaire, Zola, and Rousseau. It was here that Socialist François Mitterrand held his first large rally after winning the presidency in 1981. The intellectual, book-loving Mitterrand makes his home in this neighborhood on nearby Rue de Bièvre. In fact, the French president often can be seen strolling the narrow streets here.

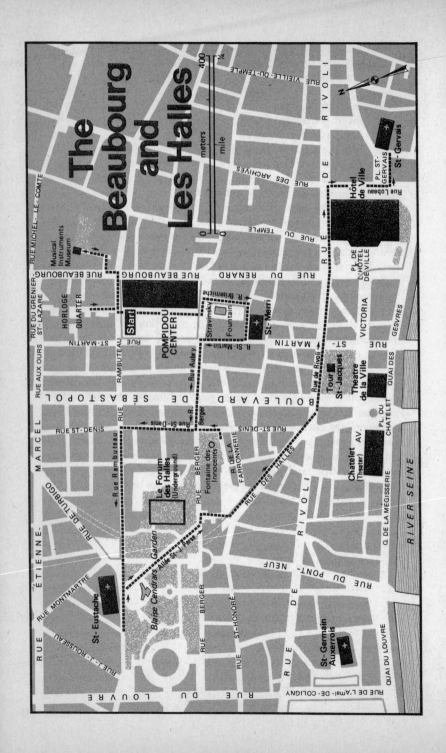

The Beaubourg and Les Halles

RUE ÉTIENNE-

RUE DE TURBIGO

RUE MONTMARTRE

RUE J.-J.-ROUSSEAU

St-Eustache

Blaise Cendrars Garden

Allée St.-J. Perse

Rue Rambuteau

Le Forum des Halles (Underground)

RUE BERGER

BERGER

Fontaine des Innocents

RUE ST-DENIS

RUE ST-DENIS

RUE ST-HONORÉ

RUE DE LA FERRONNERIE

RUE DES HALLES

RUE DE RIVOLI

RUE DU PONT-NEUF

QUAI DU LOUVRE

RUE DE L'AMAI.-DE-COLIGNY

St-Germain Auxerrois

Q. DE LA MÉGISSERIE

RIVER SEINE

PL. DU CHATELET

Chatelet (Theater)

CHATELET AV.

QUAI DES

Théatre de la Ville

Tour St-Jacques

Rue de Rivoli

ST- MARTIN

RUE DE RIVOLI

BOULEVARD DE SÉBASTOPOL

RUE RAMBUTEAU

RUE AUX OURS

RUE ST-DENIS

M A R C E L

RUE ST-MARTIN

RUE ST-MARTIN

RUE ST-MARTIN

R. St-Martin

Rue St-Denis

R. Berger

Rue Aubry

POMPIDOU CENTER

Start

HORLOGE QUARTER

RUE DU GRENIER- ST-LAZARE

RUE MICHEL- LE- COMTE

Musical Instruments Museum

RUE BEAUBOURG

RUE BEAUBOURG

R. Brisemiche

Stravinsky Fountain

St- Merri

RUE DU RENARD

VICTORIA

GESVRES

RUE DU TEMPLE

RUE DES ARCHIVES

RUE VIEILLE-DU-TEMPLE

D E R I V O L I

Hôtel de Ville

PL. DE L'HÔTEL DE VILLE

Rue Lobeau

PL. ST- GERVAIS

St-Gervais

N

0 ¼ mile

0 400 meters

Walk 6: The Beaubourg, Les Halles, and the Hôtel de Ville

Le Centre Georges-Pompidou and the bustle of the Beaubourg, with its street entertainers, have become a center for international youth of all ages. One either loves it or detests it; there is no middle ground. The *Centre Georges-Pompidou* was built on the initiative of former President Georges Pompidou, to create a multipurpose cultural center and regenerate life into the neighborhood following the demise of the old *Les Halles* food markets. Unfortunately, one can only imagine the once colorful hustle and bustle of Paris's colorful wholesale market, the scents and sights, and especially the bowl of onion soup one could always get on a cold morning at the height of the near-dawn shopping hours.

Begin the walk by exploring the Horloge Quarter, just north of the *Centre Georges-Pompidou,* between Rue Beaubourg and Rue St-Martin. This is another pedestrian area with a lot of shops, and although the neighborhood is still experiencing transition, it is a dynamic melting pot with a real sense of street life. The landmark *horloge* (clock) is an unusual design of brass and steel that is electronically operated by a life-size figure, known as "the defender of time." Not far to the east, at the end of the Impasse Berthaud off Rue Beaubourg, is the *Musée de la Musique Méchanique* (open Saturdays, Sundays, and holidays from 2 to 7 PM), whose collection includes over 100 mechanical reproducers of music dating from the late 19th century.

The *Centre Georges-Pompidou* is a futuristic concoction of steel and glass and piping with bright colors, like a surrealistic refinery.

What you first notice are the oversize see-through escalators, which look like giant caterpillars transporting a constant flux of people up and into the building. The piazza, which is directly in front of the main entrance, is swarming with spectators and the ubiquitous fire eaters, jugglers, musicians, and mimes. Be aware that there may be pickpockets around.

Take the time to visit the center, which in addition to housing the *National Museum of Modern Art* and the *Industrial Design Center* also boasts a public information library and an Institute for Acoustic and Musical Research. The permanent collection of contemporary art traces modern art's roots back to Fauvism and Cubism. There is something for every taste, from Picasso and Matisse to Mondrian, Rauschenberg, and Warhol. The temporary exhibitions are always quite spectacular, and the bookstore and poster shop are also worth a visit. Go up the escalator to the fifth floor and step outside for a view of Paris's distinctive rooftops. The café is a nice place to relax before moving on, or stay awhile for one of the classic films shown at the center.

Once back at the entrance, leave the building and walk to the left for a pleasant and peaceful diversion. Place Igor-Stravinsky is the site of a delightful pool-size fountain, a creation that is a collaboration between the playful artists Nikki de Saint-Phalle and Jean Tinguely. In homage to the works of the great composer of *The Firebird* and *Rite of Spring,* colorful Saint-Phalle creations, including water-spouting lips, twirling female torsos, and a dancing skeleton, all happily interact with the animated black steel sculptures of Tinguely.

Walk gingerly, taking care not to be sprayed by the fountain. Consider this fountain to be a little satire on the monumental fountains that have long graced Paris's boulevards. You are in the St-Merri quarter of Beaubourg, the name of the old village that stood on this site in the 12th century. At the southern end of the Place Igor-Stravinsky is the Eglise St-Merri, the name being a corruption of St. Mederic, a monk who lived in a cell until his death in 700. The church dates from 1612, when the tower was finally completed, but it was actually built in its unusual Gothic style during the reign of François I, between 1520 and 1530. If you would like to stay in a hotel in the area with bizarre furnishings, try the *St. Merri* (78 Rue de la Verrerie; phone: 42-78-14-15) just beyond the church.

After circling the Stravinsky fountain, follow the crowds on the pedestrian road west on Rue Aubry, cross the Boulevard de Sébastopol into Rue Berger, and enjoy the active street life around the Fontaine des Innocents. The fountain itself is a Renaissance work by Pierre Lescot — much altered and restored — that once adorned the old *Marché des Innocents* (which preceded the *Halles* market) and also graced the Church of Innocents.

There are several cafés along this pedestrian area, which borders *Le Forum des Halles.* One of the more popular ones is *Café Costes* (Pl. des Innocents; phone: 45-08-54-39), a post-modern–looking place designed by French wunderkind Philippe Starck. Prices are expensive, and even more so at one of the sought-after outdoor tables. Always remember that there is a three-level price structure — for dining outdoors, sitting indoors, and standing at the bar. When you sit on a terrace on a lovely day with a good vantage point, you are literally "renting" your chair. But it is worth a visit just for the contrast in design compared to other more typical French cafés. Open daily.

After leaving the café, follow Rue St-Denis north; turn left on Rue Rambuteau and continue to St-Eustache, considered to be one of Paris's most beautiful churches after Notre-Dame. A mixture of late Gothic and Renaissance architecture constructed between 1532 and 1637, the front portion of the church, with its Ionic and Doric columns, was added in 1778. The church is known for its organ, one of the finest and largest in the city; it is here that Berlioz and Liszt composed some of their finest works. The white marble altar, with its sculptured canopy, is also remarkable. The church's collection of 16th- and 17th-century paintings, sculpture, and painted glass is definitely worth noting. Across the street, visible from the church, is the underground *Forum des Halles* complex of shops, food outlets, and movie houses. The gigantic *FNAC* store sells everything from stereos and cameras to books and records at discount prices; another diversion is a walk through the Blaise Cendrars garden, which is between the church and *Le Forum des Halles*.

After passing through the gardens, cross Rue Berger and go through Passage des Lingères to get to Rue des Halles. Our favorite shop in the neighborhood is *Papeterie Moderne* (12 Rue de la Ferronnerie; phone: 42-36-21-72), which for decades has been the source of many of the city's signs. You can choose from among hundreds of typical Parisian signs or else have your own made to order: everything from the ordinary *"défense de fumer"* (no smoking) to an 18th-century saying outside a cemetery: *"De par le roi, défense à Dieu, de faire miracle en ce lieu"* (By order of the king, even God isn't allowed to work any miracles here). Open daily from 7:30 AM to noon and 1 to 7 PM; closed Sundays and two weeks in August.

For a change of scenery, walk down Rue des Halles to Rue de Rivoli. Turn left at Rue de Rivoli and continue to the Hôtel de Ville, about a 5-minute walk. On the way, notice the 16th-century Tour St-Jacques, the former belfry of a church torn down in 1802. A statue of the scientist-philosopher Blaise Pascal is in the tower. The Place de l'Hôtel de Ville, originally known as the Place du Grève until 1830, was the scene of many important historical events. From 1310 until 1832, public executions took place here, and Dr. Guillotin's machine was first put into action on humans on April 25, 1792, before being moved to the Place de la Concorde. Foulon, one of the first victims of the Revolution, was hanged here by a mob whom he had exasperated by saying that "the hungry should eat grass."

During the late 1800s it was a meeting place for men waiting in line for jobs, specifically those in the building trade. On some mornings as many as 4,000 men were assembled, with only a few gendarmes on duty to keep the road clear. The Hôtel de Ville (1533–1628), or Town Hall (city government building), has always been considered one of the city's most splendid buildings. The design of the present building is French Renaissance, with distinctive mansard windows and sculpture-adorned columns. Statues grace the courtyard and gilded figures decorate the roof. It was rebuilt between 1878 and 1882, with alterations and enlargements very much along the lines of the original Town Hall, which was burned down during the fierce street fights in the days ending the Commune in 1871.

Close to the Hôtel de Ville is the Eglise St-Gervais–St-Protais, built between 1616 and 1621, the first example of the imposing classical-style façade in Paris. The interior maintains the 17th-century theme with its finely carved stalls. The organ, said to be the oldest in Paris, was built in 1601. The elm tree that stands in the square was, according to medieval custom, the place where people came to pay their taxes. Naturally, sometimes some of them didn't show up, and the cynical expression "Wait for me under the elm tree" was born. So if you find yourself exhausted by this final walk, and longing only for a comfortable place to rest, fear not. There's no one under the elm tree — except for a few squirrels.

Walk 7: The Marais

Begin at the Place de la Bastille, a historic intersection of several important thoroughfares connecting the 4th, 11th, and 12th *arrondissements,* where many events of the 1789 Revolution took place. Until the end of the 18th century, the formidable Bastille stood here. Originally built in 1369 by Charles V as a castle to defend Old Paris against the English, it later became the infamous, dreaded state prison. For some inmates, conditions were not as horrendous as one would imagine; it is rumored that some prisoners had the privilege of inviting guests over for multi-course banquets. But then, there are as many myths as truths associated with the Bastille.

Among the detainees was the so-called Man in the Iron Mask, imprisoned by Louis XIV (his mask was actually black velvet); rumors have it that he was the twin brother of the king. The writer Voltaire, who was locked up on two different occasions for writing inflammatory pamphlets (in 1717 and 1726), is said to have spread that rumor himself. After Paris was leveled in 1682, the Bastille remained standing; it was ordered destroyed after the Revolution on July 14, 1789, an event celebrated annually as *Bastille Day*. A thousand workmen were employed to raze the prison, and trumpets proclaimed the news at all the crossroads of the city. The contractor of the demolition sold some of the stones as souvenirs, but others were used to build the Pont de la Concorde (Concorde Bridge).

Begin at the Column of July, a handsome, 154-foot-tall pillar that was built in 1840. The column, which rests on a white marble base, bears the name of 615 combatants who struggled for liberty in July of 1830 and 1848. They are interred beneath the column.

Today, on the former site of the Bastille is the controversial opera house designed by Carlos Ott, which opened in 1989. The 2,700-seat auditorium presents lyric and contemporary opera, and bears an uncanny likeness to a modern prison-fortress.

Cross the large intersection near the Column of July (opposite the opera complex) and walk down fashionable Rue St-Antoine. Look to the right down the Rue de Birague. At the end of this narrow street is a good view of the façade of the King's Pavilion and the Place des Vosges, a spot of unique historical interest. But first proceed on Rue St-Antoine to the Hôtel de Sully (No. 62), one of the most beautiful old houses in Paris. It was built in 1624 by a Monsieur Gallet, a gambler who was also the controller of finances. In 1634, Gallet lost his house in a game of cards to Count Sully, a minister of Henri IV. Enter the Hôtel de Sully's first courtyard, which is filled with sculptured wall reliefs that are allegories of the changing seasons. Take the small passageway into the garden, where you face a former *orangerie* (orange grove). Continue through the narrow door on the far right to the southwestern corner of the Place des Vosges.

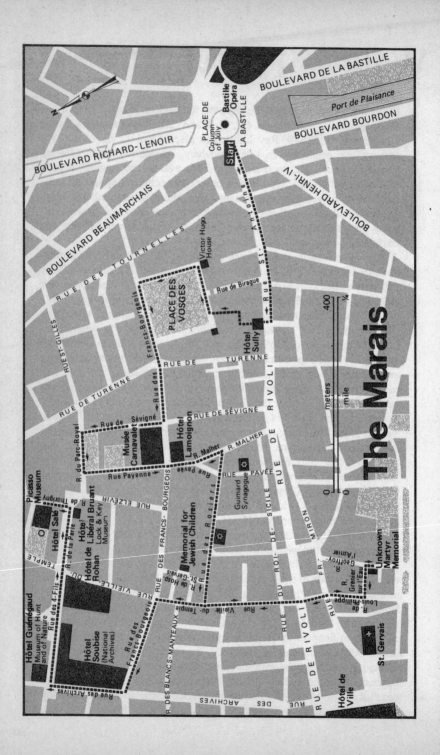

The Marais

BOULEVARD DE LA BASTILLE

Port de Plaisance

BOULEVARD BOURDON

Bastille
Opéra

PLACE DE
LA BASTILLE

Column
of July

Start

BOULEVARD RICHARD-LENOIR

BOULEVARD BEAUMARCHAIS

BOULEVARD HENRI-IV

RUE DES TOURNELLES

Victor Hugo
House

PLACE DES
VOSGES

Rue de Birague

RUE ST-GILLES

Francs-Bourgeois

RUE DE TURENNE

Hôtel
Sully

RUE DE
TURENNE

Rue des

R. du Parc-Royal

Rue de

Sévigné

RUE DE SÉVIGNÉ

RUE DE RIVOLI

Musée
Carnavalet

Hôtel
Lamoignon

R. Malher

R. MALHER

Rue Payenne

Rue Pavée

RUE
PAVÉE

Picasso
Museum

Hôtel Salé

R. de Thorigny

Rue de la Perle

Hôtel de
Libéral Bruant

Lock & Key
Museum

RUE ELZEVIR

RUE DES FRANCS-BOURGEOIS

Guimard
Synagogue

RUE DE SICILE

Hôtel Guénégaud
Museum of Hunt
and of Nature

Hôtel de
Rohan

RUE VIEILLE-DU-TEMPLE

Memorial for
Jewish Children

Rue des Rosiers

RUE DE SICILE

FR. MIRON

Unknown
Martyr
Memorial

R. des 4-Fils

Rue des
Francs-Bourgeois

RUE DES FRANCS-BOURGEOIS

R. de Hosp. St-Gervais

Rue Vieille-du-Temple

R.
Geoffroy
l'Asnier

R.
Grenier
sur l'Eau

R. de
Louis-Philippe

Hôtel
Soubise
(National
Archives)

Rue des Archives

R. DES BLANCS-MANTEAUX

RUE DU ROI-DE-SICILE

RUE DE RIVOLI

RUE DE RIVOLI

RUE
DES
ARCHIVES

Hôtel de
Ville

St. Gervais

0 meters 400 ¼

0 mile

If this door could speak, it would recount the adventures of Madame Sully, the young wife of Count Sully, who was told by her much older husband to divide her monthly household allowance into three equal parts — "for the house, yourself, and your lovers. Just be discreet and have them use the back door."

The Place des Vosges, once known as the Place Royale (it was a courtyard of a royal palace), is at the site where Henri II accidentally met his death in a tournament in 1559. When the court was removed to the *Louvre* after that tragedy, the deserted courtyard became a horse market, and was also used as a dueling ground. In an attempt to beautify Paris in 1605, Henri IV had the Place des Vosges constructed as it is today; soon it became the fashionable address of more celebrities than any other residential area in Paris — among them were Richelieu, Madame de Sévigné, Prince de Condé, and Molière. This was the center of Parisian social life, the place where some of the sophisticated residents held *ruelles,* intimate gatherings at which the elegant and witty guests attempted to rival each other in repartee and social one-upmanship. These rituals, which preceded the popular salons of the 18th century, were parodied by Molière in his play *Précieuses Ridicules.*

The fashionable neighborhood became known as Place des Vosges after a unique incident in 1800 when Lucien Bonaparte (minister of finance and Napoleon's brother) announced that the first *département* to pay its entire taxes on time would have the honor of having a street named after it. The Department of Vosges was the first to pay its full contribution, and the name was eventually changed. (Note the irony that the Rue des Francs-Bourgeois, which traverses the northern end of the square, got its name in the 15th century for the poor people who lived there in almshouses and *didn't* have to pay any taxes.) Enter the Place des Vosges from the Hôtel de Sully; follow the arcades to the right to the next corner, passing the hallway of the King's Pavilion. At the corner, at No. 6, is the house of Victor Hugo, now a museum. The objects of interest include pictures by many well-known artists illustrating the great writer's works, as well as sketches by Hugo himself, who was quite a fine draftsman. Among the collection of inkstands and pens belonging to him and his peers — Dumas, Lamartine, and George Sand — is his chest-high writing table (he wrote standing up) and the bed on which he died. As you leave the Victor Hugo home, stroll on through the arcades of the Place des Vosges. Today they are occupied by expensive shops, a popular corner café, and one of Paris's most exclusive restaurants, *L'Ambroisie* (No. 9; phone: 42-78-51-45). This is the showcase for chef Bernard Pacaud's elegant culinary talents, and has earned three Michelin stars. It is very expensive and reservations are necessary. Closed Sundays, Monday lunch, the month of August, and holidays. Enter the park, where couples stroll, children play, and busy city life seems to be suspended, and have a drink or snack at *Ma Bourgogne* (No. 19; phone: 42-78-44-64), a popular meeting place since 1920 for tourists and locals alike. Try their specialty of sausages from Auvergne with a glass of burgundy or bordeaux wine.

When leaving, turn left on Rue des Francs-Bourgeois and walk directly into the historic Marais quarter. Turn right at Rue de Sévigné; at No. 23 is the *Musée Carnavalet* (open Tuesdays through Sundays from 10 AM to 5:30 PM; admission charge; phone: 42-72-21-13), the residence of Madame de Sévigné in the 17th century. However, the museum derives its name from the widow of François de Kernevenoy (corrupted to Carnavalet), tutor to Henri III, who bought it in 1572. It was built in 1550 by the architect Pierre Lescot, and over the years had many embellishments added by other architects, especially when it was officially designated as a museum. Its collection includes mementos of Madame de Sévigné, as well as exhibitions on the history of Paris from the era of François I to the turn-of-the century Belle Epoque. The gift shop has a wealth of items, from T-shirts to interesting objets d'art.

Leave the *Carnavalet Museum* and walk left up Rue de Sévigné to the end. Turn left into the Rue du Parc-Royal. At the Square Achille on the corner, the visitor is literally surrounded by the many elegant hôtels in the area. (Note that the term "hôtel" originally referred to the large and elegant city residences of the nobility, not the French equivalent of a Hilton or Holiday Inn.) Continue down Rue Payenne; at the corner of Rue des Francs-Bourgeois is *Marais Plus* (20 Rue des Francs-Bourgeois), a delightful bookstore, gift shop, and tea salon. Still on Rue Payenne, bear left to Rue Malher, with the post office on the right and the Hôtel de Lamoignon on the left. The hotel was originally built in 1585 by Robert de Beauvais, the comptroller general of the city of Paris. It was bought in 1658 by Lamoignon, the president of the French Parliament, and was the site of many dazzling soirees.

During the 18th century, the Marais started to lose its fashionable cachet as the aristocracy and their social activities moved on to the area around the Concorde and Faubourg-St-Honoré. Many of the superb palaces were divided up into apartments, or turned over to trade. The entire area became industrialized and was a center of small businesses and crafts shops well into the early part of the 20th century. After the Second World War, the trend reversed again as Parisians who had settled in the distant suburbs sought to live within the heart of the city once more. Renewal of the Marais district began after 1972, and there was no lack of people who wanted to live here — especially at such reasonable rents. In recent years, however, with the proliferation of chic shops that have spread through the quarter, it once again has a fashionable image and is no longer a low-rent district.

Walk ahead on Rue Malher and turn right into the narrow Rue des Rosiers, the heart of Paris's Jewish quarter. It was here that the Jews came at the end of the 19th century when they fled the pogroms of Eastern Europe, and still again after fleeing the Nazis in Germany. (This is also the street down which the Nazis marched as they led 75,000 Jews to concentration camps.) As a result of the French exodus from Algeria, a third wave of Jews settled in the Marais. Like New York City's Lower East Side, it is a hectic neighborhood, whose streets are always blocked with traffic. These days, the traffic is not the fashionable carriages of years gone by, but a stubborn ballet of bicycles, motorcycle couriers, and assorted French automobiles competing for the right of way. Walk through the Rue des Rosiers and its surrounding streets with its small neighborhood synagogues, kosher meat markets (with signs that say *strictement cachère*), and shops that sell Jewish artifacts, and you are in a totally different part of Paris. (Be aware that most shops here are closed on Saturdays and open Sundays.) Walk to Rue Pavée, a tiny street off Rue des Rosiers and near Rue Malher. At 10 Rue Pavée is the synagogue built in 1913 by Hector Guimard, the famous Art Nouveau architect of the métro. The design recalls the shape of the tablets of the Ten Commandments. If you are there on a Saturday morning, the doors will be open.

Back again to Rue des Rosiers; drop in to *Le Loir dans la Théière* (The Dormouse in the Teapot; No. 3; phone: 42-72-90-61), a cozy tearoom in a loft-like space with long wooden tables and comfortable chairs. At the counter, choose from a display of delicious homemade pastries. Relax in the Alice in Wonderland ambience, then look around at their art and photo gallery. Closed Mondays. Stop at *Jo Goldenberg's* (No. 7; phone: 48-87-20-16), a traditional Jewish delicatessen with very Parisian prices, yet still a good spot to take a break; try the mushroom and barley soup. Open daily. Farther up the road on the left is *Café des Psaumes* (No. 14; phone: 48-04-74-77), which serves kosher specialties Sundays through Friday afternoons. A number of Judaica shops, stocked with gifts and artworks, are in the area; a good place to browse (or buy) is *Diasporama* (No. 20; phone: 42-78-30-50). A definite culinary experience is a falafel on pita while wandering these narrow streets. This Middle Eastern treat of mashed chick-peas fried up and served with roasted eggplant, carrots, and a tasty yogurt sauce is healthy fuel and a bargain at around $3.50. There are several stands along the road; *L'As du Falafel* (No. 34; phone: 48-87-63-60) is one of the most popular. Closed Friday evenings and Saturdays. A bit farther, at the corner of Rue des Rosiers and Rue des Hospitalières-St-Gervais, is *Chez Marianne* (No. 2; phone: 42-72-18-86), a restaurant and falafel stand that is one of our favorites. The tables upstairs and downstairs always seem to be full, but it's worth the wait for the tasty buffet. Otherwise, buy a falafel from their take-out window and continue walking. Closed Fridays.

Turn right onto Rue des Hospitalières-St-Gervais and notice a school with a placard that is a memorial to hundreds of Jewish children who were sent to war camps. There is a bench where you can sit a moment to reflect. Another memorial worth a visit is a building that serves as a tribute to the Unknown Jewish Martyr (at 17 Rue Geoffroy-l'Asnier; to get there, turn left from Rue des Rosiers down Rue Vielle-du-Temple, and left on Rue Grenier sur l'Eau). Dedicated to Jews killed in the Holocaust, it has an impressive crypt with a torch burning on the lower level; upstairs is a museum that documents the Holocaust. Closed Saturdays, Sundays (except afternoons in July and August), May 1, and Jewish holidays. Also note the trendy Soho-esque clothing shops and art galleries. If hunger strikes, stop in at *Au Gamin de Paris* (51 Rue Vielle-du-Temple; phone: 42-78-97-24), a late-night eatery where specialties include grilled salmon and *magret de canard;* for dessert, try the *crème brûlée* or *tarte tatin.*

A block to the left, down Rue des Francs-Bourgeois, is the Hôtel de Soubise, a palace with an illustrious history that today houses the National Archives, containing about 220 miles of information. In 1700, the house was acquired by François de Rohan, the Prince of Soubise, thanks to the generosity of Louis XIV. Over the next few years, extensive remodeling transformed the mansion into a palace; the best painters and artisans were brought in to enhance the classical architecture into something more formal.

On the ground floor were the apartments of the Prince of Rohan-Soubise (which can be visited by groups when arranged in advance). The princess's apartment on the first floor is now a museum, with interesting historical documents, among them the wills of Louis XIV and Napoleon, the diary of Louis XVI, and the Declaration of Human Rights. There is also a model of the Bastille that was carved from one of its original stones. Outside, turn right past the National Archives complex to Rue des Quatre-Fils. At the corner, at 60 Rue des Archives, is the Hôtel Guénégaud, still another mansion built by Mansart in 1650, regarded as one of the finest in the Marais. It has been remodeled twice since the 18th century, retaining its simple lines. Turn to the left at Rue des Quatre-Fils, and visit the small formal garden. On the same property is the *Musée de la Chasse et de la Nature,* which features a collection of hunting souvenirs and an arms collection from a Monsieur Sommer, who had restored the house in later years. There is also a collection of tapestries, ceramics, and sculptures related to the hunt. Closed Tuesdays and holidays (phone: 42-72-86-43).

Walk ahead to Rue Vieille-du-Temple and turn right. At No. 87 is the Hôtel de Rohan, converted into the imperial printing house under Napoleon, and another annex to the National Archives in 1927. It was the residence at one time of Cardinal de Rohan, who was the son of the Prince of Soubise, and became home to four other members of the Rohan family, who were also cardinals. Though the courtyard is not as elaborate as the one in the Soubise mansion, the former stables are quite interesting, simply because of the splendor of the sculptured façade, which depicts the Horses of Apollo, drinking at the trough.

If this inspires thirst, walk directly across the street to *Le Clos Follainville* (72 Rue Vieille-du-Temple; phone: 42-78-21-22), a casual and rustic tea salon/restaurant/wine bar, suitable for a light lunch and a selection of wine sold by the half glass, glass, or bottle. With their more intimate ambience, the Paris wine bars are a refreshing contrast from the hectic Paris sidewalk cafés. Open Mondays through Fridays, Saturdays after 7:30 PM; closed Sundays.

Back at the corner, turn right onto Rue de la Perle. At No. 1 is the Hôtel Libéral Bruant, built in 1685 by the architect of Les Invalides for his own residence. This stately mansion now houses the *Musée Bricard* (Lock and Key Museum; phone: 42-77-79-62). Inside is an exhibit tracing the history of the lock from the Roman Empire, as well as a collection of locks. Closed Sundays, Mondays, holidays, and the month of August.

Walk to the left to Rue de Thorigny and the former Hôtel Salé (No. 5). This house was built in 1656–59 for a gentleman who made a fortune out of the salt tax, which is how it got its name (*salé* is French for "salty"). In the 17th century, the right to collect taxes was sold by the state to private enterprises working on a percentage basis. The 3-story house has been restored over the years, and following the death of Pablo Picasso in 1973 his heirs donated an outstanding collection of the artist's works in lieu of inheritance tax; it is now the site of the *Musée Picasso* (phone: 42-71-25-21), with more than 200 paintings, 3,000 drawings and engravings, and other objets d'art. The works are arranged in chronological order, providing a fascinating insight into Picasso's various periods. Especially interesting is his private collection of paintings of other artists, with works by Cézanne, Braque, and Rousseau. There are also films on the prodigious artist's life and work. The courtyard and the museum's garden are relaxing places to pause before or after touring the museum. Be sure to see the lovely fountain by Simounet in the formal garden. Open daily except Tuesdays, from 9:15 AM to 5:15 PM (until 10 PM Wednesdays).

Index